Lexical Aids
to the Syriac New Testament

Gorgias Handbooks

61

Gorgias Handbooks provides students and scholars with reference books, textbooks and introductions to different topics or fields of study. In this series, Gorgias welcomes books that are able to communicate information, ideas and concepts effectively and concisely, with useful reference bibliographies for further study.

Lexical Aids
to the Syriac New Testament

Third Expanded Edition

Edited by

George Anton Kiraz

Timothy A. Lee

2024

Gorgias Press LLC, 954 River Road, Piscataway, NJ, 08854, USA

www.gorgiaspress.com

Copyright © 2024 by Gorgias Press LLC

All rights reserved under International and Pan-American Copyright Conventions. No part of this publication may be reproduced, stored in a retrieval system or transmitted in any form or by any means, electronic, mechanical, photocopying, recording, scanning or otherwise without the prior written permission of Gorgias Press LLC.

2024   ,

ISBN		ISSN 1935-6838
Paperback	978-1-4632-4603-7	
eBook	978-1-4632-4604-4	

Library of Congress Cataloging-in-Publication Data

A Cataloging-in-Publication Record is available from the Library of Congress.

Printed in the United States of America

Contents

Preface	vii
Introduction	ix
Abbreviations	xi
1 Word Frequency List	1
2 Proper Noun Frequency List	43
3 Greek Loanwords Frequency List	49
4 Consonantal Homographs	57
5 Verbs Arranged by Paradigm	61
6 Words Arranged by Part of Speech	77
7 Words Arranged by Root	87
8 Compound Words	177
9 Semitic Cognate List	179
Index	193

Preface

George A. Kiraz

I would like to take the opportunity to thank my Malphono Dr Sebastian P. Brock (Oriental Institute, University of Oxford), who suggested compiling this work, for his numerous valuable discussions, and for the use of his computer system to print the camera-ready copy of the first edition. His Eminence Mor Clemis Augen Kaplan, Metropolitan - then Patriarchal Assistant, kindly reviewed Section 6; Dr Andrew Criddle (Cambridge) and Ms Amanda Bowen (Peterhouse, Cambridge) kindly checked the cross references in Section 8 and Section 7, respectively. To Dr Philip Davies of Sheffield Academic Press, I give my gratitude for accepting this work for publication.

I have completed this first edition while doing research on Semitic computational morphology at the Computer Laboratory, University of Cambridge, under the direction of Dr Stephen G. Pulman (SRI International and Computer Laboratory), which was made possible by a Benefactor Studentship from St John's College.

The second edition by Gorgias Press was simply a facsimile reproduction of the first 1993 edition. This third expanded edition, published thirty years after the first edition, was produced in collaboration with Timothy A. Lee of Cambridge, for which see below.

Beth Mardutho: The Syriac Institute, Piscataway, NJ, United States
10th October, 2023.

George A. Kiraz

Timothy A. Lee

This has been a ten month project recreating, updating, and expanding Lexical Aids to the Syriac New Testament. I thank George Kiraz for access to the SEDRA database and the opportunity to mine it for useful information. From my own experience learning Hebrew and Syriac I suggested to George that we add new tables for words arranged by root, verbal paradigm, and Hebrew-Arabic cognates. The latter two lists had to be manually created. I hope these new additions will make this work even more useful that it already was.

Emmanuel College, Cambridge, England
10th October, 2023.

Timothy A. Lee

Introduction

Most students of Syriac are introduced to the text of the Syriac New Testament in their first year of studies. The main task facing the student is studying the meanings of the words which constitute the text. Learning the most frequent words, moving to the less frequent ones, the student's understanding of the text expands rapidly. *Lexical Aids to the Syriac New Testament* aims to provide the student, among other aids, with such a tool.

This work is divided into ten sections, each providing the student with a different tool. Sections 1, 2, and 3 provide three frequency lists: a word list, a proper noun list, and a list of Greek loanwords. Section 4 consists of a list of consonantal homographs which is aimed at helping the student clarify lexical ambiguities. Each of the four sections give full morphological analysis and English meanings.

Section 5 is devoted to the verb It provides lists of the most frequent verbs divided into their verbal paradigms. Section 6 lists other words (not verbs or nouns) by part of speech. These include particles and adverbs for memorization. Section 7 arranges words by base root allowing quick memorization across all words. This list also includes rarer words that a student can easily memorize alongside more their frequest relatives. Section 8 lists compound words that might help beginner students.

Section 9 lists Semitic cognate words. Learners often come to Syriac already with knowledge of another Semitic language such as Hebrew or Arabic. Therefore, through comparing common cognates between these languages the learner will realise that they already know many Syriac words. As an appendix to this section lists cognates with consonontal shifts in Hebrew. Finally, an index provides an alphabetical index of the Syriac words.

Abbreviations

abs.	absolute	impf.	imperfect
adj.	adjective	impv.	imperative
adv.	adverb	inf.	infinitive
aph.	aph^{c}el	int.	instransitive
com.	common (gender)	masc./m.	masculine
const.	construct	mp	masculine plural
denom.	denominative	ms	masculine singular
emp.	emphatic	n.	noun
eshtaph.	eshtaph^{c}al	pa.	pa^{c}el
est.	estaph^{c}al	pal.	pa^{c}li
ethaph.	ethaph^{c}el	palpa.	palpal
ethpa.	ethpa^{c}al	palpe.	palpel
ethpal.	ethpa^{c}li	pam.	pam^{c}el
ethpalp.	ethpalpal	par.	par^{c}el
ethpar.	ethpar^{c}al	pass.	passive
ethpaw.	ethpaw^{c}al	pass. ptc.	passive participle
ethpay.	ethpay^{c}al	paw.	paw^{c}el
ethpe.	ethp^{c}el	pay.	pay^{c}el
ettaph.	ettaph^{c}al	pe.	p^{c}al
fem./f.	feminine	pf.	perfect
fp	feminine plural	pl.	plural
fs	feminine singular	pr.	proper noun
Gr.	Greek	prep.	preposition

pron.	pronoun	suf.	suffix
ptc.	participle	taph.	taph^{c}el
rel.	relative	tr.	transitive
saph.	saph^{c}el	v.	verb
sg.	singular	w/	with
shaph.	shaph^{c}el		

Chapter 1

Word Frequency List

Sequence.

This list is arranged according to the frequency of occurrence of words.

Format.

The list consists of three columns:

- **Column 1: Reference No.**
  Gives each word a reference number.

- **Column 2: Syriac Lexical Entry.**
  Gives the Syriac form of the word in vocalized *Serto* (Western) script.

- **Column 3: Category.**
  Gives the grammatical (i.e. morphological) category of the lexical entry.

- **Column 4: English Meanings.**
  Gives the English meanings of the lexical entry. Main English key words are given in italic. Greek loanwords are given preceding the meanings. At the right side of this column, the frequency of the lexical entry is given in italic in parenthesis.

The list is divided into frequency-range groups to help the student plan study sessions. For example, the first group lists words of frequency higher than 1000.

How to Use the Frequency List.

It is important to review each group a few times before proceeding to the next one. It is quite difficult to establish associations between the Syriac words and their English meanings, since the Semitic language and the Indo-European one belong to two different families. In order to remember the meanings, therefore, it is crucial to understand the usage of the words. If the student has access to a copy of the updated Key Words in Context Concordance to the Syriac New Testament (Gorgias Press, 2023), the concordance can be consulted to learn the different forms of each word, and the usage of each form, as they appear in the New Testament.

Words occurring more than 1000 times

	Syriac	Cat.	Meaning	
1.	ܠ	prep.	*to, for*	(4234)
2.	ܗܘܐ	v.	*be, (as enclitic)was, turn out*	(4006)
3.	ܠܐ	particle	*no, not*	(3140)
4.	ܡܢ	prep.	*from*	(2966)
5.	ܐܡܪ	v.	*say, speak, announce, affirm*	(2553)
6.	ܗܘ	pron. m.	*he, it, (as enclitic)is*	(2141)
7.	ܕܝܢ	particle	*but, yet*	(1828)
8.	ܐܢܐ	pron. c.	*I*	(1728)
9.	ܗܢܐ	pron.	*this, these*	(1578)
10.	ܥܠ	prep.	*on, about, concerning*	(1549)
11.	ܐܢܬ	pron. m.	*thou*	(1401)
12.	ܟܠ ، ܟܠ	particle	*all, every, whole, entirely*	(1400)
13.	ܐܠܗܐ	n. m.	*God, a god.* pl. ܐܠܗܐ	(1389)
14.	ܗܘ	pron. m.	*that, those,* w/ ܃ he *who*	(1256)
15.	ܟܕ	particle	*when, after, while, where*	(1214)
16.	ܐܝܬ	sub.	*is, are*	(1100)

1. WORD FREQUENCY LIST

	Syriac	Cat.	Meaning	
17.	ܓܝܪ	particle	Gk. γάρ *for*	(1085)

Words occurring 600 – 999 times

	Syriac	Cat.	Meaning	
18.	ܐܬܐ	v.	*come*; Aph^{c}el ܐܝܬܝ *bring*	(966)
19.	ܐܝܢܐ	pron. f.	*who, what, which*	(858)
20.	ܒ	prep.	*in, by, into, among, at, with, against*	(824)
21.	ܐܠܐ	particle	*but, but rather*	(799)
22.	ܒܪܐ	n. m.	*son*. pl. ܒܢܝܐ	(786)
23.	ܐܦ	particle	*also, even*	(765)
24.	ܐܝܟ	prep.	*as, according to*	(759)
25.	ܡܪܝܐ	n. m.	*lord, master*. pl. ܡܪܘܬܐ	(755)
26.	ܡܛܠ	prep.	*because*	(740)
27.	ܚܕ	num. m.	*one*, (as adj)*certain one*, w/ ܚܕ ܚܕ *each one*	(739)
28.	ܚܙܐ	v.	*see, behold*	(734)
29.	ܥܡ	prep.	*with*	(723)
30.	ܐܢܫܐ	n. c.	*man, mankind*. pl. ܐܢܫܐ	(709)
31.	ܥܒܕ	v.	*do, make*; Shaph^{c}el ܡܫܥܒܕ *subdue, subject, act, perform, celebrate* (a feast)	(706)
32.	ܝܕܥ	v.	*know*; Aph^{c}el ܐܘܕܥ make *known*; Eshtaph^{c}al ܐܫܬܘܕܥ *recognize*	(704)
33.	ܐܢ	particle	*if*	(680)
34.	ܠܘܬ	prep.	*to, toward, against*	(602)

Words occurring 400 – 599 times

	Syriac	Cat.	Meaning	
35.	ܡܫܝܚܐ	pass. ptc. m.	*Messiah, Anointed One, Christ*	(586)

4   1. WORD FREQUENCY LIST

	Syriac	Cat.	Meaning	
36.	ܩܘܡ	v.	*rise, stand*; Pa^cel ܩܝܡ *establish*; Aph^cel ܐܩܝܡ cause to *stand*	(550)
37.	ܝܗܒ	v.	*give*	(534)
38.	ܫܡܥ	v.	*hear, obey*; Aph^cel cause to *hear*	(494)
39.	ܡܕܡ	n. c.	*something*	(492)
40.	ܪܘܚܐ	n. c.	*spirit, wind, breath.* pl. ܪܘܚܐ	(478)
41.	ܐܒܐ	n. m.	*father.* pl. ܐܒܗܐ	(453)
42.	ܐܫܟܚ	v.	*find, happen, be able*	(448)
43.	ܐܙܠ	v.	*depart, go*	(447)
44.	ܣܓܝܐܐ	adj.	*much, many*	(439)
45.	ܒܝܬܐ	n. m.	*house, abode.* pl. ܒܬܐ	(434)
46.	ܢܦܫܐ	n. f.	*soul, breath of life, self.* pl. ܢܦܫܬܐ	(422)
47.	ܥܠܡܐ	n. m.	*age, eternity, world.* pl. ܥܠܡܐ	(413)
48.	ܡܠܬܐ	n. f.	*word, case, cause, matter.* pl. ܡܠܐ	(409)
49.	ܢܦܩ	v.	*go out,* w/ ܪܘܚܐ *defend*; Ethpa^cal *be exercised*; Aph^cel ܐܦܩ *go out, make cast out, eject*	(405)

Words occurring 300 – 399 times

	Syriac	Cat.	Meaning	
50.	ܪܒܐ	adj.	*great, chief,* w/ suffix*master*	(395)
51.	ܝܘܡܐ	n. m.	*day.* pl. ܝܘܡܬܐ	(381)
52.	ܡܢ	pron.	*who,* w/ ܕ *he who*	(367)
53.	ܐܝܕܐ	n. f.	*hand,* w/ ܒ *through,* w/ ܠܘܬ *near.* pl. ܐܝܕܝܐ	(362)
54.	ܐܚܐ	n. m.	*brother.* pl. ܐܚܐ	(360)
55.	ܡܠܠ	v.	Pa^cel ܡܠܠ *speak*	(351)
56.	ܩܪܐ	v.	*call, read,* w/ ܥܠ *appeal to*	(330)
57.	ܥܡܐ	n. m.	*people, nation*; *pl. Gentiles.* pl. ܥܡܡܐ	(324)
58.	ܓܒܪܐ	n. m.	*man, husband, person.* pl. ܓܒܪܐ	(319)

1. WORD FREQUENCY LIST

	Syriac	Cat.	Meaning	
59.	ܒܥܐ	v.	*seek for, require, question, inquire into*	(313)
60.	ܫܡܝܐ	n. c.	*heaven, sky.* pl. ܫܡܝ̈ܐ	(309)
61.	ܐܝܟܢܐ	prep.	*as, how*	(308)
62.	ܗܝܡܢ	v.	*believe, trust* in	(305)

Words occurring 250 – 299 times

	Syriac	Cat.	Meaning	
63.	ܐܘ	particle	*or, else, rather than*	(296)
64.	ܐܚܪܢܐ	adj.	*another*	(295)
65.	ܩܕܡ	prep.	*before*	(290)
66.	ܡܢܐ	pron.	*why, what*	(289)
67.	ܗܟܢܐ	particle	*thus*	(282)
68.	ܬܠܡܝܕܐ	n. m.	*disciple.* pl. ܬܠܡܝ̈ܕܐ	(277)
69.	ܨܒܐ	v.	*will, desire*	(273)
70.	ܐܪܥܐ	n. f.	*earth, land, country, soil, ground.* pl. ܐܪ̈ܥܬܐ	(272)
71.	ܗܐ	particle	*lo! behold!*	(270)
72.	ܗܝܡܢܘܬܐ	n. f.	*faith, belief*	(264)
73.	ܥܠ	v.	*enter;* Aph^cel ܐܥܠ *bring in*	(264)
74.	ܒܬܪ	prep.	*after, behind*	(256)
75.	ܗܟܝܠ	particle	*therefore, hence*	(250)

Words occurring 200 – 249 times

	Syriac	Cat.	Meaning	
76.	ܫܪܐ	v.	*loosen, lodge;* Pa^cel ܫܪܝ *begin;* Ethpa^cal ܐܫܬܪܝ *be loosened, eat* a meal	(249)
77.	ܩܪܒ	v.	*draw near, touch, come;* Pa^cel ܩܪܒ *bring near, bring near, offer;* Aph^cel *fight*	(244)

1. WORD FREQUENCY LIST

	Syriac	Cat.	Meaning	
78.	ܫܡܐ	n. m.	*name.* pl. ܫܡܗܐ	(244)
79.	ܫܐܠ	v.	*ask, inquire,* w/ ܫܠܡܐ *salute;* Aph^cel *lend*	(243)
80.	ܐܢܬܬܐ	n. f.	*woman, wife.* pl. ܢܫܐ	(238)
81.	ܡܐ	pron.	*what*	(236)
82.	ܫܕܪ	v.	Pa^cel ܫܕܪ *send*	(235)
83.	ܒܪܢܫܐ	n. c.	w/ ܕ *human.* pl. ܒܢܝܢܫܐ	(231)
84.	ܟܬܒ	v.	*write*	(231)
85.	ܢܤܒ	v.	*take, receive,* w/ ܐܦܐ *be a hypocrite*	(229)
86.	ܙܒܢܐ	n. m.	*time, season, period.* pl. ܙܒܢܐ	(227)
87.	ܢܡܘܣܐ	n. m.	Gk. νομός *law.* pl. ܢܡܘܣܐ	(224)
88.	ܕܝܠ	particle	*own*	(223)
89.	ܠܝܬ	sub.	*is not*	(223)
90.	ܡܕܝܢܬܐ	n. f.	*city.* pl. ܡܕܝܢܬܐ	(223)
91.	ܥܕܡܐ	prep.	*until*	(219)
92.	ܫܒܩ	v.	*forgive, leave, allow*	(217)
93.	ܛܒܐ	adj.	*good,* w/ ܛܒ *much*	(214)
94.	ܤܡ	v.	*put, place*	(207)
95.	ܐܬܡ	particle	*there*	(206)
96.	ܝܗܘܕܝܐ	adj.	*Jew*	(205)
97.	ܬܪܝܢ	num. m.	*two*	(204)
98.	ܩܒܠ	v.	*appeal to, accuse;* Pa^cel ܩܒܠ *receive, take;* Saph^cel *be present, oppose*	(200)
99.	ܫܠܡ	v.	*die,* w/ ܠ *obey, agree, follow;* Ethp^cel ܐܫܬܠܡ *be delivered up;* Pa^cel ܫܠܡ *complete;* Aph^cel ܐܫܠܡ *deliver up, be completed*	(200)

1. WORD FREQUENCY LIST   7

Words occurring 150 – 199 times

	Syriac	Cat.	Meaning	
100.	ܗܵܫܵܐ	particle	*now*	(193)
101.	ܬܘܼܒ	particle	*again, furthermore*	(192)
102.	ܥܒܵܕܵܐ	n. m.	*deed, work.* pl. ܥܒ̣ܵܕܹ̈ܐ	(191)
103.	ܒܝܼܫܵܐ	adj.	*evil, wrong*	(185)
104.	ܡܲܠܲܐܟ̣ܵܐ	n. m.	*messenger, angel.* pl. ܡܲܠܲܐܟ̣ܹ̈ܐ	(181)
105.	ܪܹܫܵܐ	n. m.	*head, beginning; pl. chiefs.* pl. ܪܹ̈ܫܹܐ	(181)
106.	ܐܸܟ̣ܲܠ	v.	*eat, consume,* w/ ܩܲܪܨܵܐ *accuse;* Aph^cel *feed*	(178)
107.	ܟܢܵܫܵܐ	n. m.	*gathering* (of persons), *multitude, council, assembly, crowd.* pl. ܟܢܵܫܹ̈ܐ	(178)
108.	ܚܲܝܹ̈ܐ	n. m.	*life, salvation*	(177)
109.	ܦܲܓ̣ܪܵܐ	n. m.	*body.* pl. ܦܲܓ̣ܪܹ̈ܐ	(176)
110.	ܡܝܼܬ	v.	*be dead, die;* Aph^cel put to *death*	(171)
111.	ܗܵܝܕܹܝܢ	particle	*then, afterwards, next*	(169)
112.	ܐܸܚܲܕ	v.	*take, hold;* Aph^cel ܐܵܚܹܕ cause to *take, let out,* w/ ܢܘܼܪܵܐ *kindle, apprehend, maintain, close* (a door)	(168)
113.	ܠܸܒܵܐ	n. m.	*heart.* pl. ܠܸܒܵܘ̈ܵܬ̣ܵܐ	(168)
114.	ܡܲܠܟܘܼܬ̣ܵܐ	n. f.	*kingdom, realm, reign.* pl. ܡܲܠܟܘܵ̈ܬ̣ܵܐ	(167)
115.	ܢܒ̣ܝܼܵܐ	n. m.	*prophet; f. prophetess.* pl. ܢܒ̣ܝܹ̈ܐ	(167)
116.	ܡܠܵܐ	v.	*fill, complete*	(166)
117.	ܚܝܵܐ	v.	*live;* Aph^cel ܐܲܚܝܼ make *live, save*	(165)
118.	ܫܠܵܡܵܐ	n. m.	*peace,* w/ ܝܲܗ݂ܒ *salute, salutation.* pl. ܫܠܵ̈ܡܹܐ	(164)
119.	ܫܩܲܠ	v.	*take up, bear*	(160)
120.	ܥܢܵܐ	v.	*answer*	(158)
121.	ܢܦܲܠ	v.	*fall*	(157)
122.	ܥܲܝܢܵܐ	n. f.	*eye.* pl. ܥܲܝ̈ܢܹܐ	(155)
123.	ܛܲܝܒܘܼܬ̣ܵܐ	n. f.	*grace, goodness, favour, kindness, graciousuess*	(154)

	Syriac	Cat.	Meaning	
124.	ܩܳܠܐ	n. m.	*voice.* pl. ܩܳܠܐ	(153)
125.	ܚܰܝܠܐ	n. f.	*power, mighty work, strength, virtue, force.* pl. ܚܰܝܠܐ	(150)

Words occurring 125 – 149 times

	Syriac	Cat.	Meaning	
126.	ܝܺܬܶܒ	v.	*sit;* Aph^cel ܐܰܘܬܶܒ *seat, establish*	(148)
127.	ܩܰܕܝܺܫܐ	adj.	*holy, saint*	(148)
128.	ܐܰܡܺܝܢ	particle	*Amen, verily*	(147)
129.	ܝܺܠܶܦ	v.	*learn;* Pa^cel ܐܰܠܶܦ *teach*	(147)
130.	ܐܰܦ̈ܐ	n. f.	*face,* w/ ܢܣܰܒ *hypocrite,* w/ ܠܰܚܡܐ *presence-bread.* pl. ܐܰܦ̈ܐ	(143)
131.	ܫܳܥܬܐ	n.	*hour*	(142)
132.	ܥܰܒܕܐ	n. m.	*servant.* pl. ܥܰܒ̈ܕܐ	(141)
133.	ܪܡܳܐ	v.	*put, place, cast*	(136)
134.	ܣܠܶܩ	v.	*go up, ascend;* Aph^cel ܐܰܣܶܩ *make ascend*	(134)
135.	ܡܰܠܟܐ	n. m.	*king; f. queen.* pl. ܡܰܠ̈ܟܐ	(130)
136.	ܢܛܰܪ	v.	*guard, keep, reserve, observe*	(130)
137.	ܦܩܰܕ	v.	*command*	(130)
138.	ܒܶܣܪܐ	n. m.	*flesh*	(129)
139.	ܒܰܠܚܘܕ	adv.	*only, alone*	(128)
140.	ܡܺܝܬܐ	pass. ptc. m.	*dead*	(126)
141.	ܗܳܢܐ	pron. m.	w/ ܡܰܢ *who is this?*	(126)
142.	ܬܠܳܬ	num. f.	*three*	(126)
143.	ܚܘܽܒܐ	n. m.	*love, lovingkindness.* pl. ܚܘܽܒܐ	(125)
144.	ܡܰܘܬܐ	n. m.	*death.* pl. ܡܰܘ̈ܬܐ	(125)

1. WORD FREQUENCY LIST

Words occurring 110 – 124 times

	Syriac	Cat.	Meaning	
145.	ܩܛܠ	v.	*kill*	(124)
146.	ܟܘܡܪܐ	n. m.	*priest.* pl. ܟܘܡܪ̈ܐ	(121)
147.	ܛܝܒ	v.	Paᶜel ܛܰܝܶܒ *prepare*	(121)
148.	ܝܠܕ	v.	Aphᶜel ܐܰܘܠܶܕ *beget, bear* (a child)	(120)
149.	ܪܚܡ	v.	*love,* have *mercy;* Ethpaᶜal ܐܶܬܪܰܚܰܡ have *mercy;* Paᶜel ܪܰܚܶܡ have *compassion*	(119)
150.	ܕܢ	den.	*judge*	(118)
151.	ܣܗܕ	v.	*witness, testify*	(118)
152.	ܗܝܟܠܐ	n. m.	*temple, sanctuary.* pl. ܗܝ̈ܟܠܐ	(117)
153.	ܚܠܦ	prep.	*for, instead*	(117)
154.	ܐܬܪܐ	n. m.	*region, place, country, respite,* available *space or room.* pl. ܐܰܬܪ̈ܘܬܐ	(116)
155.	ܣܒܪ	den.	Paᶜel ܣܰܒܰܪ *preach, declare;* Payᶜel ܣܰܝܒܰܪ *bear, endure;* Ethpayᶜal *be nourished, be fed*	(115)
156.	ܕܚܠ	v.	*fear;* Paᶜel cause to *fear*	(114)
157.	ܥܕܬܐ	n. f.	*church, assembly, congregation.* pl. ܥܕ̈ܬܐ	(113)
158.	ܗܠܟ	v.	Paᶜel ܗܰܠܶܟ *walk*	(110)

Words occurring 100 – 109 times

	Syriac	Cat.	Meaning	
159.	ܐܝܟܐ	particle	*where*	(109)
160.	ܝܡܐ	n. m.	*sea*	(108)
161.	ܢܚܬ	v.	*descend*	(108)
162.	ܣܒܪ	v.	*think, suppose;* Paᶜel *hope, consider*	(108)
163.	ܥܒܪ	v.	*cross over,* w/ ܥܠ *transgress,* w/ ܡܢ *turn away from;* Aphᶜel ܐܰܥܒܰܪ *pass over*	(108)
164.	ܫܦܝܪܐ	adj.	*beautiful, good, well*	(108)

	Syriac	Cat.	Meaning	
165.	أُوزَملَٰا	n. f.	*way, road, highway, journeying.* pl. أَوَّتِسَكَٰا	(105)
166.	حَنَص	v.	*assemble, gather*	(105)
167.	سَجَد	v.	*be kindled;* Pa^{c}el *love*	(103)
168.	سَكْهَٰا	n. m.	*sin.* pl. سَكْهَٰا	(103)
169.	قَومَكَٰا	adj.	*first, fore*	(103)
170.	حَكْتَٰا	n. m.	*book, writing, Scripture.* pl. حَكْتَٰا	(102)
171.	فَرِيمَٰا	pass. ptc. m.	*Pharisee*	(102)
172.	وُمَٰا	n. m.	*judgement, sentence* (of judge). pl. وُمَٰا	(101)
173.	رِحْمَٰا	n. m.	*will, desire.* pl. رِحْمَٰا	(101)
174.	تَكْتَرُٰا	adj.	*more, excessive, greater, better, excelling*	(100)
175.	رَلَ	v.	*incline toward, heed;* Pa^{c}el رَكِي *pray*	(100)
176.	رِجْلَٰا	n. f.	*foot.* pl. رِجْلَٰا	(100)
177.	حَبْعَٰا	num. f.	*seven*	(100)

Words occurring 90 – 99 times

	Syriac	Cat.	Meaning	
178.	قُودِمَٰا	n. m.	*holiness.* pl. قُودِمَٰا	(99)
179.	تَمْحُومَكَٰا	n. f.	*praise, glory.* pl. تَمْحُومَكَٰا	(99)
180.	جَلَ	v.	*reveal, manifest*	(98)
181.	كَسَمَٰا	n. m.	*bread,* w/ أَفَٰا *shewbread*	(98)
182.	قَوَا	den.	Pa^{c}el قَوَّم *abide, remain*	(98)
183.	حَوَا	v.	Pa^{c}el حَوِّم *show*	(97)
184.	وَمَٰا	n. m.	*blood*	(96)
185.	قَكْحَم	n. c.	w/ كَٰ *every one*	(96)
186.	حَسَب	den.	Pa^{c}el حَسَّب *praise, glorify, commend*	(95)
187.	حَزَر	den.	Ethp^{c}el تَكَرْزِ *be preached;* Aph^{c}el أَكْرِز *preach;* Ethp^{c}el تَكَرْزِ *be proclaimed*	(94)

1. WORD FREQUENCY LIST

	Syriac	Cat.	Meaning	
188.	ܡܰܝ̈ܐ	n. m.	*water.* pl. ܡܰܝ̈ܐ	(94)
189.	ܫܪܳܪܐ	n. m.	*truth*	(94)
190.	ܐܶܡܐ	n. f.	*mother.* pl. ܐܶܡܗ̈ܬܐ	(93)
191.	ܕܒܰܪ	v.	*lead, take*; Pa^cel ܕܰܒܰܪ *rule, guide, conduct*	(93)
192.	ܦܘܩܕܳܢܐ	n. m.	*commandment, edict, decree, precept.* pl. ܦܘܩܕܳܢ̈ܐ	(92)
193.	ܗܦܰܟ	v.	*turn, return*; Ethpa^cal *conduct oneself*	(91)

Words occurring 85 – 89 times

	Syriac	Cat.	Meaning	
194.	ܚܰܝܐ	adj.	*alive, living*	(89)
195.	ܫܘܒܚܐ	n. m.	*glory, glorification, praise*	(89)
196.	ܐܒܰܕ	v.	*perish*; Aph^cel ܐܘܒܶܕ *destroy, lose*	(87)
197.	ܕܰܠܡܐ	particle	*lest*	(87)
198.	ܣܟܠܘܬܐ	n. f.	*sin*	(87)
199.	ܐܳܦܠܐ	particle	w/ ܕ *not even*	(86)
200.	ܦܘܡܐ	n. m.	*mouth, edge.* pl. ܦܘܡ̈ܐ	(86)
201.	ܫܘܐ	v.	*worthy, be equal*; Ethp^cel *agree*; Pa^cel *spread, wipe*; Aph^cel ܐܫܘܝ *smooth*	(86)
202.	ܫܠܝܚܐ	pass. ptc. m.	*apostle, sent one*	(86)

	Syriac	Cat.	Meaning	

Words occurring 80 – 84 times

	Syriac	Cat.	Meaning	
203.	ܕܶܚܠܬܳܐ	n. f.	*fear, awe.* pl. ܕܶܚܠܳܬܳܐ	(84)
204.	ܦܬܰܚ	v.	*open*	(84)
205.	ܩܰܫܺܝܫܳܐ	n. m.	*elder.* pl. ܩܰܫܺܝܫܶܐ	(84)
206.	ܝܕܐ	v.	Aphᶜel ܐܰܘܕܺܝ *confess, give* thanks; Eshtaphᶜal ܐܶܫܬܰܘܕܺܝ *profess, promise*	(83)
207.	ܟܽܠܡܶܕܶܡ	idiom	*everything*	(83)
208.	ܐܶܫܬܺܝ	v.	*drink*	(82)
209.	ܐܳܬܳܐ	n. f.	*miraculous* token, *sign.* pl. ܐܳܬܘܳܬܳܐ	(82)
210.	ܠܒܰܪ	prep.	*outside*	(82)
211.	ܢܽܘܪܳܐ	n. f.	*fire*	(81)
212.	ܦܺܐܪܳܐ	n. m.	*fruit.* pl. ܦܺܐܪܶܐ	(81)
213.	ܩܥܳܐ	v.	*cry aloud,* w/ ܥܰܠ *appeal to*	(81)
214.	ܛܰܠܝܳܐ	n. m.	*boy, youth, servant;* f. *girl;* f. *maid.* pl. ܛܠܳܝܶܐ	(80)
215.	ܝܰܬܰܪ	v.	*gain, remain over, abound;* Paᶜel *make abound,* w/ ܡܶܢ *prefer;* Aphᶜel ܐܰܘܬܰܪ *benefit*	(80)
216.	ܥܡܰܕ	v.	*be baptized;* Aphᶜel ܐܰܥܡܶܕ *baptize, sink*	(80)
217.	ܫܽܘܠܛܳܢܳܐ	n. m.	*power, authority, dominion.* pl. ܫܽܘܠܛܳܢܶܐ	(80)

Words occurring 75 – 79 times

	Syriac	Cat.	Meaning	
218.	ܝܰܬܺܝܪܳܐܝܺܬ	adv.	*abundantly, especially, exceedingly*	(78)
219.	ܪܶܥܝܳܢܳܐ	n. m.	*mind, conscience,* w/ ܣܰܟܠܳܐ *fool, thought, idea, conception.* pl. ܪܶܥܝܳܢܶܐ	(77)
220.	ܬܰܪܥܳܐ	n. m.	*door, gate, portal.* pl. ܬܰܪܥܶܐ	(77)

	Syriac	Cat.	Meaning	
221.	ܣܒܲܪ	v.	*be glad, rejoice*; Paᶜel *gladden*	(76)
222.	ܛܥܐ	v.	*wander, err, forget*; Aphᶜel ܐܛܥܝ *deceive, go astray, lead astray, delude*	(76)
223.	ܟܢܘܫܬܐ	n. f.	*synagogue, council.* pl. ܟܢܘܫ̈ܬܐ	(76)
224.	ܣܦܪܐ	n. m.	*scribe, lawyer.* pl. ܣܦܪ̈ܐ	(76)
225.	ܬܪܥܣܪ	num. m.	*twelve*	(75)

Words occurring 70 – 74 times

	Syriac	Cat.	Meaning	
226.	ܐܣܐ	v.	Paᶜel ܐܣܝ *heal*	(74)
227.	ܫܪܒܬܐ	n. f.	*generation, tribe, family, stock, line.* pl. ܫܪ̈ܒܬܐ	(74)
228.	ܟܡܐ	particle	*how much? how many?*	(73)
229.	ܬܚܝܬ	prep.	*under*	(73)
230.	ܙܒܢ	v.	*buy*; Paᶜel ܙܒܿܢ *sell*	(72)
231.	ܫܢܬܐ	n. f.	*year.* pl. ܫܢ̈ܝܐ	(72)
232.	ܕܡܐ	v.	*resemble*; Paᶜel *liken to, compare*	(70)
233.	ܛܝܒ	v.	Paᶜel ܛܝܒ *make ready*	(70)

Words occurring 65 – 69 times

	Syriac	Cat.	Meaning	
234.	ܕܘܟܬܐ	n. f.	*place.* pl. ܕܘܟ̈ܬܐ	(69)
235.	ܟܐܦܐ	n. f.	*stone, rock.* pl. ܟܐܦ̈ܐ	(69)
236.	ܩܠܝܠܐ	adj.	*little, light, swift*	(69)
237.	ܫܒܬܐ	n. f.	*Sabbath.* pl. ܫܒ̈ܐ	(69)
238.	ܕܟܐ	v.	*be pure*; Paᶜel ܕܟܝ *cleanse*	(68)
239.	ܗܘ	pron. m.	w/ ܗܘ	(68)
240.	ܠܠܝܐ	n. m.	*night*	(68)
241.	ܢܘܗܪܐ	n. m.	*light*	(68)

1. WORD FREQUENCY LIST

	Syriac	Cat.	Meaning	
242.	ܡܥܘܬܐ	n. f.	living *creature, animal.* pl. ܡܥܘܬܐ	(67)
243.	ܟܐܢܘܬܐ	n. f.	*righteousness, uprightness, godliness, rectitude, justice*	(67)
244.	ܣܗܕܘܬܐ	n. f.	*testimony.* pl. ܣܗܕܘܬܐ	(67)
245.	ܩܪܝܬܐ	n. f.	*village, field.* pl. ܩܘܪܝܐ	(67)
246.	ܐܣܪ	v.	*bind, fasten*	(66)
247.	ܙܥܘܪܐ	adj.	*little, least*	(66)
248.	ܚܫܒ	v.	*think, reckon, deliberate*	(66)
249.	ܛܘܪܐ	n. m.	*mountain, hill.* pl. ܛܘܪܐ	(66)
250.	ܝܘܠܦܢܐ	n. m.	*teaching, instruction, doctrine.* pl. ܝܘܠܦܢܐ	(66)
251.	ܡܛܐ	v.	*arrive, reach;* Pa^cel ܡܛܝ *attain*	(66)
252.	ܦܝܣ	den.	Gk. πεῖσαι Aph^cel ܐܦܝܣ *persuade, convince*	(66)
253.	ܦܠܚ	v.	*work, labour;* Aph^cel make *serve, caltivate*	(66)
254.	ܚܒܝܒܐ	adj.	*beloved*	(65)
255.	ܠܘܩܒܠ	prep.	*against, near, toward,* w/ ܩܡ *resist, opposite to*	(65)
256.	ܫܪܝܪܐ	adj.	*true, steadfast*	(65)

Words occurring 60 – 64 times

	Syriac	Cat.	Meaning	
257.	ܕܡܘܬܐ	n. f.	*form, image, similitude, type, exemplar, pattern.* pl. ܕܡܘܬܐ	(64)
258.	ܚܕܘܬܐ	n. f.	*joy, gladness*	(64)
259.	ܪܕܐ	v.	*journey, flow, chastise, instruct;* Aph^cel make *flow, supply*	(63)
260.	ܚܪ	v.	*look, behold*	(62)
261.	ܠܡܐ	pron.	*why*	(61)
262.	ܡܚܕܐ	particle	*immediately, at once*	(61)

	Syriac	Cat.	Meaning	
263.	ܣܓܶܕ	v.	*worship, pay homage*	(61)
264.	ܫܡܫ	v.	Paᶜel ܫܰܡܶܫ *minister, serve*	(60)

Words occurring 55 – 59 times

	Syriac	Cat.	Meaning	
265.	ܐܽܘܠܨܳܢܳܐ	n. m.	*oppression, affliction, tribulation.* pl. ܐܽܘܠܨܳܢ̈ܶܐ	(59)
266.	ܐܰܪܒܥܳܐ	num. f.	*four*	(59)
267.	ܚܰܕܬܳܐ	adj.	*new*	(59)
268.	ܟܽܘܪܣܝܳܐ	n. m.	*throne, seat.* pl. ܟܽܘܪ̈ܣܘܳܬܳܐ	(59)
269.	ܣܰܒܪܳܐ	n. m.	*hope*	(59)
270.	ܒܪܶܟ	v.	*kneel*; Paᶜel ܒܰܪܶܟ *bless, bow*	(58)
271.	ܙܕܩ	v.	Paᶜel ܙܰܕܶܩ *justify*; Pᶜal ܙܕܩ *it is right*, part.*fitting*; Paᶜel ܙܰܕܶܩ *approve*	(58)
272.	ܠܶܫܳܢܳܐ	n. m.	*tongue, language.* pl. ܠܶܫܳܢ̈ܶܐ	(58)
273.	ܪܳܡ	v.	*be high*; Aphᶜel ܐܰܪܺܝܡ *exalt*	(58)
274.	ܐܶܢ	particle	*if*	(57)
275.	ܐܶܡܰܬܝ	particle	*when?*	(57)
276.	ܐܰܣܺܝܪܳܐ	pass. ptc. m.	*prisoner*, w/ ܪܰܒ *sergeant, bound*	(57)
277.	ܥܡܰܪ	v.	*dwell*	(57)
278.	ܦܢܳܐ	v.	*return*; Paᶜel ܦܰܢܺܝ *answer, give back*; Aphᶜel ܐܰܦܢܺܝ cause to *turn*	(57)
279.	ܦܪܰܫ	v.	*separate, appoint*	(57)
280.	ܒܛܶܠ	v.	*be idle, cease*, w/ ܠ *care*; Paᶜel ܒܰܛܶܠ *annul*	(56)
281.	ܠܘܩܕܰܡ	particle	*before, formerly*	(56)
282.	ܡܳܐܢܳܐ	n. m.	*vessel, garment, utensil, receptacle.* pl. ܡܳܐܢ̈ܶܐ	(56)
283.	ܡܶܟܺܝܠ	particle	*therefore, now, henceforth*	(56)

	Syriac	Cat.	Meaning	
284.	ܣܥܰܪ v.		*visit, do, effect*	(55)

Words occurring 50 – 54 times

	Syriac	Cat.	Meaning	
285.	ܦܨܳܐ v.		*depart, deliver, save*; Pa^cel *rescue, pursue*; Aph^cel *go away, abstain from*	(54)
286.	ܩܰܪܺܝܒܳܐ adj.		at *hand, near, neighbour*	(54)
287.	ܐ݇ܚܪܳܝܳܐ adj.		*last, extreme*	(53)
288.	ܚܶܟܡܬܳܐ n. f.		*wisdom*	(53)
289.	ܫܰܠܺܝܛܳܐ adj.		*lawful, permitted*, (pl)*magistrates,* (pl)*rulers*	(53)
290.	ܬܡܰܗ v.		Ethpa^cal ܐܶܬܬ݁ܡܰܗ *marvel, be amazed*	(52)
291.	ܚܶܫܽܘܟܳܐ adj.		*dark, darkness* (dark place)	(52)
292.	ܝܰܡܺܝܢܳܐ n. f.		*right*	(52)
293.	ܒܟܽܠܙܒܰܢ idiom		*always*	(52)
294.	ܠܡܳܢܳܐ pron.		*why*	(52)
295.	ܩܰܕܶܡ v.		*go before*	(52)
296.	ܬܶܫܡܶܫܬܳܐ n. f.		*ministration, service, attendance.* pl. ܬܶܫܡܳܫܳܬܳܐ	(52)
297.	ܗܳܪܟܳܐ particle		*here, hence*	(51)
298.	ܙܩܰܦ v.		*crucify, lift up, elevate, erect*	(50)
299.	ܙܪܰܥ v.		*sow*	(50)
300.	ܙܰܪܥܳܐ n. m.		*seed.* pl. ܙܰܪ̈ܥܶܐ	(50)
301.	ܠܒܶܫ v.		*put on, be clothed*; Aph^cel ܐܰܠܒܶܫ *clothe*	(50)

Words occurring 48 – 49 times

	Syriac	Cat.	Meaning	
302.	ܒܰܝܢܳܬ prep.		*between*	(49)
303.	ܚܰܛܳܝܳܐ adj.		*sinner*	(49)

1. WORD FREQUENCY LIST

	Syriac	Cat.	Meaning	
304.	ܚܰܡܫܳܐ	num. f.	*five*	(49)
305.	ܝܺܕܰܥܬܳܐ	n. f.	*knowledge*	(49)
306.	ܒܥܶܠܕܒܳܒܳܐ	n. m.	*adversary*, as prop. n.*Satan*	(49)
307.	ܣܟܠ	v.	Pa^cel make *understand*; Ethpa^cal ܐܶܣܬܰܟܰܠ *understand*	(49)
308.	ܨܠܽܘܬܳܐ	n. f.	*prayer*. pl. ܨܠܰܘ̈ܳܬܳܐ	(49)
309.	ܐܰܠܦܳܐ	num.	*thousand*	(48)
310.	ܘܳܝ	particle	*woe! alas for!*	(48)
311.	ܚܽܘܒ	v.	*be condemned, owe*; Pa^cel ܚܰܝܶܒ *condemn*	(48)
312.	ܛܽܘܒܳܐ	n. m.	*blessedness, beatitude, happiness*. pl. ܛܽܘ̈ܒܶܐ	(48)
313.	ܣܒܰܪܬܳܐ	n. f.	good *tidings*, *Gospel*, *message*	(48)
314.	ܫܺܐܕܳܐ	n. m.	*demon*, evil *spirit*. pl. ܫܺܐܕ̈ܶܐ	(48)

Words occurring 45 – 47 times

	Syriac	Cat.	Meaning	
315.	ܒܢܳܐ	v.	*build*	(47)
316.	ܙܰܕܺܝܩܳܐ	adj.	*righteous, just, worthy*	(47)
317.	ܦܠܰܓ	v.	*divide, distribute*; Ethp^cel ܐܶܬܦܠܶܓ *divide, doubt*	(47)
318.	ܒܰܝܢܰܝ	prep.	*between*	(46)
319.	ܡܗܰܝܡܢܳܐ	n. m.	*believer, believing*. pl. ܡܗܰܝ̈ܡܢܶܐ	(46)
320.	ܡܰܘܗܰܒܬܳܐ	n. f.	*gift*. pl. ܡܰܘ̈ܗܒܳܬܳܐ	(46)
321.	ܡܰܬܠܳܐ	n. m.	*parable, proverb, similitude*. pl. ܡܰܬ̈ܠܶܐ	(46)
322.	ܣܡܰܟ	v.	*support, recline* to eat; Aph^cel *cause to recline*	(46)
323.	ܪܗܶܛ	v.	*run*	(46)
324.	ܐܶܕܢܳܐ	n. f.	*ear*. pl. ܐܶܕ̈ܢܶܐ	(45)
325.	ܐܶܠܦܳܐ	n. f.	*ship, boat*. pl. ܐܶܠ̈ܦܶܐ	(45)

	Syriac	Cat.	Meaning	
326.	ܕܗܘܪ	den.	Shaph^{c}el *glorify*; Eshtaph^{c}al *pride oneself*	(45)
327.	ܚܰܝܳܒܳܐ	adj.	*debtor*	(45)
328.	ܡܚܳܐ	v.	*strike, gird*	(45)
329.	ܡܶܩܰܕܡܳܐ	pass. ptc. m.	*before*, w/ ܩܡ *before, formerly*	(45)

Words occurring 43 – 44 times

	Syriac	Cat.	Meaning	
330.	ܒܰܥܠܳܐ	n. m.	*lord, husband, master.* pl. ܒܰܥܠܶܐ	(44)
331.	ܓܒܳܐ	v.	*choose*; Pa^{c}el *gather, elect, collect* (tribute or tax)	(44)
332.	ܗܳܢܰܘ	pron.	w/ ܗܘ *i.e. that is to say*	(44)
333.	ܙܳܥ	v.	*be shaken, be confused*; Aph^{c}el ܐܰܙܺܝܥ *stir up, trouble, stir*	(44)
334.	ܟܦܰܪ	v.	*deny, refuse*	(44)
335.	ܡܰܠܦܳܢܳܐ	n. m.	*teacher.* pl. ܡܰܠܦܳܢܶܐ	(44)
336.	ܪܢܳܐ	den.	Ethpa^{c}al ܐܶܬܪܰܢܺܝ *think*	(43)

Words occurring 40 – 42 times

	Syriac	Cat.	Meaning	
337.	ܝܰܘܡܳܢܳܐ	n. m.	*to-day*	(42)
338.	ܡܠܰܟ	v.	*counsel, promise*; Ethpa^{c}al *deliberate*; Aph^{c}el ܐܰܡܠܶܟ *reign*	(42)
339.	ܣܢܳܐ	v.	*hate*	(42)
340.	ܥܪܰܩ	v.	*flee*	(42)
341.	ܐܰܠܶܨ	v.	*urge, constrain*	(41)
342.	ܒܟܳܐ	v.	*weep*	(41)
343.	ܒܰܪܬܐ	n. f.	w/ ܡܠܳܐ *utterance, daughter, word.* pl. ܒܢܳܬܐ	(41)

1. WORD FREQUENCY LIST

	Syriac	Cat.	Meaning	
344.	ܙܗܪ	v.	Ethpᶜel take *heed*, w/ ܡܢ *beware of*, w/ ܠ take *care of*; Paᶜel ܙܗܰܪ *warn*	(41)
345.	ܣܳܟܐ	n. f.	*end*	(41)
346.	ܝܩܰܪ	v.	*be heavy, be precious*; Paᶜel *honour*; Aphᶜel make *heavy*	(41)
347.	ܡܫܰܡܫܳܢܐ	n. m.	*minister, servant, attendant.* pl. ܡܫܰܡܫܳܢܐ	(41)
348.	ܢܩܶܦ	v.	*cleave to, follow, adhere*	(41)
349.	ܣܰܡܝܐ	adj.	*blind*	(41)
350.	ܥܝܪ	v.	Ettaphᶜal ܐܬܬܥܺܝܪ *be awake*; Aphᶜel *wake up*; Ettaphᶜal ܐܬܬܥܺܝܪ *watch*; Aphᶜel *arouse*	(41)
351.	ܓܡܰܪ	v.	*perfect, accomplish, mature, fulfil*	(40)
352.	ܕܰܗܒܐ	n. m.	*gold*	(40)
353.	ܙܰܕܺܝܩܽܘܬܐ	n. f.	*righteousness, justness, uprightness*	(40)
354.	ܢܳܚ	v.	*cease, rest*; Aphᶜel ܐܢܺܝܚ *give rest, put off, refresh*	(40)
355.	ܢܰܣܝ	v.	Paᶜel *tempt, prove, try*	(40)
356.	ܫܰܪܟܐ	n. m.	*residue, rest, remainder*	(40)

Words occurring 38 – 39 times

	Syriac	Cat.	Meaning	
357.	ܐܺܝܩܳܪܐ	n. m.	*honour, glory, majesty.* pl. ܐܺܝܩܳܪܐ	(39)
358.	ܐܶܡܪܐ	n. m.	*lamb,* young *sheep.* pl. ܐܶܡܪܐ	(39)
359.	ܣܟܰܠ	v.	*sin, err*	(39)
360.	ܣܺܐܡܐ	n. m.	*silver, money*	(39)
361.	ܟܪܰܟ	v.	*wrap*; Ethpᶜel ܐܬܟܪܰܟ *go around*; Aphᶜel *lead about*	(39)
362.	ܣܦܺܝܢܬܐ	n. f.	*boat, ship, sailing vessel.* pl. ܣܦܺܝܢܬܐ	(39)
363.	ܥܰܘܠܐ	n. m.	*unrighteousness, iniquity.* pl. ܥܰܘܠܐ	(39)

	Syriac	Cat.	Meaning	
364.	ܪ̈ܲܚܡܹܐ	n. m.	*bowels, mercy.* pl. ܪ̈ܲܚܡܹܐ	(39)
365.	ܪܵܡܵܐ	adj.	*high*, w/ ܩܵܠܵܐ *loud voice*	(39)
366.	ܒܥܸܠܕܒܵܒܵܐ	adj.	*enemy*	(38)
367.	ܕܲܓܵܠܵܐ	adj.	*false, liar*	(38)
368.	ܗܲܕܵܡܵܐ	n. m.	*member, limb.* pl. ܗܲܕܵܡܹܐ	(38)
369.	ܡܘܼܠܟܵܢܵܐ	n. m.	*promise.* pl. ܡܘܼܠܟܵܢܹܐ	(38)
370.	ܡܸܣܟܹܢܵܐ	adj.	*poor*	(38)
371.	ܪܘܼܓܙܵܐ	n. m.	*anger, wrath, indignation*	(38)
372.	ܪܡܵܐ	v.	*throw, cast*	(38)
373.	ܬܵܒ	v.	*return, repent*; Aph^cel ܐܲܬܸܒ *answer, vomit*	(38)

Words occurring 35 – 37 times

	Syriac	Cat.	Meaning	
374.	ܒܗܸܬ	v.	*be ashamed*; Aph^cel ܐܲܒܗܸܬ *shame*	(37)
375.	ܚܲܡܪܵܐ	n. m.	*wine*	(37)
376.	ܚܲܟܝܼܡܵܐ	adj.	*wise, prudent, cunning* (words)	(36)
377.	ܦܪܲܥ	v.	*recompense*	(36)
378.	ܩܝܵܡܬܵܐ	n. f.	*resurrection*	(36)
379.	ܫܲܪܝܼܪܵܐܝܼܬ	adv.	*truly*	(36)
380.	ܚܲܒܸܠ	v.	Pa^cel *corrupt, destroy, alter*	(35)
381.	ܚܲܫ	v.	*feel, suffer*	(35)
382.	ܥܗܲܕ	v.	*remember*; Aph^cel *cause to remember*	(35)
383.	ܥܲܬܝܼܪܵܐ	adj.	*rich, wealthy*	(35)
384.	ܦܲܪܨܘܿܦܵܐ	n. m.	Gk. πρόσωπον *face, countenance, person, aspect.* pl. ܦܲܪܨܘܿܦܹܐ	(35)
385.	ܪܒܵܐ	v.	*grow up, increase*; Pa^cel ܪܲܒܝܼ *nourish, cause increase*	(35)
386.	ܫܢܵܐ	v.	*be mad*; Pa^cel ܫܲܢܝܼ *depart, remove*	(35)

1. WORD FREQUENCY LIST

	Syriac	Cat.	Meaning	
387.	ܚܣܢ	v.	*be strong*; Pa^cel ܚܰܣܶܢ *establish*; Aph^cel ܐܰܚܣܶܢ *strengthen, believe*	(35)

Words occurring 33 – 34 times

	Syriac	Cat.	Meaning	
388.	ܐܺܝܢ	particle	*yes, so, truly, yea*	(34)
389.	ܓܕܦ	v.	Pa^cel ܓܰܕܶܦ *blaspheme*	(34)
390.	ܝܛܫ	v.	*sleep*	(34)
391.	ܝܡܐ	v.	*swear*; Aph^cel make *swear*, take an oath	(34)
392.	ܠܟ	pron. m.	w/ ܠܐ *no, not*	(34)
393.	ܦܣܩ	v.	*cut off, cut down*; Pa^cel *break*	(34)
394.	ܪܕܦ	v.	*follow, persecute*	(34)
395.	ܓܙܘܪܬܐ	n. f.	*circumcision*	(33)
396.	ܕܟܪ	v.	Ethp^cel ܐܶܬܕܟܰܪ *remember*; Aph^cel ܐܰܘܕܟܰܪ *remind, make mention of*	(33)
397.	ܟܣܐ	n. m.	*cup*. pl. ܟܳܣܶܐ	(33)
398.	ܥܶܠܬܐ	n. f.	*cause, occasion*	(33)
399.	ܨܒܘܬܐ	n. f.	*thing, matter, affair*. pl. ܨܶܒܘܳܬܐ	(33)
400.	ܫܡܫܐ	n. c.	*sun*	(33)

Words occurring 31 – 32 times

	Syriac	Cat.	Meaning	
401.	ܐܳܦܶܢ	particle	*even if*	(32)
402.	ܕܶܝܢ	particle	*nevertheless, but, yet*	(32)
403.	ܒܰܓܶܠ	particle	*quickly*	(32)
404.	ܩܰܒܪܐ	n. m.	*tomb, sepulchre*. pl. ܩܰܒܪ̈ܐ	(32)
405.	ܐܰܓܪܐ	n. m.	*pay, reward, recompense*. pl. ܐܰܓܪ̈ܐ	(31)
406.	ܕܝܘܐ	n. m.	*devil, demon*. pl. ܕܰܝܘ̈ܐ	(31)

	Syriac	Cat.	Meaning	
407.	ܕܝܰܬܩܺܐ	n. f.	Gk. διαθήκη *testament, covenant*	(31)
408.	ܙܟܐ	v.	*overcome*	(31)
409.	ܛܰܡܐܐ	adj.	*defiled, unclean, impure, filthy*	(31)
410.	ܟܣܐ	v.	*cover, conceal, hide*	(31)
411.	ܡܣܰܝܒܪܳܢܘܬܐ	n. f.	*patience, endurance*	(31)
412.	ܡܰܥܡܘܕܺܝܬܐ	n. f.	*baptism, washing.* pl. ܡܰܥܡܘܕܝܳܬܐ	(31)
413.	ܩܘܪܒܳܢܐ	n. m.	*offering, gift.* pl. ܩܘܪܒܳܢܐ	(31)
414.	ܩܘܫܬܐ	n. m.	*truth, verity*	(31)
415.	ܫܦܰܪ	v.	*please*	(31)

Words occurring 30 times

	Syriac	Cat.	Meaning	
416.	ܐܘܰܢܓܶܠܝܘܢ	n. m.	Gk. εὐαγγέλιον *Gospel*	(30)
417.	ܐܺܝܡܳܡܐ	n. m.	*daytime*	(30)
418.	ܓܰܘ	prep.	*in, within*	(30)
419.	ܚܘܪܒܐ	n. m.	*wilderness, plain, desolation*	(30)
420.	ܝܨܶܦ	v.	*be careful, be anxious, be solicitous*	(30)
421.	ܝܩܶܕ	v.	*burn;* Aph^cel ܐܰܘܩܶܕ *set* (on fire)	(30)
422.	ܟܪܰܗ	v.	*be sick, be weak*	(30)
423.	ܟܫܠ	v.	Ethp^cel *be offended;* Aph^cel *make stumble*	(30)
424.	ܣܓܺܝ	v.	*increase;* Aph^cel ܐܰܣܓܝ *multiply, be great*	(30)
425.	ܣܳܗܕܐ	n. m.	*witness, martyr.* pl. ܣܳܗܕܐ	(30)
426.	ܥܕܰܟܺܝܠ	particle	*yet, still*	(30)
427.	ܫܥܐ	v.	Ethp^cel *play;* Ethpa^cal ܐܶܫܬܰܥܝ *narrate*	(30)

Words occurring 28 – 29 times

	Syriac	Cat.	Meaning	
428.	ܡܲܚܒܪܵܐ	n. m.	*friend, companion, associate, comrade, neighbour.* pl. ܡܲܚܒܪ̈ܐ	(29)
429.	ܟܐܐ	v.	*rebuke, reprove*	(29)
430.	ܟܪܝܗܐ	pass. ptc. m.	*sick, weak* (in faith), *infirm*	(29)
431.	ܡܨܥܬܐ	n. f.	*middle, midst*	(29)
432.	ܢܒܐ	v.	Ethpaᶜal ܐܬܢܲܒܝ *prophesy*	(29)
433.	ܢܓܕ	v.	*lead, drag;* Paᶜel ܢܲܓܸܕ *beat, scourge;* Ethpaᶜal *be beaten, draw, withdraw*	(29)
434.	ܢܗܪ	v.	*shine;* Paᶜel *bring to* light, *explain;* Aphᶜel ܐܲܢܗܲܪ *light*	(29)
435.	ܢܘܢܐ	n. m.	*fish.* pl. ܢܘܼܢ̈ܐ	(29)
436.	ܥܕ	particle	*while, until*	(29)
437.	ܪܵܚܡܵܐ	n. m.	*friend.* pl. ܪ̈ܚܡܐ	(29)
438.	ܐܓܪܬܐ	n. f.	*letter, epistle.* pl. ܐܓܪ̈ܬܐ	(28)
439.	ܐܪܙܐ	n. m.	*mystery.* pl. ܐܪ̈ܙܐ	(28)
440.	ܒܝܐ	v.	Paᶜel ܒܲܝܐ *comfort, encourage*	(28)
441.	ܚܙܘܐ	n. m.	*appearance, aspect, apparition*	(28)
442.	ܟܘܟܒܐ	n. m.	*star, planet.* pl. ܟܘܟܒ̈ܐ	(28)
443.	ܟܘܡܪܐ	n. m.	*priest.* pl. ܟܘܡܪ̈ܐ	(28)
444.	ܟܪܐ	v.	*sorrow;* Paᶜel ܟܲܪܝ *shorten;* Aphᶜel ܐܲܟܪܝ *make* sorry	(28)
445.	ܠܥܣ	v.	*eat, chew*	(28)
446.	ܡܐܟܘܠܬܐ	n. f.	*food.* pl. ܡܐܟܘ̈ܠܬܐ	(28)
447.	ܣܟܐ	v.	Paᶜel *expect, look for*	(28)
448.	ܥܢܢܐ	n. f.	*cloud.* pl. ܥܢ̈ܢܐ	(28)
449.	ܥܪܣܐ	n. f.	*bed, pallet, bier.* pl. ܥܪ̈ܣܬܐ	(28)
450.	ܦܨܚܐ	n. m.	Feast of *Passover*	(28)
451.	ܪܫܝܬܐ	n. f.	*beginning,* (pl)first *fruits.* pl. ܪ̈ܫܝܬܐ	(28)

1. Word Frequency List

Words occurring 26 – 27 times

	Syriac	Cat.	Meaning	
452.	ܐܪܡܠܬܐ	n. f.	*widow.* pl. ܐܪܡܠܬܐ	(27)
453.	ܓܠܝܢܐ	n. m.	*manifestation, revelation, assurance, the* Apocalypse. pl. ܓܠܝܢܐ	(27)
454.	ܕܝܢܐ	n. m.	*judge.* pl. ܕܝܢܐ	(27)
455.	ܟܪܣܐ	n. f.	*belly, womb.* pl. ܟܪܣܬܐ	(27)
456.	ܠܒܘܫܐ	n. m.	*garment.* pl. ܠܒܘܫܐ	(27)
457.	ܡܥܒܪܐ	n. m.	*crossing.* pl. ܡܥܒܪܐ	(27)
458.	ܥܣܪܐ	num.	*ten*	(27)
459.	ܦܬܓܡܐ	n. m.	*word.* pl. ܦܬܓܡܐ	(27)
460.	ܫܘܩܐ	n. m.	*street, marketplace, square, bazaar.* pl. ܫܘܩܐ	(27)
461.	ܫܘܬܦ	v.	*be partaker*	(27)
462.	ܬܐܪܬܐ	n. f.	*conscience.* pl. ܬܐܪܬܐ	(27)
463.	ܐܝܠܢܐ	n. m.	*tree.* pl. ܐܝܠܢܐ	(26)
464.	ܐܡܟܐ	particle	*whence?*	(26)
465.	ܙܩܝܦܐ	n. m.	*cross, the* Cross. pl. ܙܩܝܦܐ	(26)
466.	ܟܪܡܐ	n. m.	*vineyard*	(26)
467.	ܠܐܐ	v.	*toil, labour;* Aphᶜel *tire*	(26)
468.	ܡܟܣܐ	n. m.	*tax collector, publican.* pl. ܡܟܣܐ	(26)
469.	ܥܕܪ	v.	*help, be of* profit, advantage	(26)
470.	ܫܒܩ	v.	Aphᶜel ܐܫܒܩ *allow, permit*	(26)
471.	ܨܠܡܐ	n. m.	*idol, image.* pl. ܨܠܡܐ	(26)
472.	ܩܒܪܐ	n. m.	*tomb, sepulchre, grave.* pl. ܩܒܪܐ	(26)
473.	ܩܕܫ	v.	Paᶜel ܩܕܫ *consecrate, sanctify*	(26)
474.	ܪܓܬܐ	n. f.	*lust.* pl. ܪܓܬܐ	(26)
475.	ܫܬܐ	num. f.	*six*	(26)
476.	ܬܗܪ	v.	*be astonished;* Aphᶜel ܐܬܗܪ *astonish*	(26)

1. Word Frequency List

Words occurring 25 times

	Syriac	Cat.	Meaning	
477.	ܐܟܚܕܐ	particle	*as one, together*	(25)
478.	ܐܪܒܥܝܢ	num.	*forty*	(25)
479.	ܐܫܕ	v.	*pour out*	(25)
480.	ܕܒܚܐ	n. m.	*sacrifice, victim.* pl. ܕܒܚ̈ܐ	(25)
481.	ܕܟܝܐ	adj.	*clean, pure*	(25)
482.	ܙܢܝܘܬܐ	n. f.	*fornication, adultery, harlotry*	(25)
483.	ܝܣܦ	v.	Aph^{c}el ܐܘܣܦ *add, increase*	(25)
484.	ܟܠܐ	v.	*hinder, forbid, restrain*	(25)
485.	ܡܐܐ	num.	*one hundred*	(25)
486.	ܣܝܡܬܐ	n. f.	*treasure, store.* pl. ܣܝ̈ܡܬܐ	(25)
487.	ܥܘܕܪܢܐ	adj.	*expedient, profitable, better*	(25)
488.	ܩܢܛܪܘܢܐ	n. m.	Gk. κεντυρίων *centurion.* pl. ܩܢܛܪ̈ܘܢܐ	(25)

Words occurring 24 times

	Syriac	Cat.	Meaning	
489.	ܓܒܝܐ	pass. ptc. m.	*chosen, elect, approved*	(24)
490.	ܝܒܠ	v.	Aph^{c}el ܐܘܒܠ *conduct, take, lead away;* Ethpa^{c}al ܐܬܝܒܠ *be transmitted*	(24)
491.	ܝܩܝܪܐ	adj.	*heavy, precious*	(24)
492.	ܟܘܪܗܢܐ	n. m.	*sickness, infirmity, ailment, disease.* pl. ܟܘܪ̈ܗܢܐ	(24)
493.	ܡܐܬܝܬܐ	n. f.	*coming, advent*	(24)
494.	ܡܕܒܚܐ	n. m.	*altar.* pl. ܡܕܒ̈ܚܐ	(24)
495.	ܡܚܘܬܐ	n. f.	*wound, plague, stroke.* pl. ܡܚ̈ܘܬܐ	(24)
496.	ܥܕܢܐ	n. m.	*moment, season, time, opportunity.* pl. ܥܕ̈ܢܐ	(24)
497.	ܥܕܥܐܕܐ	n. m.	*feast, festival*	(24)
498.	ܨܡ	v.	*fast*	(24)

25

1. WORD FREQUENCY LIST

	Syriac	Cat.	Meaning	
499.	ܪܰܓ	v.	*desire, covet, lust*	(24)
500.	ܡܥ	v.	Aph{c}el ܐܰܡܥܝ *wash*	(24)
501.	ܫܽܘܒܗܳܪܳܐ	n. m.	*glorying, vainglory, vaunting*	(24)
502.	ܫܬܶܩ	v.	keep *silent, be still*; Pa{c}el ܫܰܬܶܩ *silence*	(24)

Words occurring 22 – 23 times

	Syriac	Cat.	Meaning	
503.	ܒܽܘܝܳܐܳܐ	n. m.	*comfort, encouragement*	(23)
504.	ܟܺܐܢܳܐ	adj.	*upright, just, righteous*	(23)
505.	ܡܰܚܫܰܒܬܳܐ	n. f.	*thought, reasoning, counsel.* pl. ܡܰܚܫܒܳܬܳܐ	(23)
506.	ܣܦܰܩ	v.	*be sufficient, be able, suffice*	(23)
507.	ܥܶܪܒܳܐ	n. m.	*sheep.* pl. ܥܶܪ̈ܒܶܐ	(23)
508.	ܦܽܘܪܩܳܢܳܐ	n. m.	*redemption, salvation, deliverance*	(23)
509.	ܨܰܦܪܳܐ	n. m.	*daybreak, morning.* pl. ܨܰܦܪ̈ܶܐ	(23)
510.	ܪܰܚܺܝܩܳܐ	adj.	*far, distant, remote*	(23)
511.	ܬܝܳܒܽܘܬܳܐ	n. f.	*repentance*	(23)
512.	ܬܟܰܠ	v.	Ethp{c}el *be confident*	(23)
513.	ܒܰܝܢܰܬ	prep.	*between, among*	(22)
514.	ܒܪܺܝܬܳܐ	n. f.	*creation.* pl. ܒܶܪ̈ܝܳܬܳܐ	(22)
515.	ܓܰܒܳܐ	n. m.	*party, side, sect, part* (of a ship)	(22)
516.	ܗܳܟܘܳܬ	particle	*likewise, so*	(22)
517.	ܣܚܽܘܪܳܐ	n. m.	*surroundings, circle, vagrancy*	(22)
518.	ܚܶܪܝܳܢܳܐ	n. m.	*contention, strife, dispute, altercation, contradiction.* pl. ܚܶܪ̈ܝܳܢܶܐ	(22)
519.	ܚܳܬܳܐ	n. f.	*sister.* pl. ܐܰܚܘܳܬܳܐ	(22)
520.	ܛܥܰܡ	v.	*taste*; Ethp{c}el ܐܶܬܛܥܶܡ *be grafted*; Aph{c}el *graft, partake* (of)	(22)
521.	ܛܫܳܐ	v.	*hide oneself, be hidden*; Pa{c}el ܛܰܫܝ *hide*	(22)
522.	ܣܢܶܩ	v.	*need*	(22)

	Syriac	Cat.	Meaning	
523.	ܦܲܠܚܵܐ	n. m.	*servant, worshipper, soldier.* pl. ܦܲܠܚܹ̈ܐ	(22)
524.	ܦܲܫܸܩ	v.	Pa^cel *interpret, expound*	(22)
525.	ܩܲܪܢܵܐ	n. f.	*horn, corner.* pl. ܩܲܪ̈ܢܵܬܵܐ	(22)
526.	ܫܸܬܐܸܣܬܵܐ	n. f.	*foundation.* pl. ܫܸܬܐܸܣ̈ܬܵܐ	(22)
527.	ܬܵܩܸܢ	v.	*be restored*; Pa^cel *restore, prepare*; Aph^cel ܐܲܬܩܸܢ *establish*	(22)

Words occurring 21 times

	Syriac	Cat.	Meaning	
528.	ܐܲܒܕܵܢܵܐ	n. m.	*loss, perdition, waste*	(21)
529.	ܐܸܣܛܪܵܛܝܘܿܛܵܐ	n. m.	Gk. στρατιώτης *soldier.* pl. ܐܸܣܛܪ̈ܵܛܝܘܿܛܹܐ	(21)
530.	ܒܸܣܡܵܐ	n. m.	*ointment, unguent, incense* (censings). pl. ܒܸܣ̈ܡܹܐ	(21)
531.	ܒܚܲܢ	v.	*prove, examine*; Ethpa^cal *consider*	(21)
532.	ܚܸܘܵܪܵܐ	adj.	*white*	(21)
533.	ܚܲܣܝܼܪܵܐ	adj.	*lacking, deficient*	(21)
534.	ܝܲܪܚܵܐ	n. m.	*month.* pl. ܝܲܪ̈ܚܹܐ	(21)
535.	ܟܠܝܘܿܡ	idiom	*everyday*	(21)
536.	ܟܦܸܢ	v.	*hunger*	(21)
537.	ܠܒܘܿܫܵܐ	n. m.	*clothing, dress, apparel.* pl. ܠܒܘܿ̈ܫܹܐ	(21)
538.	ܡܲܟܝܼܟܵܐ	adj.	*humble, lowly, mild, gentle*	(21)
539.	ܢܘܼܟܪܵܝܵܐ	adj.	*strange, foreign, alien*	(21)
540.	ܢܸܣܝܘܿܢܵܐ	n. m.	*trial, temptation.* pl. ܢܸܣ̈ܝܘܿܢܹܐ	(21)
541.	ܣܘܿܓܵܐܐ	n. m.	*multitude, abundance*	(21)
542.	ܣܲܐܸܒ	v.	Pa^cel ܣܲܐܸܒ *defile*	(21)
543.	ܣܲܟܠܘܼܬܵܐ	n. f.	*foolishness, transgression, error,* *trespass, wrong-doing, sin.* pl. ܣܲܟ̈ܠܘܵܬܵܐ	(21)
544.	ܥܘܼܬܪܵܐ	n. m.	*wealth, riches*	(21)
545.	ܦܪܲܝ	v.	Pa^cel ܦܲܪܝܼ *deliver*	(21)

	Syriac	Cat.	Meaning	
546.	ܬܹܬܐ	n. f.	*fig, fig tree.* pl. ܬܐܢܹܐ	(21)

Words occurring 20 times

	Syriac	Cat.	Meaning	
547.	ܐܝܟܡܐ	prep.	*like as*	(20)
548.	ܐܣܘܪܐ	n. m.	*bond, fetter, chain.* pl. ܐܣܘ̈ܪܐ	(20)
549.	ܒܢܝܢܐ	n. m.	*edification, building.* pl. ܒܢܝ̈ܢܐ	(20)
550.	ܚܕܝ	v.	*be merry;* Paᶜel *anoint;* Ethpaᶜal ܐܬܚܕܝ *live merrily, live joyfully, be rejoice*	(20)
551.	ܓܙܪ	v.	*cut, circumcise*	(20)
552.	ܕܝܢܪܐ	n. m.	Gk. δηνάριον *denarius.* pl. ܕܝ̈ܢܪܐ	(20)
553.	ܗܓܡܘܢܐ	n. m.	Gk. ἡγεμών *governor, prefect.* pl. ܗܓ̈ܡܘܢܐ	(20)
554.	ܚܣܝܢܐ	adj.	*strong, mighty, robust, potentate*	(20)
555.	ܚܠܝܡܐ	adj.	*whole, healthy, sound, strong*	(20)
556.	ܚܠܦ	v.	Paᶜel *change, transmute;* Shaphᶜel *change, alter*	(20)
557.	ܚܡܬܐ	n. f.	*anger, wrath, fury*	(20)
558.	ܚܨܕ	v.	*reap*	(20)
559.	ܣܦܩ	pron. m.	w/ ܕ *it suffices*	(20)
560.	ܟܝܠܝܪܟܐ	n. m.	Gk. χιλίαρχος *capt of a thousand.* pl. ܟܝ̈ܠܝܪܟܐ	(20)
561.	ܡܬܘܡ	particle	*always, ever*	(20)
562.	ܢܒܝܘܬܐ	n. f.	*prophecy.* pl. ܢܒܝ̈ܘܬܐ	(20)
563.	ܣܠܐ	v.	*despise, reject*	(20)
564.	ܣܪܩ	v.	Paᶜel ܣܪܩ *make empty, make void*	(20)
565.	ܥܘܪܠܘܬܐ	n. f.	*uncircumcision*	(20)
566.	ܥܩܪܐ	n. m.	*root.* pl. ܥܩ̈ܪܐ	(20)
567.	ܪܓܡ	v.	*stone*	(20)
568.	ܪܥܝܐ	n. m.	*shepherd, pastor.* pl. ܪ̈ܥܘܬܐ	(20)

	Syriac	Cat.	Meaning	
569.	ܫܠܐ	v.	*cease, be quiet*; Paᶜel ܫܰܠܺܝ *quiet, stop*	(20)

Words occurring 19 times

	Syriac	Cat.	Meaning	
570.	ܐܳܟܶܠ ܩܰܪܨܳܐ	n. m.	*accuser, calumniator*	(19)
571.	ܒܰܕܰܪ	v.	*scatter, disperse, spend, waste, scare away*	(19)
572.	ܓܽܘܕܳܦܳܐ	n. m.	*blasphemy.* pl. ܓܽܘܕܳܦ̈ܶܐ	(19)
573.	ܓܳܪ	v.	commit *adultery*	(19)
574.	ܙܰܝܬܳܐ	n. m.	*olive,* w/ ܛܽܘܪܳܐ *Mount of Olives.* pl. ܙܰܝ̈ܬܶܐ	(19)
575.	ܚܒܳܠܳܐ	n. m.	*corruption, decay.* pl. ܚܒ̈ܳܠܶܐ	(19)
576.	ܚܦܛ	v.	Paᶜel ܚܰܦܶܛ *exhort, incite, encourage*	(19)
577.	ܗܘܐ	v.	*exist*; Paᶜel *reprove, rebuke*; Aphᶜel *create*	(19)
578.	ܟܠܺܝܠܳܐ	n. m.	*crown, wreath.* pl. ܟܠܺܝ̈ܠܶܐ	(19)
579.	ܡܰܕܒܪܳܐ	n. m.	*wilderness, desert*	(19)
580.	ܡܟ	v.	*be humble*; Paᶜel ܡܰܟܶܟ *humble*	(19)
581.	ܥܠܰܝܡܳܐ	n. m.	young *man, young man, youth.* pl. ܥܠܰܝ̈ܡܶܐ	(19)
582.	ܦܳܬܽܘܪܳܐ	n. m.	*table.* pl. ܦܳܬܽܘܖ̈ܶܐ	(19)
583.	ܩܶܢܝܳܢܳܐ	n. m.	*possession, goods, property, substance.* pl. ܩܶܢܝ̈ܳܢܶܐ	(19)
584.	ܩܪܳܒܳܐ	n. m.	*war, battle, fighting.* pl. ܩܖ̈ܳܒܶܐ	(19)
585.	ܪܰܡܫܳܐ	n. m.	*evening*	(19)
586.	ܪܥܳܐ	v.	*feed, tend*	(19)
587.	ܫܰܒܛܳܐ	n. m.	*rod, sceptre, tribe,* w/ ܒ̈ܶܝܬ ܕܰܝ̈ܢܶܐ *magistrates, staff.* pl. ܫܰܒ̈ܛܶܐ	(19)
588.	ܫܽܘܒܩܳܢܳܐ	n. m.	*remission, forgiveness, repudiation, release*	(19)

1. WORD FREQUENCY LIST

Words occurring 17 – 18 times

	Syriac	Cat.	Meaning	
589.	ܒܘܪܟܬܐ	n. f.	*blessing, benediction.* pl. ܒܘܪܟܬܐ	(18)
590.	ܕܪܟ	v.	Aphᶜel ܐܕܪܟ *overtake, comprehend*	(18)
591.	ܚܐܪܐ	adj.	*free, noble, freedman*	(18)
592.	ܚܣܢ	den.	Paᶜel ܚܣܢ *strengthen, confirm*	(18)
593.	ܚܨܐ	n. m.	*back* (of the body), *loins.* pl. ܚܨܝܢ	(18)
594.	ܝܪܬ	v.	*inherit, heir*	(18)
595.	ܡܕܥܐ	n. m.	*knowledge, understanding, mind.* pl. ܡܕܥܐ	(18)
596.	ܡܘܡܬܐ	n. f.	*oath, curse.* pl. ܡܘܡܬܐ	(18)
597.	ܡܢܝܢܐ	n. m.	*number*	(18)
598.	ܡܪܚ	den.	Aphᶜel ܐܡܪܚ *dare*	(18)
599.	ܢܟܠܐ	n. m.	*deceit, guilt, trickery, guile, craft.* pl. ܢܟܠܐ	(18)
600.	ܣܒܥ	v.	*be full, be satisfied;* Paᶜel ܣܒܥ *satisfy*	(18)
601.	ܣܟܠܐ	adj.	*foolish*	(18)
602.	ܦܠܚܐ	n. m.	*husbandman, tiller, cultivator.* pl. ܦܠܚܐ	(18)
603.	ܦܫܛ	v.	Tr. *stretch out,* Int. *be straight*	(18)
604.	ܨܝܕ	prep.	*near, with, at*	(18)
605.	ܩܨܐ	v.	*break* (bread)	(18)
606.	ܪܒܐ	n. m.	*rabbi, master*	(18)
607.	ܪܓܬܐ	n. f.	*desire, lust*	(18)
608.	ܫܕܪ	v.	*send*	(18)
609.	ܐܘ	particle	*O! Oh!*	(17)
610.	ܒܨܪ	v.	*decrease, be less, be inferior*	(17)
611.	ܓܢܒܐ	n. m.	*thief.* pl. ܓܢܒܐ	(17)
612.	ܚܛܦ	v.	*seize, snatch*	(17)
613.	ܝܪܬܘܬܐ	n. f.	*inheritance*	(17)
614.	ܟܒܪ	particle	*perhaps, long ago*	(17)

1. Word Frequency List

	Syriac	Cat.	Meaning	
615.	ܟܝܢܐ	n. m.	*nature.* pl. ܟܝܢ̈ܐ	(17)
616.	ܡܫܟܢܐ	n. m.	*tabernacle, habitation, tent.* pl. ܡܫܟ̈ܢܐ	(17)
617.	ܥܛܦ	v.	*turn;* Paᶜel *clothe*	(17)
618.	ܫܛ	v.	*be despised;* Paᶜel ܫܛ *despise*	(17)
619.	ܩܢܐ	v.	*obtain*	(17)
620.	ܪܓܙ	v.	*be angry;* Aphᶜel *provoke*	(17)
621.	ܙܝܥ	v.	*stir up, trouble*	(17)
622.	ܬܒܥ	v.	*avenge, require*	(17)
623.	ܬܘܕܝܬܐ	n. f.	*confession, thanksgiving, avowal.* pl. ܬܘܕ̈ܝܬܐ	(17)

Words occurring 16 times

	Syriac	Cat.	Meaning	
624.	ܒܙܚ	den.	Paᶜel *mock, deride*	(16)
625.	ܒܣܬܪܐ	particle	the *back, behind, backwards*	(16)
626.	ܚܕ̈ܕܐ	pron. m.	*one another*	(16)
627.	ܚܣ	particle	*God forbid, let it not be*	(16)
628.	ܚܣܡܐ	n. m.	*envy, emulation, jealousy*	(16)
629.	ܚܪܫܐ	adj.	*dumb, mute, deaf*	(16)
630.	ܚܫܐ	n. m.	*feeling, suffering, experience, affection, passion, lust.* pl. ܚܫ̈ܐ	(16)
631.	ܝܪܬܐ	n. m.	*heir.* pl. ܝܪ̈ܬܐ	(16)
632.	ܟܝ	particle	*now, indeed, perhaps*	(16)
633.	ܡܟܝܠ	particle	*then, therefore*	(16)
634.	ܡܚܝܢܐ	adj.	*life-giving, Saviour, preserver*	(16)
635.	ܡܢܘ	pron. m.	w/ ܡܢܐ *what is this?*	(16)
636.	ܡܢܬܐ	n. f.	*part, portion.* pl. ܡܢ̈ܬܐ	(16)
637.	ܡܨܝܕܬܐ	n. f.	*net.* pl. ܡܨܝܕ̈ܬܐ	(16)
638.	ܢܗܝܪܐ	adj.	*light, bright, (pl.)luminaries, illumined*	(16)

	Syriac	Cat.	Meaning	
639.	ܣܥܪܐ	n. m.	*hair.* pl. ܣܥ̈ܪܐ	(16)
640.	ܓܙܪܐ	n. f.	*flock*	(16)
641.	ܦܨܚܐ	n. f.	*bird.* pl. ܦܨܚܐ	(16)
642.	ܩܒܪ	v.	*bury;* Pa‘el *heap up*	(16)
643.	ܪܒܘܬܐ	n. f.	*greatness,* w/ ܟܗܢܘ *high priesthood.* pl. ܪ̈ܒܘܬܐ	(16)
644.	ܫܘܠܡܐ	n. m.	*end, consummation, fulfilment, fulness*	(16)
645.	ܫܘܬܦܘܬܐ	n. f.	*partnership, fellowship, participation, communion*	(16)
646.	ܫܠܝܐ	n. m.	*calm, silence,* w/ ܡܢ *suddenly, cessation, lull, quietness*	(16)
647.	ܫܢܩ	v.	Pa‘el *torment*	(16)
648.	ܫܪܓܐ	n. m.	*light, lamp, wick.* pl. ܫܪ̈ܓܐ	(16)

Words occurring 15 times

	Syriac	Cat.	Meaning	
649.	ܐܟܣܢܝܐ	adj.	Gk. ξένος *guest, stranger*	(15)
650.	ܒܪܐ	v.	*create, make*	(15)
651.	ܒܬܪܟܢ	particle	*afterwards*	(15)
652.	ܓܢܒ	v.	*steal*	(15)
653.	ܕܪܬܐ	n. f.	*court, atrium*	(15)
654.	ܗܪ	v.	*suffer harm;* Aph‘el *harm, hurt*	(15)
655.	ܚܫܡܝܬܐ	n. f.	*supper;* pl. *feasts.* pl. ܚܫܡ̈ܝܬܐ	(15)
656.	ܚܬܢܐ	n. m.	*bridegroom*	(15)
657.	ܝܘܒܠܐ	n. m.	*kin, family, birth, nationality*	(15)
658.	ܛܠܡ	v.	*reject, deny, wrong*	(15)
659.	ܡܟܝܟܘܬܐ	n. f.	*humility, meekness, lowliness, condescension, courtesy*	(15)
660.	ܡܥܡܕܢܐ	n. m.	*baptizer*	(15)
661.	ܢܗܪܐ	n. m.	*river.* pl. ܢܗܪ̈ܘܬܐ	(15)

1. WORD FREQUENCY LIST

	Syriac	Cat.	Meaning	
662.	ܨܗܝ	v.	*be thirsty*	(15)
663.	ܨܠܡܐ	n. m.	*image, portrait, figure*	(15)
664.	ܩܝܣܐ	n. m.	*timber, tree, wood.* pl. ܩܝܣ̈ܐ	(15)
665.	ܩܢܘܡܐ	n. m.	*person, individual* (self), *substance*	(15)
666.	ܩܪܨܐ	n. m.	w/ ܐܟܠ *accuse.* pl. ܩܪ̈ܨܐ	(15)
667.	ܩܫܝܐ	adj.	*hard, strong, rough*	(15)
668.	ܪܘܚܩܐ	n. m.	*far place, far place,* w/ ܡܢ *from afar*	(15)
669.	ܪܢܐ	v.	*meditate, think, consider, plan*	(15)
670.	ܫܝܘܠ	n. f.	*sheol, place of the dead*	(15)
671.	ܬܕܡܘܪܬܐ	n. f.	*wonder, marvel, prodigy.* pl. ܬܕܡܪ̈ܬܐ	(15)
672.	ܬܠܝܬܝܐ	n. m.	*third*	(15)
673.	ܬܚܘܡܐ	n. m.	*boundary, border, confine.* pl. ܬܚܘܡ̈ܐ	(15)
674.	ܬܫܥ	num.	*nine*	(15)

Words occurring 14 times

	Syriac	Cat.	Meaning	
675.	ܐܪܟܘܢܐ	n. m.	Gk. ἄρχων *ruler, magistrate, captain.* pl. ܐܪ̈ܟܘܢܐ	(14)
676.	ܒܘܪܟܐ	n. f.	*knee.* pl. ܒܘܪ̈ܟܐ	(14)
677.	ܒܬܘܠܬܐ	n. f.	*virgin.* pl. ܒܬܘ̈ܠܬܐ	(14)
678.	ܓܙܪܬܐ	n. f.	*island*	(14)
679.	ܕܡܝܐ	n. m.	*price.* pl. ܕܡ̈ܝܐ	(14)
680.	ܙܒܘܪܐ	n. m.	*bowl, platter*	(14)
681.	ܙܕܘܩܝܐ	adj.	*Sadducee*	(14)
682.	ܙܕܩܬܐ	n. f.	*alms, almsgiving, charity.* pl. ܙܕܩ̈ܬܐ	(14)
683.	ܚܕܪ	v.	*surround, wander, beg;* Aphᶜel ܐܚܕܪ *hedge*	(14)
684.	ܚܙܝܪܐ	n. m.	*swine.* pl. ܚܙܝܪ̈ܐ	(14)
685.	ܚܠܡ	v.	Ethpᶜel ܐܬܚܠܡ *be cured;* Aphᶜel ܐܚܠܡ *cure*	(14)

34   1. WORD FREQUENCY LIST

	Syriac	Cat.	Meaning	
686.	ܣܥܪܐ	n. m.	*leaven*	(14)
687.	ܚܣܪ	v.	*lack, lose*	(14)
688.	ܣܝܦܐ	n. c.	*sword, slaughter, ploughshare*	(14)
689.	ܛܢܦܘܬܐ	n. f.	*uncleaness, impurity.* pl. ܛܢܦ̈ܘܬܐ	(14)
690.	ܥܘܠܐ	n. m.	*infant, child, babe.* pl. ܥܘ̈ܠܐ	(14)
691.	ܟܐܒܐ	n. m.	*pain, suffering, disease.* pl. ܟܐ̈ܒܐ	(14)
692.	ܟܘܒܐ	n. m.	*thorn.* pl. ܟ̈ܘܒܐ	(14)
693.	ܟܦܢܐ	n. m.	*hunger, famine.* pl. ܟ̈ܦܢܐ	(14)
694.	ܟܘܬܡܐ	n. m.	*spot, blemish.* pl. ܟ̈ܘܬܡܐ	(14)
695.	ܡܨܐ	v.	*be able*	(14)
696.	ܡܫܚ	v.	*anoint*	(14)
697.	ܡܫܚܐ	n. m.	*ointment, oil, unguent*	(14)
698.	ܡܫܪܝܐ	pass. ptc. m.	*sick, paralytic*	(14)
699.	ܡܫܬܘܬܐ	n. f.	*festivity,* wedding *feast, symposium*	(14)
700.	ܣܝܦܐ	n. m.	*sword.* pl. ܣ̈ܝܦܐ	(14)
701.	ܣܟܠ	den.	Aphᶜel ܐܣܟܠ *offend, wrong*	(14)
702.	ܣܡܟܐ	n. m.	*seat* at a meal, *feast, company* at a meal. pl. ܣܡ̈ܟܐ	(14)
703.	ܣܦܪܐ	n. m.	*book, scroll, roll.* pl. ܣܦܖ̈ܐ	(14)
704.	ܥܘܠܐ	adj.	*unjust, unrighteous*	(14)
705.	ܦܠܐܬܐ	n. f.	*comparison, parable.* pl. ܦܠܐ̈ܬܐ	(14)
706.	ܩܕܝܫܘܬܐ	n. f.	*holiness, sanctification*	(14)
707.	ܩܘܟܐ	n. m.	*rock.* pl. ܩܘ̈ܟܐ	(14)
708.	ܫܘܬܦܐ	n. m.	*partaker, partner.* pl. ܫܘܬ̈ܦܐ	(14)
709.	ܫܝܢܐ	n. m.	*peace, tranquility*	(14)
710.	ܫܢܐ	n. f.	*tooth, ivory, tusk.* pl. ܫ̈ܢܐ	(14)
711.	ܫܩܐ	v.	Aphᶜel ܐܫܩܝ *water,* give to *drink*	(14)
712.	ܬܘܩܠܬܐ	n. f.	*offense, stumbling block*	(14)
713.	ܬܘܪܐ	n. m.	*ox, steer.* pl. ܬܘܖ̈ܐ	(14)

	Syriac	Cat.	Meaning	
714.	ܬܰܢܺܝܢܳܐ	n. m.	*dragon, monster*	(14)
715.	ܬܰܢܳܢ	particle	*here*	(14)
716.	ܬܰܪܥܺܝܬܳܐ	n. f.	*mind, thought, imagination.* pl. ܬܰܪ̈ܥܝܳܬܳܐ	(14)

Words occurring 13 times

	Syriac	Cat.	Meaning	
717.	ܒܺܝܫܽܘܬܳܐ	n. f.	*wickedness, wrong-doing*	(13)
718.	ܒܣܳܐ	v.	*despise*; Aph^cel *despise, neglect*	(13)
719.	ܒܰܣܺܝܡܽܘܬܳܐ	n. f.	*pleasantness, gentleness, kindliness, pleasure, gladness*	(13)
720.	ܕܪܰܫ	v.	Pa^cel *train, debate, argue, question, dispute*	(13)
721.	ܙܰܘܥܳܐ	n. m.	*earthquake, shaking, agitation, commotion.* pl. ܙܰܘ̈ܥܶܐ	(13)
722.	ܙܥܰܩ	v.	*cry out*	(13)
723.	ܚܶܘܝܳܐ	n. m.	*serpent.* pl. ܚܶܘܘܳܬܳܐ	(13)
724.	ܚܰܣܺܝܪܽܘܬܳܐ	n. f.	*want, need, defect*	(13)
725.	ܚܪܐ	v.	Ethp^cel *hold on to, affirm, strive, argue, contend*	(13)
726.	ܚܪܪ	v.	Pa^cel ܚܪܪ set *free*	(13)
727.	ܚܫܰܚ	v.	*be useful*; Ethpa^cal ܐܶܬܚܰܫܰܚ *use, adapt, apply*	(13)
728.	ܛܰܒܥܳܐ	n. m.	*seal, stamp.* pl. ܛܰܒ̈ܥܶܐ	(13)
729.	ܡܐܶܠ	v.	*be tired, be weary*; Aph^cel *neglect, tedious*	(13)
730.	ܡܫܽܘܚܬܳܐ	n. f.	*measure, proportion*	(13)
731.	ܢܨܰܒ	v.	*plant*	(13)
732.	ܢܫܰܩ	v.	*kiss*	(13)
733.	ܣܰܘܟܳܐ	n. f.	*branch.* pl. ܣܰܘ̈ܟܶܐ	(13)
734.	ܣܽܘܥܪܳܢܳܐ	n. m.	*deed, visitation, event, happening, matter, affair.* pl. ܣܽܘܥܪ̈ܳܢܶܐ	(13)

	Syriac	Cat.	Meaning	
735.	ܐܠܚܽܡܟܐ	n. f.	*food, sustenance*	(13)
736.	ܣܡܳܠܐ	n. f.	*left*	(13)
737.	ܐܡܒܘܕܽܐ	n. f.	*service, bondage*	(13)
738.	ܥܺܝܠܐ	n. m.	*colt, young animal*	(13)
739.	ܥܰܡܠܐ	n. m.	*toil, labour.* pl. ܥܡܠܐ̈	(13)
740.	ܦܳܥܠܐ	n. m.	*labourer, worker.* pl. ܦܥܠܐ̈	(13)
741.	ܩܰܝܳܡܐ	adj.	*remaining, abiding, lasting, valid*	(13)
742.	ܪܛܶܢ	v.	*murmur*	(13)
743.	ܪܶܫܝܳܢܐ	n. m.	*accusation, blame,* w/ ܕܠܐ *blameless.* pl. ܪܫܝܢܐ̈	(13)
744.	ܫܓܽܘܫܝܐ	n. m.	*riot, uproar, tumult, commotion.* pl. ܫܓܘܫܝܐ̈	(13)
745.	ܫܽܘܘܕܳܝܐ	n. m.	*promise.* pl. ܫܘܘܕܝܐ̈	(13)
746.	ܬܰܪܢܳܓܠܐ	n. m.	*cock*	(13)

Words occurring 12 times

	Syriac	Cat.	Meaning	
747.	ܐܶܣܟܺܡܐ	n. m.	Gk. σχῆμα *form, fashion, figure*	(12)
748.	ܒܺܝܫܳܐܝܬ	adv.	*badly, sorely*	(12)
749.	ܒܠܰܥ	v.	*swallow up, be struck, be beaten, be smitten*	(12)
750.	ܒܳܥܽܘܬܐ	n. f.	*prayer, petition.* pl. ܒܥܘܬܐ̈	(12)
751.	ܒܰܪܳܝܐ	adj.	*outer, without*	(12)
752.	ܕܢܰܚ	v.	*rise, shine;* Aph^cel *make rise, dawn*	(12)
753.	ܙܳܢܺܝܬܐ	n. f.	*harlot, prostitute.* pl. ܙܢܝܬܐ̈	(12)
754.	ܙܶܩܐ	n. f.	*wineskin, leather bag.* pl. ܙܩܐ̈	(12)
755.	ܚܶܛܬܐ	n. f.	*wheat.* pl. ܚܛܐ̈	(12)
756.	ܚܰܢܦܐ	adj.	*godless, Gentile, heathen, foreigner, profane*	(12)
757.	ܚܢܰܩ	v.	*choke, strangle;* Pa^cel *drown*	(12)

1. WORD FREQUENCY LIST

	Syriac	Cat.	Meaning	
758.	ܣܪܘܿܐ	n. m.	*harvest*	(12)
759.	ܛܢ	v.	*be eager, be jealous*; Aph^cel *provoke jealousy*	(12)
760.	ܛܢܢܐ	n. m.	*jealousy, zeal.* pl. ܛܢܢܐ	(12)
761.	ܛܥܢ	v.	*bear, carry*; Aph^cel *make carry*	(12)
762.	ܝܒܫ	v.	*dry up, wither*; Aph^cel *cause to wither*	(12)
763.	ܝܕܝܥܐ	pass. ptc. m.	*apparent, known, certain* (one), *notable*	(12)
764.	ܝܘܬܪܢܐ	n. m.	*lucre, advantage, profit, gain, abundance.* pl. ܝܘܬܪܢܐ	(12)
765.	ܝܠܕܐ	n. m.	*birth, offspring, fruit* (of the vine). pl. ܝܠܕܐ	(12)
766.	ܝܡܛ	v.	Aph^cel ܐܘܫܛ *stretch out*	(12)
767.	ܟܟܪܐ	n. f.	*talent.* pl. ܟܟܪܐ	(12)
768.	ܟܣܣ	v.	Ethp^cel *be reproved*; Aph^cel *rebuke, admonish, convict*	(12)
769.	ܟܬܫ	v.	*strike*; Ethpa^cal *strive, endeavor, fight*	(12)
770.	ܡܚܪ	adv.	*tomorrow*	(12)
771.	ܡܛܪܐ	n. m.	*rain*	(12)
772.	ܡܟܐ	particle	of place:*hence,* w/ ܘܡܟܐ *here and there,* w/ ܡܢ *from this time*	(12)
773.	ܡܢܪܬܐ	n. f.	*candlestick, lamp-stand.* pl. ܡܢܪܬܐ	(12)
774.	ܡܣܒܐ	n. m.	*taking,* w/ ܐܦܐ *hypocrisy, acceptance*	(12)
775.	ܢܓܪ	v.	Aph^cel ܐܢܓܪ *be prolonged, make long,* w/ ܪܘܚܐ *be patient*	(12)
776.	ܢܝܚܬܐ	n. f.	*rest, repose, leisure, recreation.* pl. ܢܝܚܬܐ	(12)
777.	ܩܕܡ	particle	*before*	(12)
778.	ܥܝܕܐ	n. m.	*custom, manner.* pl. ܥܝܕܐ	(12)
779.	ܥܬܝܩܐ	adj.	*old, ancient*	(12)
780.	ܥܬܪ	v.	*grow rich*; Aph^cel *make rich*	(12)

	Syriac	Cat.	Meaning	
781.	ܦܽܘܠܳܓܳܐ	n. f.	*division, portion, separation.* pl. ܦܽܘܠܳܓ̈ܶܐ	(12)
782.	ܩܛܺܝܪܳܐ	n. m.	*violence, necessity, force*	(12)
783.	ܩܰܢܝܳܐ	n. m.	*pen, cane, reed*	(12)
784.	ܩܪܶܐ	pass. ptc. m.	*called, being by vocation*	(12)
785.	ܪܶܒܽܘܬܳܐ	n. f.	*myriad, thousand.* pl. ܪܶܒܘܳܬ̈ܳܐ	(12)
786.	ܪܰܥܡܳܐ	n. m.	*thunder.* pl. ܪܰܥܡ̈ܶܐ	(12)
787.	ܫܽܘܪܳܝܳܐ	n. m.	*beginning*	(12)
788.	ܫܺܫܰܠܬܳܐ	n. f.	*chain.* pl. ܫܺܫܠ̈ܳܬܳܐ	(12)
789.	ܬܡܳܢܝܳܐ	num. m.	*eight*	(12)
790.	ܬܶܢܳܢܳܐ	n. m.	*smoke*	(12)

Words occurring 11 times

	Syriac	Cat.	Meaning	
791.	ܐܰܚܺܝܕܳܐ	pass. ptc. m.	*holder, closed*	(11)
792.	ܐܰܡܶܢ	v.	Aphᶜel ܐܰܡܶܢ *tarry, delay*	(11)
793.	ܐܰܪܰܥ	v.	*encounter, meet*	(11)
794.	ܒܶܗܬܬܳܐ	n. f.	*shame*	(11)
795.	ܒܺܝܡ	n. f.	Gk. βῆμα *judgement-seat, tribunal*	(11)
796.	ܓܺܗܰܢܳܐ	n.	*hell, Gehenna*	(11)
797.	ܓܡܺܝܪܳܐ	pass. ptc. m.	*perfect, mature*	(11)
798.	ܕܰܟܡܳܐ	n. m.	*guard, attendant, servant, officer.* pl. ܕܰܟܡ̈ܶܐ	(11)
799.	ܕܶܟܪܳܐ	adj.	*male*	(11)
800.	ܕܶܡܥܬܳܐ	n. f.	*tear.* pl. ܕܶܡ̈ܥܶܐ	(11)
801.	ܕܽܘܘܳܟܳܐ	n. m.	*conduct, behavior, ways, manner of life.* pl. ܕܽܘܘܳܟ̈ܶܐ	(11)

1. WORD FREQUENCY LIST   39

	Syriac	Cat.	Meaning	
802.	ܡܢܚܡܢܐ	n. m.	*compassion, mercy, favour*	(11)
803.	ܚܣ	v.	*spare, pity*	(11)
804.	ܚܫܟ	v.	grow *dark*; Aph^cel *darken*; Ettaph^cal *be darkened*	(11)
805.	ܛܡܐܐ	adj.	*unclean, impure*	(11)
806.	ܝܐܝܐ	adj.	*due, becoming, seemly, congruous, decorous*	(11)
807.	ܝܡܬܐ	n. f.	*lake*	(11)
808.	ܟܐ	particle	*here*	(11)
809.	ܟܘܬܝܢܐ	n. f.	*coat*, linen *garment, tunic.* pl. ܟܘܬܝܢܝܬܐ	(11)
810.	ܟܬܢܐ	n. m.	*linen sheet.* pl. ܟܬܢ̈ܐ	(11)
811.	ܟܬܪ	v.	Pa^cel ܟܬܰܪ *remain, abide, continue, wait*	(11)
812.	ܡܓܪܢܘܬܐ	n. f.	*long suffering*	(11)
813.	ܡܠܟܐ	n. m.	*counsel.* pl. ܡܠܟ̈ܐ	(11)
814.	ܡܦܩܐ	n. m.	w/ ܡܠܬܐ *defense, answer*	(11)
815.	ܡܫܚܠܦܐ	pass. ptc. m.	*different, diverse, various*	(11)
816.	ܡܬܘܡ	particle	*always, ever*	(11)
817.	ܢܩܫ	v.	*knock*	(11)
818.	ܣܩܘܒܠܐ	adj.	*contrary, adverse*	(11)
819.	ܣܪܝܩܐ	pass. ptc. m.	*vain, empty, vacant, void*	(11)
820.	ܥܒܪܐܝܬ	adv.	in *Aramaic*, only in Rev.in *Hebrew*	(11)
821.	ܥܡܘܪܐ	n. m.	*dweller, inhabitant.* pl. ܥܡ̈ܘܪܐ	(11)
822.	ܥܣܪܝܢ	num.	*twenty*	(11)
823.	ܦܪܘܩܐ	n. m.	*Saviour, deliverer*	(11)
824.	ܩܪܙ	v.	*rend, burst*; Ethpa^cal w/ ܥܠ *break out against*	(11)
825.	ܩܛܠܐ	n. m.	*murder, slaughter.* pl. ܩܛ̈ܠܐ	(11)
826.	ܩܝܢܕܘܢܘܣ	n. f.	Gk. κίνδυνος *peril, danger*	(11)
827.	ܩܪܩܦܬܐ	n. f.	*head, skull.* pl. ܩܪ̈ܩܦܬܐ	(11)

40   1. WORD FREQUENCY LIST

	Syriac	Cat.	Meaning	
828.	زەد	v.	agitate; Ethp^cel be frightened; Saph^cel hurry	(11)
829.	زجّد	v.	mount, ride; Ethpa^cal be constructed; Aph^cel make ride	(11)
830.	زَهِمُا	adj.	impious, wicked, ungodly	(11)
831.	ݲلحݝ	num.	thirty	(11)

Words occurring 10 times

	Syriac	Cat.	Meaning	
832.	أَجُونَا	n. m.	Gk. ἀγών contest, conflict	(10)
833.	أَجَّا	n. m.	roof, housetop. pl. أَجّا	(10)
834.	أُومحَا	n. c.	people, nation. pl. أُمَّحَا	(10)
835.	اِسُنُا	adj.	cousin; f. kinswoman, kinsman	(10)
836.	أَكَه	particle	w/ اَكَا where is (he)?	(10)
837.	أَهِسُا	adj.	constant	(10)
838.	أَهِسَانَيڬ	adv.	assiduously, constantly	(10)
839.	أَحجَا	n. f.	handmaid, female bond-servant. pl. أَهجَوهِا	(10)
840.	دَرّا	v.	search, examine	(10)
841.	حلد	den.	Ethp^cel أِلحَند be entrusted; Aph^cel commit, commend	(10)
842.	دلي	v.	Pa^cel lie, speak falsely	(10)
843.	وَحَـر	v.	go out (fire); Pa^cel quench, extinguish	(10)
844.	وُمـ	v.	trample	(10)
845.	زَنُـا	adj.	fornicator, adulterer	(10)
846.	حَاوَوهِا	n. f.	freedom, liberty	(10)
847.	حَصُنَا	adj.	strong, mighty	(10)
848.	سجُهِهِا	n. f.	diligence, zest, earnestness, perseverance	(10)
849.	سكَم	v.	seal, stamp, impress	(10)

	Syriac	Cat.	Meaning	
850.	ܛܥܝܘܬܐ	n. f.	*error, deception, mistake*	(10)
851.	ܝܒܫܐ	n. m.	dry *land, earth*	(10)
852.	ܝܘܢܐ	n. c.	*dove.* pl. ܝܘ̈ܢܐ	(10)
853.	ܟܢܬܐ	n. m.	*companion, fellow* servant. pl. ܟܢܘ̈ܬܐ	(10)
854.	ܟܪܝܗܘܬܐ	n. f.	*sickness, infirmity, frailty, weakness*	(10)
855.	ܟܪܝܘܬܐ	n. f.	*sorrowfulness, sadness*	(10)
856.	ܠܒܒ	den.	Pa^cel ܠܒܒ *encourage*	(10)
857.	ܠܘܐ	v.	*accompany*; Pa^cel *escort*	(10)
858.	ܡܗܝܡܢܐ	n. m.	*eunuch, faithful.* pl. ܡܗܝܡܢ̈ܐ	(10)
859.	ܡܢܝܐ	n. m.	*mina* (monetary unit)	(10)
860.	ܡܣܢܐ	n. m.	*sandal, shoe.* pl. ܡܣܢ̈ܐ	(10)
861.	ܡܥܕܪܢܐ	n. m.	*help, helper.* pl. ܡܥܕܪ̈ܢܐ	(10)
862.	ܡܫܠܡܢܐ	n. m.	*betrayer, traitor.* pl. ܡܫܠܡ̈ܢܐ	(10)
863.	ܡܫܡܥܬܐ	n. f.	*hearing, obedience*	(10)
864.	ܡܫܪܝܬܐ	n. f.	*encampment.* pl. ܡܫܪ̈ܝܬܐ	(10)
865.	ܣܐܡܐ	n. m.	Gk. ἄσημον *silver, money*	(10)
866.	ܣܗܪܐ	n. c.	*moon*	(10)
867.	ܣܦܣܪܐ	n. f.	*sword.* pl. ܣܦܣܪ̈ܐ	(10)
868.	ܣܪܝܩܐܝܬ	adv.	*vainly*	(10)
869.	ܥܘܡܩܐ	n. m.	*depth, deep.* pl. ܥܘܡ̈ܩܐ	(10)
870.	ܥܪܛܠܝܐ	adj.	*naked, bare, exposed*	(10)
871.	ܦܘܠܚܢܐ	n. m.	*trade, occupation, work*	(10)
872.	ܦܠܓܐ	n. m.	*half, middle*	(10)
873.	ܨܚܐ	v.	Pa^cel *revile*	(10)
874.	ܩܛܪܓ	v.	Gk. κατηγορεῖν *accuse*	(10)
875.	ܩܨܝܐ	n. m.	*fragment.* pl. ܩܨ̈ܝܐ	(10)
876.	ܩܪܝܢܐ	n. m.	*calling, vocation, reading, lesson*	(10)
877.	ܪܘܐ	v.	become *drunk*	(10)
878.	ܪܟܫܐ	n. m.	*horse.* pl. ܪ̈ܟܫܐ	(10)

	Syriac	Cat.	Meaning	
879.	ܪܩܕ	v.	*dance*; Aph^cel *mourn*	(10)
880.	ܫܛ	v.	*despise*, treat w/ *contempt*	(10)
881.	ܬܘܟܠܢܐ	n. m.	*trust, confidence*	(10)
882.	ܬܩܠ	v.	*stumble, hinder*	(10)
883.	ܬܪܣܝ	v.	*nourish, support, feed*	(10)

Chapter 2

Proper Noun Frequency List

Sequence.

This list is arranged according to the frequency of occurrence of proper nouns.

Format.

The list consists of three columns:

- **Column 1: Sequential No.**
  Gives a sequential number.

- **Column 2: Syriac Lexical Entry.**
  Gives the Syriac form of the proper noun in vocalized *Serto* (Western) script.

- **Column 4: English Meanings.**
  Gives the English meanings of the lexical entry. Main English key words are given in italic. At the right side of this column, the frequency of the lexical entry is given in italic in parenthesis.

The list is divided into frequency-range parts to help the student plan study sessions.

2. Proper Noun Frequency List

How to Use the Frequency List.

Same as Section 1.

Words occurring more than 1000 times

	Syriac	Meaning	
1.	ܝܶܫܽܘܥ *Jesus*		(1113)
2.	ܦܰܘܠܳܘܣ *Paul*		(171)
3.	ܐܽܘܪܶܫܠܶܡ *Jerusalem*		(143)
4.	ܫܶܡܥܽܘܢ *Simon* (Peter)		(141)

Words occurring 40 – 99 times

	Syriac	Meaning	
5.	ܝܽܘܚܰܢܳܢ *John* (the Baptist)		(95)
6.	ܟܺܐܦܳܐ *Cephas*		(89)
7.	ܡܽܘܫܶܐ *Moses*		(82)
8.	ܐܺܝܣܪܳܐܝܶܠ *Israel*		(77)
9.	ܐܰܒܪܳܗܳܡ *Abraham*		(75)
10.	ܘܳܠܶܐ it is *right*, part.it *proper*		(75)
11	ܓܠܺܝܠܳܐ *Galilee*		(63)
12.	ܕܰܘܺܝܕ *David*		(60)
13	ܦܶܢܛܺܝܳܘܣ *Pontius Pilate*		(58)
14.	ܝܺܗܽܘܕ *Judea*		(49)

Words occurring 20 – 39 times

	Syriac	Meaning	
15	ܝܽܘܚܰܢܳܢ *John* (the disciple)		(35)
16.	ܩܶܣܰܪ Gk. χαῖσαρ *Caesar*		(35)
17	ܐܺܠܺܝܳܐ *Elijah*		(31)
18.	ܒܰܪܢܰܒܰܐ *Barnabas*		(28)

2. Proper Noun Frequency List

	Syriac	Meaning	
19	ܗܶܪܳܘܕܶܣ	*Herod Antipas*	(26)
20.	ܝܰܘܣܶܦ	*Joseph* (Mary's husband)	(25)
21	ܝܰܥܩܽܘܒ	*Jacob*	(25)
22.	ܡܶܨܪܶܝܢ	*Egypt*	(25)
23	ܛܺܝܡܳܬܶܐܳܘܣ	*Timotheus*	(24)
24.	ܝܺܗܽܘܕܳܐ	*Judas* (Iscariot)	(24)
25	ܫܳܐܘܳܠ	*Saul*	(23)
26.	ܐܶܫܰܥܝܳܐ	*Isaiah*	(22)
27	ܝܰܥܩܽܘܒ	*James* (John's brother)	(21)
28.	ܢܳܨܪܳܝܳܐ	*Nazarene*	(21)
29	ܐܺܝܣܚܳܩ	*Isaac*	(20)
30.	ܐܳܪܳܡܳܝܳܐ	*Gentile, Aramaean* (Syrian)	(20)
31	ܡܰܪܝܰܡ	*Mary* (Jesus' mother)	(20)
32.	ܫܳܡܪܳܝܳܐ	*Samaritan*	(20)

Words occurring 15 – 19 times

	Syriac	Meaning	
33	ܐܰܣܺܝܰܐ	*Asia*	(19)
34.	ܡܰܩܶܕܳܘܢܺܝܰܐ	*Macedonia*	(18)
35	ܐܶܦܶܣܳܘܣ	*Ephesus*	(16)
36.	ܟܦܰܪܢܰܚܽܘܡ	*Capernaum*	(16)
37	ܦܺܝܠܺܝܦܳܘܣ	*Philip* (the apostle)	(16)
38.	ܕܰܪܡܣܽܘܩ	*Damascus*	(15)
39	ܝܽܘܪܕܢܳܢ	*Jordan*	(15)
40.	ܩܶܣܰܪܺܝܰܐ	*Caesarea*	(15)
41	ܪܽܗܘܡܳܝܳܐ	*Roman*	(15)

Words occurring 12 – 14 times

	Syriac	Meaning	
42	ܐܲܓܪܸܦܘܣ	*Agrippa*	(14)
43.	ܐܲܢܛܝܘܟܝܵܐ	*Antioch of Syria*	(14)
44	ܛܹܛܘܣ	*Titus*	(14)
45.	ܡܲܪܝܲܡ	*Mary* (Magdalene)	(14)
46	ܦܸܣܛܘܣ	(Porcius) *Festus*	(14)
47.	ܦܝܠܝܦܘܣ	*Philip* (one of the seven)	(14)
48	ܐܲܢܕܪܹܐܘܣ	*Andrew*	(13)
49.	ܒܹܝܬ ܥܲܢܝܵܐ	*Bethany*	(13)
50	ܗܹܪܘܕܸܣ	*Herod the Great*	(13)
51.	ܡܲܪܝܲܡ	*Mary* (Lazarus' sister)	(13)
52	ܡܵܪܬܵܐ	*Martha*	(13)
53.	ܢܵܨܪܲܬ	*Nazareth*	(13)
54	ܫܝܠܵܐ	*Silas*	(13)
55.	ܒܵܒܹܠ	*Babylon*	(12)
56	ܙܲܒܕܲܝ	*Zebedee*	(12)
57.	ܡܲܓܕܠܵܝܬܵܐ	*Magdelene*	(12)
58	ܣܟܲܪܝܘܛܵܐ	*Iscariot*	(12)
59.	ܫܠܹܝܡܘܢ	*Solomon*	(12)

Words occurring 10 – 11 times

	Syriac	Meaning	
60	ܐܲܟܲܐܝܵܐ	*Achaia*	(11)
61.	ܒܲܪ ܐܲܒܵܐ	*Barabbas*	(11)
62	ܙܲܟܲܪܝܵܐ	*Zacharias* (John's father)	(11)
63.	ܠܵܥܵܙܲܪ	*Lazarus* (of Bethany)	(11)
64	ܨܘܪ	*Tyre*	(11)
65.	ܨܲܝܕܵܢ	*Sidon*	(11)
66	ܬܵܐܘܡܵܐ	*Thomas*	(11)

2. Proper Noun Frequency List

	Syriac	Meaning	
67.	ܐܠܝܫܒܥ	*Elizabeth*	(10)
68	ܐܦܠܘ	*Apollos*	(10)
69.	ܓܠܝܠܝܐ	*Galilean*	(10)
70	ܝܥܩܘܒ	*James* (Jesus' brother)	(10)
71.	ܡܠܟܝܙܕܩ	*Melchisedec*	(10)
72	ܡܩܕܘܢܝܐ	*Macedonian*	(10)
73.	ܣܕܘܡ	*Sodom*	(10)
74	ܩܝܦܐ	*Caiaphas*	(10)

Chapter 3

Greek Loanwords Frequency List

Sequence.

This list is arranged according to the frequency of occurrence of Greek loanwords. All Greek loanwords are included, irrespective of their frequency.

Format.

The list consists of four columns:

- **Column 1: Syriac Lexical Entry.**
  Gives the Syriac form of the proper noun in vocalized *Serto* (Western) script.

- **Column 2: Category.**
  Gives the grammatical category of the lexical entry.

- **Column 3: Greek form.**
  Gives the Greek form from which the Syriac word derives.

- **Column 4: English Meanings.**
  Gives the English meanings of the lexical entry. At the right side of this column, the frequency of the lexical entry is given in italic in parenthesis.

50   3. GREEK LOANWORDS FREQUENCY LIST

How to use the list.

Same as Section 1.

Syriac	Cat.	Greek	Meaning	
ܓܶܝܪ	particle	γάρ	for	(1085)
ܢܳܡܽܘܣܳܐ	n. m.	νομός	law	(224)
ܚܣܣ	den.	πεῖσαι	persuade, convince	(66)
ܦܰܪܨܽܘܦܳܐ	n. m.	πρόσωπον	face, countenance, person, aspect	(35)
ܩܶܣܰܪ	pr. n.	καῖσαρ	Caesar	(35)
ܕܺܝܰܬܺܩܺܐ	n. f.	διαθήκη	testament, covenant	(31)
ܐܶܘܰܢܓܶܠܝܳܘܢ	n. m.	εὐαγγέλιον	Gospel	(30)
ܩܶܢܛܪܽܘܢܳܐ	n. m.	κεντυρίων	centurion	(25)
ܐܶܣܛܪܰܛܺܝܽܘܛܳܐ	n. m.	στρατιώτης	soldier	(21)
ܕܺܝܢܳܪܳܐ	n. m.	δηνάριον	denarius	(20)
ܗܺܓܡܽܘܢܳܐ	n. m.	ἡγεμών	governor, prefect	(20)
ܟܺܠܝܰܪܟܳܐ	n. m.	χιλίαρχος	capt of a thousand	(20)
ܐܰܟܣܢܳܝܳܐ	adj.	ξένος	guest, stranger	(15)
ܐܰܪܟܽܘܢܳܐ	n. m.	ἄρχων	ruler, magistrate, captain	(14)
ܐܶܣܟܺܡܳܐ	n. m.	σχῆμα	form, fashion, figure	(12)
ܒܺܡ	n. f.	βῆμα	judgement-seat, tribunal	(11)
ܩܺܢܕܽܘܢܳܘܣ	n. f.	κίνδυνος	peril, danger	(11)
ܐܰܓܽܘܢܳܐ	n. m.	ἀγών	contest, conflict	(10)
ܐܰܣܺܡܳܐ	n. m.	ἄσημον	silver, money	(10)
ܩܰܛܪܓ	v.	κατηγορεῖν	accuse	(10)
ܡܰܪܓܳܢܺܝܬܳܐ	n. f.	μαργαρίτης	pearl	(9)
ܐܶܣܛܠܳܐ	n. f.	στολή	robe	(8)
ܦܪܶܛܽܘܪܺܝܢ	n. f.	πραιτώριον	judgement hall, praetorium	(8)
ܐܶܣܦܺܝܪܳܐ	n. f.	σπεῖρα	cohort	(7)
ܒܰܪܒܪܳܝܳܐ	adj.	βάρβαρος	foreigner, barbarian	(7)
ܠܰܡܦܺܐܕܳܐ	n. m.	λαμπάς	lamp, light	(7)

3. GREEK LOANWORDS FREQUENCY LIST

Syriac	Cat.	Greek	Meaning	
ܠܶܣܛܳܝܳܐ	n. m.	λῃστής	robber, brigand	(7)
ܦܝܳܣܳܐ	n. m.	πεῖσαι	compliance, persuasion, assurance, persuasiveness	(7)
ܐܐܰܪ	n. c.	ἀήρ	air	(6)
ܐܶܟܶܕܢܳܐ	n. f.	ἔχιδνα	viper	(6)
ܐܰܢܬܽܘܦܰܛܳܘܣ	n. m.	ἀνθύπατος	proconsul	(6)
ܐܶܣܛܽܘܟܣܳܐ	n. m.	στοιχεῖον	element, body	(6)
ܐܰܪܟܳܐ	n. f.	ἀρχή	principality	(6)
ܙܘܓ	den.	ζεῦγος	join together, marry, unite	(6)
ܛܽܘܦܣܳܐ	n. m.	τύπος	type, example	(6)
ܦܰܪܶܗܣܺܝܰܐ	n. f.	παρρησία	boldness, liberty of speech, assurance	(6)
ܩܽܘܦܺܝܢܳܐ	n. m.	κόφινος	basket	(6)
ܩܠܺܝܕܳܐ	n. m.	κλείς	key	(6)
ܐܰܢܰܢܩܺܐ	n. f.	ἀνάγκη	necessity	(5)
ܐܰܣܽܘܛܽܘܬܳܐ	n. f.	ἄσωτος	luxury, profligacy	(5)
ܐܶܣܛܪܰܛܺܓܳܐ	n. m.	στρατηγός	prefect, praetor	(5)
ܐܶܣܦܺܪܺܝܕܳܐ	n. m.	σπυρίς	basket	(5)
ܣܶܕܽܘܢܳܐ	n. m.	σινδών	cloth	(5)
ܦܺܝܢܟܳܐ	n. m.	πίναξ	dish, platter	(5)
ܦܰܪܰܩܠܺܛܳܐ	n. m.	παράκλητος	comforter, advocate	(5)
ܩܺܝܬܳܪܳܐ	n. m.	κιθάρα	harp, instrument	(5)
ܬܶܐܰܛܪܽܘܢ	n. f.	θέατρον	theatre	(5)
ܐܰܓܪܽܘܣܳܐ	n. m.	ἀγρός	land, field, farms	(4)
ܐܽܘܢܩܺܢܳܐ	n. m.	ὄγκινος	anchor	(4)
ܐܺܝܩܺܐ	particle	εἰκῆ	vain, cause	(4)
ܐܽܘܟܠܽܘܣ	n. m.	ὄχλος	crowd, multitude	(4)
ܐܶܣܛܘܳܐ	n. m.	στοά	portico, arcade	(4)
ܐܶܣܛܰܣܺܝܣ	n. f.	στάσις	riot, strife	(4)
ܓܶܢܣܳܐ	n. m.	γένος	kind, offspring	(4)

3. GREEK LOANWORDS FREQUENCY LIST

Syriac	Cat.	Greek	Meaning	
ܗܕܝܘܛܐ	adj.	ἰδιώτης	vulgar, ignorant, plebeian	(4)
ܙܘܓܐ	n. m.	ζυγόν	yoke, pair, couple	(4)
ܙܛܡܐ	n. m.	ζήτημα	investigation, inquiry	(4)
ܛܛܪܪܟܐ	n. m.	τετράρχης	tetrarch	(4)
ܛܟܣܐ	n. m.	τάξις	order, arrangement	(4)
ܠܓܝܘܢܐ	n. f.	λεγιών	legion	(4)
ܡܡܘܢܐ	n. m.	μαμμωνᾶς	Mamon	(4)
ܩܐܪܘܣ	n. m.	καιρός	time, opportunity, war, season	(4)
ܩܛܓܪܢܐ	n. m.	(κατηγορεῖν)	accuser	(4)
ܩܒܘܬܐ	n. f.	κιβωτός	ark	(4)
ܩܘܣܛܘܢܪܐ	n. m.	κουεστιονάριος	guard	(4)
ܐܘܪܡܐ	n. m.	εἶδος	profit, fruit	(3)
ܐܘ	particle	εὖ	well	(3)
ܐܣܦܘܓܐ	n. f.	σπόγγος	sponge	(3)
ܒܘܪܣܝܐ	n. m.	βυρσεύς	tanner	(3)
ܗܪܘܡܐ	n. m.	ἄρωμα	spice	(3)
ܟܪܣܛܝܢܐ	adj.	χριστιανός	Christian	(3)
ܠܡܐܢܐ	n. m.	λιμήν	port, haven	(3)
ܣܘܕܪܐ	n. m.	σουδάριον	cloth	(3)
ܦܢܛܩܘܣܛܐ	pr. n.	πεντηκοστή	Pentecost	(3)
ܩܣܛܐ	n. f.	ξέστης	pint, pitcher, jug	(3)
ܩܪܩܘܪܐ	n. f.	κέρκουρος	boat	(3)
ܪܗܒܘܢܐ	n. m.	ἀρραβών	security, earnest, pledge	(3)
ܐܘܟܪܣܛܝܐ	n. f.	εὐχαριστία	Eucharist	(2)
ܐܣܪܐ	n. m.	ἀσσάριον	coin	(2)
ܐܦܣܢܬܝܢ	n. m.	ἄψινθος	wormwood	(2)
ܐܪܡܢܘܢ	n. m.	ἄρμενον	foresail, tackle	(2)
ܒܘܠܘܛܐ	n. m.	βουλευτής	senator, councillor	(2)
ܓܠܘܣܩܡܐ	n. m.	γλωσσόκομον	bag, box, chest	(2)

3. GREEK LOANWORDS FREQUENCY LIST

Syriac	Cat.	Greek	Meaning	
ܗܓܡܘܢܐ	n. f.	ἡγεμών	governorship, perfecture	(2)
ܙܡܪܓܕܐ	n. m.	σμάραγδος	emerald	(2)
ܛܝܡܐ	n. m.	τιμή	price	(2)
ܟܠܡܘܣ	n. f.	χλαμύς	robe, mantle	(2)
ܡܢ	particle	μέν	indeed	(2)
ܡܛܪܛܐ	n. f.	μετρητής	measure	(2)
ܦܝܪܡܐ	n. m.	πύρωμα	censer, thurible	(2)
ܦܪܓܠܐ	n. m.	φραγέλλιον	whip, scourge	(2)
ܩܘܪܝܐ	n. f.	κυρία	lady	(2)
ܩܛܓܪܢܘܬܐ	n. f.	(κατηγορεῖν)	accusation	(2)
ܩܪܟܕܢܐ	n. m.	καρχηδόνιος	chalcedony	(2)
ܬܪܘܢܘܣ	n. m.	θρόνος	throne	(2)
ܐܘܪܩܠܝܕܘܢ	pr. n.	εὐροκλύδων	Euraquilo, wind	(1)
ܐܡܬܘܣܛܘܣ	n. c.	ἀμέθυστος	amethyst	(1)
ܐܣܛܕܝܐ	n. m.	στάδιον	stadium, arena	(1)
ܐܣܛܘܐܝܩܘ	adj.	στωικός	Stoics	(1)
ܐܣܛܘܡܟܐ	n. m.	στόμαχος	stomach	(1)
ܐܣܛܪܛܝܐ	n. f.	στρατεία	army, soldiery, band	(1)
ܐܣܛܪܢܐ	n.	στρῆνος	luxury, wantonness, excess	(1)
ܐܣܟܘܠܐ	n. f.	σχολή	school, lecture-hall	(1)
ܐܣܦܘܩܠܛܪܐ	n. m.	σπεκουλάτωρ	executioner, spy, scout	(1)
ܐܣܦܣ	n. f.	ἀσπίς	asp, snake	(1)
ܐܣܬܪܐ	n. f.	στατήρ	shekel	(1)
ܐܦܛܪܘܦܐ	n. m.	ἐπίτροπος	guardian, tutor	(1)
ܐܦܣܩܘܦܐ	n. m.	ἐπίσκοπος	bishop, overseer	(1)
ܐܦܣܘܢܝܐ	n. f.	ὀψόνια	rations, pay	(1)
ܕܘܡܣܐ	n. f.	δόμος	building	(1)
ܗܘܦܪܟܝܐ	n. f.	ἐπαρχεία	province	(1)
ܗܪܣܝܣ	n. f.	αἵρεσις	heresy, sect	(1)

3. GREEK LOANWORDS FREQUENCY LIST

Syriac	Cat.	Greek	Meaning	
ܛܘܦܰܙܝܳܢ	n. m.	τοπάζιον	topaz	(1)
ܛܘܦܰܢܝܩܳܐ	adj.	τυφωνικός	tempestuous	(1)
ܛܟ	particle	τάχα	perhaps, peradventure	(1)
ܛܟܣ	den.	(τάξις)	order, arrange	(1)
ܝܘܩܢܬܘܣ	n. m.	ὑάκινθος	jacinth	(1)
ܟܘܪܐ	n. c.	χώρα	region, district	(1)
ܟܝܡܘܢܐ	n. m.	χειμών	storm, tempest	(1)
ܟܪܘܣܘܦܪܣܘܢ	n. m.	χροσόπρασον	chrysoprase	(1)
ܟܪܛܝܣܐ	n. c.	χάρτης	paper, papyrus	(1)
ܠܘܢܟܬܐ	n. f.	λόγχη	spear, pike	(1)
ܠܝܛܪܐ	n. m.	λίτρα	pound	(1)
ܡܘܪܘܢ	n. m.	μύρον	ointment, unguent, perfume	(1)
ܡܛܟܣܘܬܐ	n. f.	(τάξις)	orderliness	(1)
ܡܩܠܘܢ	n. m.	μάκελλον	marketplace	(1)
ܢܘܓܝܐ	n. m.	ναυαγία	shipwreck	(1)
ܢܘܡܐ	n. f.	νομή	hold	(1)
ܢܘܣܐ	n. m.	ναός	shrine, temple	(1)
ܢܦܛܝܪܐ	n. m.	λαμπτήρ	lantern	(1)
ܣܡܝܕܐ	n. m.	σεμίδαλις	flour	(1)
ܦܝܓܢܐ	n. m.	πήγανον	rue	(1)
ܦܘܪܘܣܐ	n. m.	πόρος	way, means, trick	(1)
ܦܘܢܕܩܐ	n. m.	πανδοκεῖον	inn, hostelry	(1)
ܦܘܢܕܩܐ	n. m.	(πανδοκεῖον)	innkeeper, host	(1)
ܦܝܠܘܣܘܦܐ	n. m.	φιλόσοφος	philosopher	(1)
ܦܝܠܘܣܦܘܬܐ	n. f.	(φιλόσοφος)	philosophy	(1)
ܦܝܢܩܝܬܐ	n. f.	πινακίδιον	writing tablet	(1)
ܩܘܒܪܢܛܐ	n. m.	κυβερνήτης	shipmaster, captain	(1)
ܩܘܠܘܢܝܐ	n. f.	κολωνία	colony	(1)
ܩܘܢܡܘܢ	n. m.	κιννάμωμον	cinnamon	(1)

3. Greek Loanwords Frequency List

Syriac	Cat.	Greek	Meaning	
ܩܝܬܪܘܕܐ	n. m.	κιθαρῳδός	harpist, musician	(1)
ܩܪܘܣܛܠܘܢ	n. m.	κρύσταλλος	crystal	(1)
ܪܗܘܡܝܘܬܐ	n. f.	(Ῥωμαῖος)	Roman citizenship	(1)
ܪܗܛܪܐ	n. m.	ῥήτωρ	orator, rhetorician, barrister	(1)

Chapter 4

Consonantal Homographs

Sequence.

This list is arranged in alphabetical order.

Format.

The list consists of three columns:

- **Column 1: Syriac Lexical Entry.**
  Gives the Syriac form of the word in vocalized *Serto* (Western) script.

- **Column 2: Category.**
  Gives the grammatical category of the lexical entry.

- **Column 3: English Meanings.**
  Gives the English meanings of the lexical entry. Main English key words are given in italic. At the right side of this column, the frequency of the lexical entry is given in italic in parenthesis.

How to use the list.

The student should pay attention to the vocalization, for it is the only way, in most cases, to distinguish between each pair of consonantal homographs. Note that some pairs belong to different grammatical categories. In most pairs there is one entry whose frequency is much higher than the other. It is worthwhile remembering which one is more frequent.

Notice that in verbal forms, the following pairs are consonantal homographs:

- Perfect sing. 3 masc., and active participle sing. 3 masc.

- Perfect sing. 3 fem., sing. 2 masc., and sing. 1 com.

Also notice that in verbal forms, the following are identical homographs:

- Imperfect: sing. 3 masc. and pl. 1 com.

- Imperfect: sing. 3 fem. and sing 2 masc.

Syriac	Cat.	Meaning	
ܐܓܪܐ	n.	*pay, reward, recompense*	(31)
ܐܓܪܐ	n.	*roof, housetop*	(10)
ܐܘ	particle	*or, else, rather than*	(296)
ܐܘ	particle	*O! Oh!*	(17)
ܐܠܦܐ	num.	*thousand*	(48)
ܐܠܦܐ	n.	*ship, boat*	(45)
ܐܬܐ	n.	*miraculous* token, *sign*	(82)
ܐܬܐ	v.	*come*; Aph^cel ܐܝܬܝ *bring*	(966)
ܒܪܐ	n.	*son*	(786)
ܒܪܐ	v.	*create, make*	(15)
ܓܒܐ	v.	*choose*; Pa^cel *gather, elect, collect* (tribute or tax)	(44)
ܓܒܐ	n.	*party, side, sect, part* (of a ship)	(22)
ܕܝܢܐ	n.	*judge*	(27)
ܕܝܢܐ	n.	*judgement, sentence* (of judge)	(101)
ܕܡܐ	n.	*blood*	(96)
ܕܡܐ	v.	*resemble*; Pa^cel *liken to, compare*	(70)

4. CONSONANTAL HOMOGRAPHS

Syriac	Cat.	Meaning	
ܗܘ	pron.	*that, those*, w/ ܕ he *who*	(1256)
ܗܘ	pron.	*he, it*, (as enclitic)*is*	(2141)
ܝܒ	v.	*be kindled*; Paᶜel *love*	(103)
ܝܒ	v.	*be condemned, owe*; Paᶜel ܡܚܝܒ *condemn*	(48)
ܚܝܐ	v.	*live*; Aphᶜel ܐܚܝ make *live, save*	(165)
ܚܝܐ	n.	*life, salvation*	(177)
ܚܝܐ	adj.	*alive, living*	(89)
ܚܠܦ	v.	Paᶜel *change, transmute*; Shaphᶜel *change, alter*	(20)
ܚܠܦ	prep.	*for, instead*	(117)
ܚܣ	v.	*spare, pity*	(11)
ܚܣ	particle	*God forbid, let it not be*	(16)
ܝܡܐ	n.	*sea*	(108)
ܝܡܐ	v.	*swear*; Aphᶜel make *swear*, take an *oath*	(34)
ܟܐܦܐ	n.	*stone, rock*	(69)
ܟܐܦܐ	pr. n.	*Cephas*	(89)
ܟܣܐ	v.	*cover, conceal, hide*	(31)
ܟܣܐ	n.	*cup*	(33)
ܡܠܟܐ	n.	*king*; f. *queen*	(130)
ܡܠܟܐ	n.	*counsel*	(11)
ܡܢ	pron.	*who*, w/ ܕ he *who*	(367)
ܡܢ	prep.	*from*	(2966)
ܡܢܘ	pron.	w/ ܡܢ *who is this?*	(126)
ܡܢܘ	pron.	w/ ܡܢܐ *what is this?*	(16)
ܣܒܪ	v.	*think, suppose*; Paᶜel *hope, consider*	(108)
ܣܒܪ	den.	Paᶜel ܣܒܪ *preach, declare*; Payᶜel ܣܝܒܪ *bear, endure*; Ethpayᶜal *be nourished, be fed*	(115)

4. Consonantal Homographs

Syriac	Cat.	Meaning	
ܣܟܠ	v.	Pa^cel make *understand*; Ethpa^cal ܐܣܬܟܠ *understand*	(49)
ܣܟܠ	den.	Aph^cel ܐܣܟܠ *offend, wrong*	(14)
ܣܦܪܐ	n.	*scribe, lawyer*	(76)
ܣܦܪܐ	n.	*book, scroll, roll*	(14)
ܥܒܕܐ	n.	*deed, work*	(191)
ܥܒܕܐ	n.	*servant*	(141)
ܥܘܠܐ	n.	*unrighteousness, iniquity*	(39)
ܥܘܠܐ	adj.	*unjust, unrighteous*	(14)
ܥܠ	v.	*enter*; Aph^cel ܐܥܠ *bring in*	(264)
ܥܠ	prep.	*on, about, concerning*	(1549)
ܥܢܐ	v.	*answer*	(158)
ܥܢܐ	n.	*flock*	(16)
ܦܠܚܐ	n.	*husbandman, tiller, cultivator*	(18)
ܦܠܚܐ	n.	*servant, worshipper, soldier*	(22)
ܩܕܡ	v.	*go before*	(52)
ܩܕܡ	prep.	*before*	(290)
ܪܒܐ	v.	*grow up, increase*; Pa^cel ܪܒܝ *nourish, cause increase*	(35)
ܪܒܐ	adj.	*great, chief*, w/ suffix*master*	(395)
ܪܒܘܬܐ	n.	*greatness*, w/ ܟܗܢܘܬܐ *high priesthood*	(16)
ܪܒܘܬܐ	n.	*myriad, thousand*	(12)
ܪܚܡܬܐ	n.	*bowels, mercy*	(39)
ܪܚܡܐ	n.	*friend*	(29)
ܪܡܐ	v.	*put, place, cast*	(136)
ܪܡܐ	adj.	*high*, w/ ܩܠܐ *loud voice*	(39)
ܪܥܐ	v.	*feed, tend*	(19)
ܪܥܐ	den.	Ethpa^cal ܐܬܪܥܝ *think*	(43)
ܫܢܐ	v.	*be mad*; Pa^cel ܫܢܝ *depart, remove*	(35)
ܫܢܐ	n.	*tooth, ivory, tusk*	(14)

Chapter 5

Verbs Arranged by Paradigm

Sequence.

These lists are arranged by verbal paradigm.

Format.

The lists consist of two columns:

- **Column 1: Syriac Lexical Entry.**
  Gives the Syriac form of the word in vocalized *Serto* (Western) script.

- **Column 2: English Meanings.**
  Gives the English meanings of the lexical entry. Main English key words are given in italic. At the right side of this column, the frequency of the lexical entry is given in italic in parenthesis.

How to use the list.

This list is useful for reference or learning verbs by paradigm.

Strong verbs with imperfects in u

Syriac	Imperfect	Meaning	
ܓܢܒ	ܢܓܢܘܒ	steal	(15)
ܗܦܟ	ܢܗܦܘܟ	turn, return; Ethpaʿal *conduct oneself*	(91)
ܙܩܦ	ܢܙܩܘܦ	crucify, lift up, elevate, erect	(50)
ܚܛܦ	ܢܚܛܘܦ	seize, snatch	(17)
ܚܨܕ	ܢܚܨܘܕ	reap	(20)
ܚܫܒ	ܢܚܫܘܒ	think, reckon, deliberate	(66)
ܚܬܡ	ܢܚܬܘܡ	seal, stamp, impress	(10)
ܛܠܡ	ܢܛܠܘܡ	reject, deny, wrong	(15)
ܟܬܒ	ܢܟܬܘܒ	write	(231)
ܣܓܕ	ܢܣܓܘܕ	worship, pay homage	(61)
ܣܡܟ	ܢܣܡܘܟ	support, recline to eat; Aphʿel *cause to recline*	(46)
ܥܪܩ	ܢܥܪܘܩ	flee	(42)
ܦܠܓ	ܢܦܠܘܓ	divide, distribute; Ethpʿel ܐܬܦܠܓ *divide, doubt*	(47)
ܦܣܩ	ܢܦܣܘܩ	cut off, cut down; Paʿel *break*	(34)
ܦܩܕ	ܢܦܩܘܕ	command	(130)
ܦܪܩ	ܢܦܪܘܩ	depart, deliver, save; Paʿel *rescue, pursue*; Aphʿel *go away, abstain from*	(54)
ܦܪܫ	ܢܦܪܘܫ	separate, appoint	(57)
ܦܫܛ	ܢܦܫܘܛ	Tr. *stretch out*, Int. *be straight*	(18)
ܩܒܠ	ܢܩܒܘܠ	appeal to, accuse; Paʿel ܩܲܒܠ *receive, take*; Saphʿel *be present, oppose*	(200)
ܩܛܠ	ܢܩܛܘܠ	kill	(124)
ܩܪܒ	ܢܩܪܘܒ	draw *near, touch, come*; Paʿel ܩܲܪܒ *bring near, bring near, offer*; Aphʿel *fight*	(244)

Syriac	Imperfect	Meaning	
ܪܓܡ	ܢܪܓܘܡ	*stone*	(20)
ܪܕܦ	ܢܪܕܘܦ	*follow, persecute*	(34)
ܫܒܩ	ܢܫܒܘܩ	*forgive, leave, allow*	(217)
ܫܩܠ	ܢܫܩܘܠ	*take up, bear*	(160)
ܫܬܩ	ܢܫܬܘܩ	keep *silent, be still*; Paᶜel ܫܰܬܶܩ *silence*	(24)

Strong verbs with imperfects in a

Syriac	Imperfect	Meaning	
ܒܗܬ	ܢܒܗܬ	*be ashamed*; Aphᶜel ܐܒܗܶܬ *shame*	(37)
ܕܚܠ	ܢܕܚܠ	*fear*; Paᶜel cause to *fear*	(114)
ܕܡܟ	ܢܕܡܟ	*sleep*	(34)
ܚܫܟ	ܢܚܫܟ	grow *dark*; Aphᶜel *darken*; Ettaphᶜal *be darkened*	(11)
ܛܥܡ	ܢܛܥܡ	*taste*; Ethpᶜel ܐܬܛܥܡ *be grafted*; Aphᶜel *graft, partake* (of)	(22)
ܛܥܢ	ܢܛܥܢ	*bear, carry*; Aphᶜel make *carry*	(12)
ܟܦܢ	ܢܟܦܢ	*hunger*	(21)
ܠܒܫ	ܢܠܒܫ	*put on, be clothed*; Aphᶜel ܐܠܒܶܫ *clothe*	(50)
ܠܥܣ	ܢܠܥܣ	*eat, chew*	(28)
ܣܗܕ	ܢܣܗܕ	*witness, testify*	(118)
ܣܠܩ	ܢܣܩ	*go up, ascend*; Aphᶜel ܐܣܶܩ *make ascend*	(134)
ܣܦܩ	ܢܣܦܩ	*be sufficient, be able, suffice*	(23)
ܥܗܕ	ܢܥܗܕ	*remember*; Aphᶜel cause to *remember*	(35)
ܥܡܕ	ܢܥܡܕ	*be baptized*; Aphᶜel ܐܥܡܶܕ *baptize, sink*	(80)

Syriac	Imperfect	Meaning	
ܪܓܙ	ܢܪܓܙ	be angry; Aphᶜel provoke	(17)
ܪܗܛ	ܢܪܗܛ	run	(46)
ܪܚܡ	ܢܪܚܡ	love, have mercy; Ethpaᶜal ܐܬܪܚܡ have mercy; Paᶜel ܪܚܡ have compassion	(119)
ܪܛܢ	ܢܪܛܢ	murmur	(13)
ܫܠܡ	ܢܫܠܡ	die, w/ ܠ obey, agree, follow; Ethpᶜel ܐܫܬܠܡ be delivered up; Paᶜel ܫܠܡ complete; Aphᶜel ܐܫܠܡ deliver up, be completed	(200)

Strong verbs with imperfects in e

Syriac	Imperfect	Meaning	
ܙܒܢ	ܢܙܒܢ	buy; Paᶜel ܙܒܢ sell	(72)
ܥܒܕ	ܢܥܒܕ	do, make; Shaphᶜel ܫܥܒܕ subdue, subject, act, perform, celebrate (a feast)	(706)
ܬܩܠ	ܢܬܩܠ	stumble, hinder	(10)

Strong verbs without imperfect peal in New Testament

Syriac	Imperfect	Meaning	
ܒܪܟ		kneel; Paᶜel ܒܪܟ bless, bow	(58)
ܒܛܠ		be idle, cease, w/ ܠ care; Paᶜel ܒܛܠ annul	(56)
ܚܕܝ		be merry; Paᶜel anoint; Ethpaᶜal ܐܬܚܕܝ live merrily, live joyfully, be rejoice	(20)

Syriac	Imperfect	Meaning	
ܓܕܦ		Pa^{c}el ܓܰܕܶܦ *blaspheme*	(34)
ܕܓܠ		Pa^{c}el *lie, speak falsely*	(10)
ܕܥܟ		*go out* (fire); Pa^{c}el *quench, extinguish*	(10)
ܕܪܟ		Aph^{c}el ܐܰܕܪܶܟ *overtake, comprehend*	(18)
ܕܪܫ		Pa^{c}el *train, debate, argue, question, dispute*	(13)
ܗܠܟ		Pa^{c}el ܗܰܠܶܟ *walk*	(110)
ܙܕܩ		Pa^{c}el ܙܰܕܶܩ *justify*; P^{c}al ܙܕܶܩ *it is right*, part.*fitting*; Pa^{c}el ܙܰܕܶܩ *approve*	(58)
ܙܥܩ		*cry out*	(13)
ܚܒܠ		Pa^{c}el *corrupt, destroy, alter*	(35)
ܚܠܡ		Ethp^{c}el ܐܶܬ݂ܚܠܶܡ *be cured*; Aph^{c}el ܐܰܚܠܶܡ *cure*	(14)
ܚܠܦ		Pa^{c}el *change, transmute*; Shaph^{c}el *change, alter*	(20)
ܚܢܩ		*choke, strangle*; Pa^{c}el *drown*	(12)
ܚܦܛ		Pa^{c}el ܚܰܦܶܛ *exhort, incite, encourage*	(19)
ܛܝܒ		Pa^{c}el ܛܰܝܶܒ make *ready*	(70)
ܟܘܢ		*exist*; Pa^{c}el *reprove, rebuke*; Aph^{c}el *create*	(19)
ܟܢܫ		*assemble, gather*	(105)
ܟܪܟ		*wrap*; Ethp^{c}el ܐܶܬ݂ܟܪܶܟ *go around*; Aph^{c}el *lead about*	(39)
ܟܫܠ		Ethp^{c}el *be offended*; Aph^{c}el make *stumble*	(30)
ܟܬܫ		*strike*; Ethpa^{c}al *strive, endeavor, fight*	(12)
ܡܠܟ		*counsel, promise*; Ethpa^{c}al *deliberate*; Aph^{c}el ܐܰܡܠܶܟ *reign*	(42)
ܣܝܒ		Pa^{c}el ܣܰܝܶܒ *defile*	(21)

Syriac	Imperfect	Meaning	
ܣܟܠ		Pa‘el make *understand*; Ethpa‘al ܐܣܬܟܠ *understand*	(49)
ܣܢܩ		*need*	(22)
ܣܪܩ		Pa‘el ܣܪܩ make *empty*, make *void*	(20)
ܥܛܦ		*turn*; Pa‘el *clothe*	(17)
ܥܬܕ		Pa‘el ܥܬܕ *prepare*	(121)
ܦܫܩ		Pa‘el *interpret, expound*	(22)
ܩܕܡ		*go before*	(52)
ܩܕܫ		Pa‘el ܩܕܫ *consecrate, sanctify*	(26)
ܙܘܥ		*agitate*; Ethp‘el *be frightened*; Saph‘el *hurry*	(11)
ܪܟܒ		*mount, ride*; Ethpa‘al *be constructed*; Aph‘el make *ride*	(11)
ܪܩܕ		*dance*; Aph‘el *mourn*	(10)
ܫܓܫ		*stir up, trouble*	(17)
ܫܡܫ		Pa‘el ܫܡܫ *minister, serve*	(60)
ܫܢܩ		Pa‘el *torment*	(16)
ܬܟܠ		Ethp‘el *be confident*	(23)
ܬܩܢ		*be restored*; Pa‘el *restore, prepare*; Aph‘el ܐܬܩܢ *establish*	(22)

Pe-ālaph verbs

Syriac	Imperfect	Meaning	
ܐܒܕ	ܢܐܒܕ	*perish*; Aph‘el ܐܘܒܕ *destroy, lose*	(87)
ܐܙܠ	ܢܐܙܠ	*depart, go*	(447)
ܐܚܕ	ܢܐܚܘܕ	*take, hold*; Aph‘el ܐܘܚܕ *cause to take, let out*, w/ ܢܘܪܐ *kindle, apprehend, maintain, close* (a door)	(168)

5. Verbs Arranged by Paradigm

Syriac	Imperfect	Meaning	
ܐ݁ܟܲܠ	ܢܐܟܘܠ	eat, consume, w/ ܩܪܨܐ accuse; Aphᶜel feed	(178)
ܐ݁ܟܲܪ	ܢܐܚܕܲܪ	urge, constrain	(41)
ܐ݁ܡܲܪ	ܢܐܡܲܪ	say, speak, announce, affirm	(2553)
ܐܣܐ		Paᶜel ܐܲܣܝ heal	(74)
ܐ݁ܣܲܪ	ܢܐܣܘܲܪ	bind, fasten	(66)
ܐ݁ܘܲܥ	ܢܐܘܥܲ	encounter, meet	(11)
ܐ݁ܫܲܕ	ܢܐܫܘܲܕ	pour out	(25)
ܐ݁ܬܐ		come; Aphᶜel ܐܲܝܬܝ bring	(966)
ܐܡܢ		Aphᶜel ܐܲܡܢ tarry, delay	(11)

Pe-nun verbs

Syriac	Imperfect	Meaning	
ܢܒܐ		Ethpaᶜal ܐܸܬܢܲܒܝ prophesy	(29)
ܢܓܲܕ	ܢܸܓܘܲܕ	lead, drag; Paᶜel ܢܲܓܸܕ beat, scourge; Ethpaᶜal be beaten, draw, withdraw	(29)
ܢܓܲܪ	ܢܸܓܘܲܪ	Aphᶜel ܐܲܓܲܪ be prolonged, make long, w/ ܪܘܚܐ be patient	(12)
ܢܘܲܪ	ܢܸܢܗܲܪ	shine; Paᶜel bring to light, explain; Aphᶜel ܐܲܢܗܲܪ light	(29)
ܢܚܲܬ	ܢܸܚܘܬ	descend	(108)
ܢܛܲܪ	ܢܸܛܲܪ	guard, keep, reserve, observe	(130)
ܢܣܲܒ	ܢܸܣܲܒ	take, receive, w/ ܐ݁ܦܐ be a hypocrite	(229)
ܢܣܐ		Paᶜel tempt, prove, try	(40)
ܢܦܲܠ	ܢܸܦܸܠ	fall	(157)
ܢܦܲܩ	ܢܸܦܘܩ	go out, w/ ܪܘܚܐ defend; Ethpaᶜal be exercised; Aphᶜel ܐܲܦܸܩ go out, make cast out, eject	(405)
ܢܨܲܒ		plant	(13)

Syriac	Imperfect	Meaning	
ܢܩܦ	ܢܶܩܰܦ	cleave to, follow, adhere	(41)
ܢܩܫ	ܢܶܩܽܘܫ	knock	(11)
ܢܫܩ		kiss	(13)

Pe-yod verbs

Syriac	Imperfect	Meaning	
ܝܒܠ		Aph^cel ܐܘܒܶܠ *conduct, take, lead away*; Ethpa^cal ܐܶܬܝܰܒܰܠ *be transmitted*	(24)
ܝܒܫ		*dry up, wither*; Aph^cel *cause to wither*	(12)
ܝܕܐ		Aph^cel ܐܰܘܕܺܝ *confess, give thanks*; Eshtaph^cal ܐܶܫܬܰܘܕܺܝ *profess, promise*	(83)
ܝܕܥ	ܢܶܕܰܥ	*know*; Aph^cel ܐܰܘܕܰܥ *make known*; Eshtaph^cal ܐܶܫܬܰܘܕܰܥ *recognize*	(704)
ܝܗܒ	ܢܶܬܶܠ	*give*	(534)
ܝܠܕ	ܢܺܐܠܰܕ	Aph^cel ܐܰܘܠܶܕ *beget, bear* (a child)	(120)
ܝܠܦ	ܢܺܐܠܰܦ	*learn*; Pa^cel ܐܰܠܶܦ *teach*	(147)
ܝܡܐ	ܢܺܐܡܶܐ	*swear*; Aph^cel *make swear, take an oath*	(34)
ܝܣܦ		Aph^cel ܐܰܘܣܶܦ *add, increase*	(25)
ܝܨܦ	ܢܺܐܨܰܦ	*be careful, be anxious, be solicitous*	(30)
ܝܩܕ	ܢܺܐܩܰܕ	*burn*; Aph^cel ܐܰܘܩܶܕ *set* (on fire)	(30)
ܝܩܪ	ܢܺܐܩܰܪ	*be heavy, be precious*; Pa^cel *honour*; Aph^cel *make heavy*	(41)
ܝܪܬ	ܢܺܐܪܰܬ	*inherit, heir*	(18)
ܝܫܛ		Aph^cel ܐܰܘܫܶܛ *stretch out*	(12)
ܝܬܒ	ܢܶܬܶܒ	*sit*; Aph^cel ܐܰܘܬܶܒ *seat, establish*	(148)

5. Verbs Arranged by Paradigm

Syriac	Imperfect	Meaning	
ܝܬܰܪ	ܢܺܐܬܰܪ	gain, remain over, abound; Pa^{c}el make abound, w/ ܥܰܠ prefer; Aph^{c}el ܐܘܬܰܪ benefit	(80)

^{c}E-ālaph verbs

Syriac	Imperfect	Meaning	
ܐܰܐܒ		rebuke, reprove	(29)
ܠܐܺܝ	ܢܶܠܐܶܐ	toil, labour; Aph^{c}el tire	(26)
ܡܐܶܢ	ܢܶܡܐܰܢ	be tired, be weary; Aph^{c}el neglect, tedious	(13)
ܫܐܶܠ	ܢܶܫܐܰܠ	ask, inquire, w/ ܒܰܫܠܳܡ salute; Aph^{c}el lend	(243)

Lomad-ālaph (originally yod) verbs

Syriac	Imperfect	Meaning	
ܒܟܳܐ	ܢܶܒܟܶܐ	weep	(41)
ܒܢܳܐ	ܢܶܒܢܶܐ	build	(47)
ܒܣܳܐ	ܢܶܒܣܶܐ	despise; Aph^{c}el despise, neglect	(13)
ܒܥܳܐ	ܢܶܒܥܶܐ	seek for, require, question, inquire into	(313)
ܒܨܳܐ	ܢܶܒܨܶܐ	search, examine	(10)
ܒܩܳܐ		prove, examine; Ethpa^{c}al consider	(21)
ܒܪܳܐ	ܢܶܒܪܶܐ	create, make	(15)
ܓܒܳܐ	ܢܶܓܒܶܐ	choose; Pa^{c}el gather, elect, collect (tribute or tax)	(44)
ܓܠܳܐ	ܢܶܓܠܶܐ	reveal, manifest	(98)

5. Verbs Arranged by Paradigm

Syriac	Imperfect	Meaning	
ܘܕܐ		be pure; Pacel ܘܕܨ cleanse	(68)
ܘܡܕܐ	ܢܕܡܐ	resemble; Pacel liken to, compare	(70)
ܗܘܐ	ܢܗܘܐ	be, (as enclitic)was, turn out	(4006)
ܙܟܐ	ܢܙܟܐ	overcome	(31)
ܚܕܝ	ܢܚܕܐ	be glad, rejoice; Pacel gladden	(76)
ܚܘܐ		Pacel ܚܘܝ show	(97)
ܚܙܐ	ܢܚܙܐ	see, behold	(734)
ܚܛܐ	ܢܚܛܐ	sin, err	(39)
ܚܝܐ	ܢܚܐ	live; Aphcel ܐܚܝ make live, save	(165)
ܚܝܕ		Ethpcel hold on to, affirm, strive, argue, contend	(13)
ܛܥܐ	ܢܛܥܐ	wander, err, forget; Aphcel ܐܛܥܝ deceive, go astray, lead astray, delude	(76)
ܛܫܐ	ܢܛܫܐ	hide oneself, be hidden; Pacel ܛܫܝ hide	(22)
ܟܠܐ	ܢܟܠܐ	hinder, forbid, restrain	(25)
ܟܣܐ		cover, conceal, hide	(31)
ܟܪܐ	ܢܟܪܐ	sorrow; Pacel ܟܪܝ shorten; Aphcel ܐܟܪܝ make sorry	(28)
ܠܘܐ		accompany; Pacel escort	(10)
ܡܚܐ	ܢܡܚܐ	strike, gird	(45)
ܡܛܐ	ܢܡܛܐ	arrive, reach; Pacel ܡܛܝ attain	(66)
ܡܠܐ	ܢܡܠܐ	fill, complete	(166)
ܡܨܐ		be able	(14)
ܣܓܐ	ܢܣܓܐ	increase; Aphcel ܐܣܓܝ multiply, be great	(30)
ܣܟܐ		Pacel expect, look for	(28)
ܣܠܐ		despise, reject	(20)
ܣܢܐ	ܢܣܢܐ	hate	(42)
ܥܢܐ	ܢܥܢܐ	answer	(158)

5. Verbs Arranged by Paradigm

Syriac	Imperfect	Meaning	
ܥܢܐ	ܢܥܢܐ	*return*; Pa‘el ܥܲܢܝ *answer, give back*; Aph‘el ܐܲܥܢܝ *cause to* turn	(57)
ܐܪܥ		Pa‘el ܦܲܪܝ *deliver*	(21)
ܨܒܐ	ܢܨܒܐ	*will, desire*	(273)
ܨܗܐ	ܢܨܗܐ	*be thirsty*	(15)
ܨܥܪ		Pa‘el *revile*	(10)
ܨܪܐ		*rend, burst*; Ethpa‘al w/ ܥܠ *break out against*	(11)
ܩܢܐ	ܢܩܢܐ	*obtain*	(17)
ܩܥܐ	ܢܩܥܐ	*cry aloud*, w/ ܩܕܡ *appeal to*	(81)
ܩܨܐ	ܢܩܨܐ	*break* (bread)	(18)
ܩܪܐ	ܢܩܪܐ	*call, read*, w/ ܩܕܡ *appeal to*	(330)
ܪܒܐ		*grow up, increase*; Pa‘el ܪܲܒܝ *nourish, cause* increase	(35)
ܪܕܐ	ܢܪܕܐ	*journey, flow, chastise, instruct*; Aph‘el make *flow, supply*	(63)
ܪܘܐ		*become* drunk	(10)
ܪܡܐ		*put, place, cast*	(136)
ܪܢܐ	ܢܪܢܐ	*meditate, think, consider, plan*	(15)
ܪܥܐ	ܢܪܥܐ	*feed, tend*	(19)
ܫܕܐ	ܢܫܕܐ	*throw, cast*	(38)
ܫܘܐ	ܢܫܘܐ	*worthy, be equal*; Ethp‘el *agree*; Pa‘el *spread, wipe*; Aph‘el ܐܲܫܘܝ *smooth*	(86)
ܫܠܐ		*cease, be quiet*; Pa‘el ܫܲܠܝ *quiet, stop*	(20)
ܫܢܐ		*be mad*; Pa‘el ܫܲܢܝ *depart, remove*	(35)
ܫܥܐ		Ethp‘el *play*; Ethpa‘al ܐܸܫܬܲܥܝ *narrate*	(30)
ܫܩܐ		Aph‘el ܐܲܫܩܝ *water, give to* drink	(14)

Syriac	Imperfect	Meaning	
ܫܪܐ	ܢܫܪܐ	*loosen, lodge*; Pa^cel ܫܲܪܝ *begin*; Ethpa^cal ܐܸܫܬܲܪܝ *be loosened, eat* a meal	(249)

Lāmad-ālaph verbs

Syriac	Imperfect	Meaning	
ܒܝܐ		Pa^cel ܒܝܐ *comfort, encourage*	(28)
ܨܠܐ	ܢܨܠܐ	*incline toward, heed*; Pa^cel ܨܲܠܝ *pray*	(100)

Lāmad-guttural or rish verbs

Syriac	Imperfect	Meaning	
ܒܲܕܲܪ		*scatter, disperse, spend, waste, scare away*	(19)
ܒܠܲܥ	ܢܒܠܲܥ	*swallow* up, *be struck, be beaten, be smitten*	(12)
ܒܨܲܪ		*decrease, be less, be inferior*	(17)
ܓܙܲܪ	ܢܸܓܙܘܿܪ	*cut, circumcise*	(20)
ܓܡܲܪ	ܢܸܓܡܘܿܪ	*perfect, accomplish, mature, fulfil*	(40)
ܕܒܲܪ	ܢܕܒܲܪ	*lead, take*; Pa^cel ܕܲܒܲܪ *rule, guide, conduct*	(93)
ܕܟܲܪ		Ethp^cel ܐܸܬܕܟܲܪ *remember*; Aph^cel ܐܲܕܟܲܪ *remind, make mention of*	(33)
ܕܡܪ		Ethpa^cal ܐܸܬܕܲܡܲܪ *marvel, be amazed*	(52)
ܕܢܲܚ	ܢܕܢܲܚ	*rise, shine*; Aph^cel make *rise, dawn*	(12)
ܙܗܪ		Ethp^cel take *heed*, w/ ܡܢ *beware of*, w/ ܒ take *care of*; Pa^cel ܙܲܗܲܪ *warn*	(41)

5. Verbs Arranged by Paradigm

Syriac	Imperfect	Meaning	
ܙܪܰܥ	ܢܶܙܪܽܘܥ	sow	(50)
ܣܪܰܚ		Pa‘el ܣܰܪܰܚ set *free*	(13)
ܣܚܰܪ	ܢܶܣܚܰܪ	surround, wander, beg; Aph‘el ܐܰܣܚܰܪ *hedge*	(14)
ܣܪܶܩ	ܢܶܣܪܰܩ	lack, lose	(14)
ܚܫܰܚ		be useful; Ethpa‘al ܐܶܬܚܰܫܰܚ *use, adapt, apply*	(13)
ܟܦܰܪ	ܢܶܟܦܽܘܪ	deny, refuse	(44)
ܟܪܶܗ		be sick, be weak	(30)
ܟܬܰܪ		Pa‘el ܟܰܬܰܪ remain, abide, continue, wait	(11)
ܡܫܰܚ	ܢܶܡܫܽܘܚ	anoint	(14)
ܣܒܰܥ	ܢܶܣܒܰܥ	be full, be satisfied; Pa‘el ܣܰܒܰܥ *satisfy*	(18)
ܣܒܰܪ	ܢܶܣܒܰܪ	think, suppose; Pa‘el *hope, consider*	(108)
ܣܥܰܪ	ܢܶܣܥܽܘܪ	visit, do, effect	(55)
ܥܒܰܪ	ܢܶܥܒܰܪ	cross over, w/ ܥܰܠ transgress, w/ ܡܶܢ turn away from; Aph‘el ܐܰܥܒܰܪ pass over	(108)
ܥܕܰܪ		help, be of *profit, advantage*	(26)
ܥܡܰܪ	ܢܶܥܡܰܪ	dwell	(57)
ܥܬܰܪ	ܢܶܥܬܰܪ	grow *rich*; Aph‘el make *rich*	(12)
ܦܠܰܚ	ܢܶܦܠܽܘܚ	work, *labour*; Aph‘el make *serve, caltivate*	(66)
ܦܪܰܥ	ܢܶܦܪܽܘܥ	recompense	(36)
ܦܬܰܚ	ܢܶܦܬܰܚ	open	(84)
ܨܚܰܪ		be despised; Pa‘el ܨܰܚܰܪ *despise*	(17)
ܩܒܰܪ	ܢܶܩܒܽܘܪ	bury; Pa‘el *heap up*	(16)
ܫܕܰܪ		Pa‘el ܫܰܕܰܪ *send*	(235)
ܫܟܰܚ	ܢܶܫܟܰܚ	find, happen, be able	(448)
ܫܠܰܚ		send	(18)

5. Verbs Arranged by Paradigm

Syriac	Imperfect	Meaning	
ܫܡܥ	ܢܫܡܥ	hear, obey; Aph^cel cause to *hear*	(494)
ܫܦܪ	ܢܫܦܪ	please	(31)
ܬܒܥ	ܢܬܒܥ	avenge, require	(17)
ܬܡܗ	ܢܬܡܗ	be astonished; Aph^cel ܐܬܡܗ *astonish*	(26)

Hollow verbs

Syriac	Imperfect	Meaning	
ܓܪ	ܢܓܘܪ	commit *adultery*	(19)
ܕܫ	ܢܕܘܫ	trample	(10)
ܙܥ	ܢܙܘܥ	be shaken, be confused; Aph^cel ܐܙܝܥ stir up, trouble, stir	(44)
ܚܒ	ܢܚܘܒ	be condemned, owe; Pa^cel ܚܝܒ condemn	(48)
ܚܣ	ܢܚܘܣ	spare, pity	(11)
ܚܪ	ܢܚܘܪ	look, behold	(62)
ܟܣ		Ethp^cel be reproved; Aph^cel rebuke, admonish, convict	(12)
ܡܬ	ܢܡܘܬ	be dead, die; Aph^cel put to *death*	(171)
ܡܠ		Pa^cel ܡܠܠ *speak*	(351)
ܢܚ		cease, rest; Aph^cel ܐܢܝܚ give *rest*, put off, refresh	(40)
ܣܡ	ܢܣܝܡ	put, place	(207)
ܥܪ		Ettaph^cal ܐܬܬܥܝܪ be awake; Aph^cel wake up; Ettaph^cal ܐܬܬܥܝܪ watch; Aph^cel arouse	(41)
ܦܣ		Aph^cel ܐܦܣ allow, permit	(26)
ܨܡ	ܢܨܘܡ	fast	(24)
ܩܡ	ܢܩܘܡ	rise, stand; Pa^cel ܩܝܡ establish; Aph^cel ܐܩܝܡ cause to *stand*	(550)

5. VERBS ARRANGED BY PARADIGM

Syriac	Imperfect	Meaning	
ܪܳܡ		*be high*; Aph^cel اܪܝܡ *exalt*	(58)
		Aph^cel ܐܫܝܓ *wash*	(24)
ܫܳܛ	ܢܫܘܛ	*despise*, treat w/ *contempt*	(10)
ܬܳܒ	ܢܬܘܒ	*return, repent*; Aph^cel ܐܬܝܒ *answer, vomit*	(38)

Geminate verbs

Syriac	Imperfect	Meaning	
ܢܟܺܝ	ܢܢܟܐ	*suffer harm*; Aph^cel *harm, hurt*	(15)
ܚܰܡ	ܢܚܡ	*be kindled*; Pa^cel *love*	(103)
ܚܰܫ	ܢܚܫ	*feel, suffer*	(35)
ܛܰܢ		*be eager, be jealous*; Aph^cel *provoke jealousy*	(12)
ܡܰܟ		*be humble*; Pa^cel ܡܟܟ *humble*	(19)
ܥܰܠ	ܢܥܘܠ	*enter*; Aph^cel ܐܥܠ *bring in*	(264)
ܪܰܓ	ܢܪܓ	*desire, covet, lust*	(24)
ܥܫܶܢ		*be strong*; Pa^cel ܥܫܢ *establish*; Aph^cel ܐܥܫܢ *strengthen, believe*	(35)

Quadrilateral verbs

Syriac	Imperfect	Meaning	
ܗܰܝܡܶܢ		*believe, trust* in	(305)
ܐܟܠܩܪܨܐ		*accuse*	(10)
ܫܰܘܬܶܦ		*be partaker*	(27)
ܐܶܫܬܺܝ	ܢܫܬܐ	*drink*	(82)

Syriac	Imperfect	Meaning	
ܬܐܘܨܒ		*nourish, support, feed*	(10)

Chapter 6

Words Arranged by Part of Speech

Sequence.

These lists are arranged by parts of speech.

Format.

The lists consist of two columns:

- **Column 1: Syriac Lexical Entry.**
  Gives the Syriac form of the word in vocalized *Serto* (Western) script.

- **Column 2: English Meanings.**
  Gives the English meanings of the lexical entry. Main English key words are given in italic. At the right side of this column, the frequency of the lexical entry is given in italic in parenthesis.

How to use the list.

These lists are useful for reference or learning verbs by part of speech.

Pronouns

Syriac	Meaning	
ܐܲܝܢܵܐ	who, what, which	(858)
ܐܲܢ̱ܬ	thou	(1401)
ܐܸܢܵܐ	I	(1728)
ܗܵܘ	that, those, w/ ܕ he who	(1256)
ܗܵܘܗܘ	w/ ܗܵܘ	(68)
ܗܵܢܵܐ	this, these	(1578)
ܗܘ	he, it, (as enclitic) is	(2141)
ܗܘܝܘ	w/ ܗܘ i.e. that is to say	(44)
ܚ̈ܕܵܕܹܐ	one another	(16)
ܣܵܦܹܩ	w/ ܣ it suffices	(20)
ܠܡܵܢܐ	why	(61)
ܠܡܵܢܵܐ	why	(52)
ܟܠ	w/ ܠܐ no, not	(34)
ܡܲܢ	who, w/ ܕ he who	(367)
ܡܲܢܘ	w/ ܡܲܢ who is this?	(126)
ܡܵܐ	what	(236)
ܡܵܢܘ	w/ ܡܵܢܐ what is this?	(16)
ܡܵܢܵܐ	why, what	(289)

Prepositions

Syriac	Meaning	
ܐܲܝܟܲܢܵܐ	as, how	(308)
ܐܲܝܟ	as, according to	(759)
ܐܲܝܟܡܵܐ	like as	(20)

6. Words Arranged by Part of Speech

Syriac	Meaning	
ܒ	in, by, into, among, at, with, against	(824)
ܒܝܢܬ	between, among	(22)
ܒܝܢܝ	between	(49)
ܒܬܪ	after, behind	(256)
ܒܝܢ	between	(46)
ܓܘ	in, within	(30)
ܚܠܦ	for, instead	(117)
ܠ	to, for	(4234)
ܠܒܪ	outside	(82)
ܠܘܬ	to, toward, against	(602)
ܠܩܘܒܠ	against, near, toward, w/ ܩܡ resist, opposite to	(65)
ܡܛܠ	because	(740)
ܡܢ	from	(2966)
ܥܕܡܐ	until	(219)
ܥܠ	on, about, concerning	(1549)
ܥܡ	with	(723)
ܨܝܕ	near, with, at	(18)
ܩܕܡ	before	(290)
ܬܚܝܬ	under	(73)

Particles

Syriac	Meaning	
ܐܘ	or, else, rather than	(296)
ܐܝܟܐ	w/ ܐܝܟܐ where is (he)?	(10)
ܐܝܟܐ	where	(109)
ܐܝܡܟܐ	whence?	(26)
ܐܟܚܕܐ	as one, together	(25)

6. WORDS ARRANGED BY PART OF SPEECH

Syriac	Meaning	
ܐܡܝܢ	Amen, verily	(147)
ܐܘ	O! Oh!	(17)
ܐܦ	also, even	(765)
ܐܦܠܐ	w/ ܐܘ not even	(86)
ܐܦܢ	even if	(32)
ܐܠܐ	but, but rather	(799)
ܐܠܘ	if	(57)
ܐܡܬܝ	when?	(57)
ܐܢ	if	(680)
ܐܝܢ	yes, so, truly, yea	(34)
ܐܝܬ	is, are	(1100)
ܒܪܡ	nevertheless, but, yet	(32)
ܒܬܪܟܢ	afterwards	(15)
ܒܣܬܪܐ	the back, behind, backwards	(16)
ܓܝܪ	for	(1085)
ܕܠܡܐ	lest	(87)
ܕܝܢ	but, yet	(1828)
ܕܝܠ	own	(223)
ܗܐ	lo! behold!	(270)
ܗܝܕܝܢ	then, afterwards, next	(169)
ܗܟܘܬ	likewise, so	(22)
ܗܟܢܐ	thus	(282)
ܗܟܝܠ	therefore, hence	(250)
ܗܪܟܐ	here, hence	(51)
ܗܫܐ	now	(193)
ܘܝ	woe! alas for!	(48)
ܚܣ	God forbid, let it not be	(16)
ܟܒܪ	perhaps, long ago	(17)
ܟܡܐ	how much? how many?	(73)

6. WORDS ARRANGED BY PART OF SPEECH

Syriac	Meaning	
ܟܲܕ	*when, after, while, where*	(1214)
ܟܲܝ	*now, indeed, perhaps*	(16)
ܟܵܐ	*here*	(11)
ܟܿܠܵܗ، ܟܿܠ	*all, every, whole, entirely*	(1400)
ܠܲܝܬ	*is not*	(223)
ܠܵܐ	*no, not*	(3140)
ܠܘܿܩܕܲܡ	*before, formerly*	(56)
ܡܲܕܝܢ	*then, therefore*	(16)
ܡܬܘܿܡ	*always, ever*	(11)
ܡܚܕܵܐ	*immediately, at once*	(61)
ܡܟܵܐ	*of place:hence,* w/ ܡܟܵܐ ܘܡܟܵܐ *here and there,* w/ ܡܢ *from this time*	(12)
ܡܟܝܠ	*therefore, now, henceforth*	(56)
ܡܬܘܿܡܐܝܼܬ	*always, ever*	(20)
ܥܓܲܠ	*quickly*	(32)
ܥܕܲܟܝܠ	*yet, still*	(30)
ܥܲܕ	*while, until*	(29)
ܥܲܕܠܵܐ	*before*	(12)
ܗܵܪܟܵܐ	*here*	(14)
ܗܲܡܢ	*there*	(206)
ܬܘܿܒ	*again, furthermore*	(192)

Adjectives

Syriac	Meaning	
ܐܲܚܝܵܢܵܐ	*cousin; f. kinswoman, kinsman*	(10)
ܐܚܪܵܝܵܐ	*last, extreme*	(53)
ܐܚܪܹܢܵܐ	*another*	(295)

Syriac	Meaning	
ܐܰܡܝܼܪܐ	holder, closed	(11)
ܐܟܣܢܳܝܐ	guest, stranger	(15)
ܐܰܡܝܼܢܐ	constant	(10)
ܐܰܣܝܼܪܐ	prisoner, w/ ܪܒ sergeant, bound	(57)
ܐܳܪܡܳܝܐ	Gentile, Aramaean (Syrian)	(20)
ܒܥܶܠܕܒܳܒܐ	enemy	(38)
ܒܰܪܳܝܐ	outer, without	(12)
ܒܝܼܫܐ	evil, wrong	(185)
ܓܠܝܼܠܳܝܐ	Galilean	(10)
ܓܡܝܼܪܐ	perfect, mature	(11)
ܓܒܰܝܐ	chosen, elect, approved	(24)
ܕܰܓܳܠܐ	false, liar	(38)
ܕܰܟܝܐ	clean, pure	(25)
ܕܶܟܪܐ	male	(11)
ܘܳܠܶܐ	it is *right*, part.it *proper*	(75)
ܙܥܘܿܪܐ	little, least	(66)
ܙܰܕܝܼܩܐ	righteous, just, worthy	(47)
ܙܰܕܘܿܩܳܝܐ	Sadducee	(14)
ܙܰܢܳܝܐ	fornicator, adulterer	(10)
ܚܠܝܼܡܐ	whole, healthy, sound, strong	(20)
ܚܰܒܝܼܒܐ	beloved	(65)
ܚܰܕܬܐ	new	(59)
ܚܰܛܳܝܐ	sinner	(49)
ܚܰܣܝܼܢܐ	strong, mighty, robust, potentate	(20)
ܚܰܝܐ	alive, living	(89)
ܚܰܝܳܒܐ	debtor	(45)
ܚܰܟܝܼܡܐ	wise, prudent, cunning (words)	(36)
ܚܰܢܦܐ	godless, Gentile, heathen, foreigner, profane	(12)
ܚܰܨܝܼܢܐ	strong, mighty	(10)

6. WORDS ARRANGED BY PART OF SPEECH

Syriac	Meaning	
ܡܰܚܣܪܳܐ	lacking, deficient	(21)
ܡܟܰܢܐ	dumb, mute, deaf	(16)
ܚܶܘܳܪܐ	white	(21)
ܚܶܫܽܘܟܳܐ	dark, darkness (dark place)	(52)
ܚܺܐܪܳܐ	free, noble, freedman	(18)
ܛܰܡܐܳܐ	unclean, impure	(11)
ܛܰܢܦܳܐ	defiled, unclean, impure, filthy	(31)
ܛܳܒܳܐ	good, w/ ܛܳܒ much	(214)
ܝܰܩܺܝܪܳܐ	heavy, precious	(24)
ܝܰܬܺܝܪܳܐ	more, excessive, greater, better, excelling	(100)
ܝܳܐܐ	due, becoming, seemly, congruous, decorous	(11)
ܝܺܕܺܝܥܳܐ	apparent, known, certain (one), notable	(12)
ܝܺܗܽܘܕܳܝܳܐ	Jew	(205)
ܟܪܺܝܗܳܐ	sick, weak (in faith), infirm	(29)
ܟܺܐܢܳܐ	upright, just, righteous	(23)
ܡܫܰܚܠܦܳܐ	different, diverse, various	(11)
ܡܫܰܪܝܳܐ	sick, paralytic	(14)
ܡܫܺܝܚܳܐ	Messiah, Annointed One, Christ	(586)
ܡܰܓܕܠܳܝܬܳܐ	Magdelene	(12)
ܡܰܚܝܳܢܳܐ	life-giving, Saviour, preserver	(16)
ܡܰܟܺܝܟܳܐ	humble, lowly, mild, gentle	(21)
ܡܰܩܶܕܳܘܢܳܝܳܐ	Macedonian	(10)
ܡܶܣܟܺܢܳܐ	poor	(38)
ܡܺܝܬܳܐ	dead	(126)
ܢܰܗܺܝܪܳܐ	light, bright, (pl.)luminaries, illumined	(16)
ܢܳܨܪܳܝܳܐ	Nazarene	(21)
ܢܽܘܟܪܳܝܳܐ	strange, foreign, alien	(21)
ܣܪܺܝܩܳܐ	vain, empty, vacant, void	(11)
ܣܰܓܺܝܳܐܐ	much, many	(439)

6. Words Arranged by Part of Speech

Syriac	Meaning	
ܣܰܟ݈ܠܐ	foolish	(18)
ܥܘܝܪܐ	blind	(41)
ܣܰܩܘܒ݈ܠܐ	contrary, adverse	(11)
ܥܰܘܳܠܐ	unjust, unrighteous	(14)
ܥܰܪܛܶܠܳܝܐ	naked, bare, exposed	(10)
ܥܰܬܝܩܐ	old, ancient	(12)
ܥܰܬܝܪܐ	rich, wealthy	(35)
ܦܪܝܫܐ	Pharisee	(102)
ܦܰܩܳܚܐ	expedient, profitable, better	(25)
ܩܰܕܡܳܝܐ	before, w/ ܩܕܡ before, formerly	(45)
ܩܰܕܝܫܐ	holy, saint	(148)
ܩܰܕܡܳܝܐ	first, fore	(103)
ܩܰܝܳܡܐ	remaining, abiding, lasting, valid	(13)
ܩܰܠܝܠܐ	little, light, swift	(69)
ܩܪܝܐ	called, being by vocation	(12)
ܩܰܪܝܒ݈ܐ	at hand, near, neighbour	(54)
ܩܰܫܝܐ	hard, strong, rough	(15)
ܪܰܒܐ	great, chief, w/ suffix master	(395)
ܪܰܚܝܩܐ	far, distant, remote	(23)
ܪܰܫܝܥܐ	impious, wicked, ungodly	(11)
ܪܳܡܐ	high, w/ ܩܳܠܐ loud voice	(39)
ܪܗܘܡܳܝܐ	Roman	(15)
ܫܠܝܚܐ	apostle, sent one	(86)
ܫܰܠܝܛܐ	lawful, permitted, (pl) magistrates, (pl) rulers	(53)
ܫܰܦܝܪܐ	beautiful, good, well	(108)
ܫܰܪܝܪܐ	true, steadfast	(65)
ܫܳܡܪܳܝܐ	Samaritan	(20)

6. Words Arranged by Part of Speech

Adverbs

Syriac	Meaning	
ܐܡܝܢܐܝܬ	*assiduously, constantly*	(10)
ܒܠܚܘܕ	*only, alone*	(128)
ܒܝܫܐܝܬ	*badly, sorely*	(12)
ܝܬܝܪܐܝܬ	*abundantly, especially, exceedingly*	(78)
ܡܚܪ	*tomorrow*	(12)
ܣܪܝܩܐܝܬ	*vainly*	(10)
ܪܒܘܠܝܬ	in *Aramaic*, only in Rev.in *Hebrew*	(11)
ܫܪܝܪܐܝܬ	*truly*	(36)

Chapter 7

Words Arranged by Root

Sequence.

This list is arranged according to root.

Format.

The list consists of three columns:

- **Column 1: Syriac Lexical Entry.**
  Gives the Syriac form of the word in vocalized *Serto* (Western) script.

- **Column 2: Category.**
  Gives the grammatical category of the lexical entry.

- **Column 3: English Meanings.**
  Gives the English meanings of the lexical entry. Main English key words are given in italic. At the right side of this column, the frequency of the lexical entry is given in italic in parenthesis.

How to use the list.

This lists all the words that etymologically share a root where that root occurs at least 10 times in the Syriac New Testament. The list excludes proper nouns

87

88   7. WORDS ARRANGED BY ROOT

and gentilic adjectives. Learning groups of words under the same root helps the student save time expanding their vocabulary. This list also alerts students to similarities and differences between entries under the same root.

Syriac	Cat.	Meaning	
		ܐܒ	
ܐܒܐ	n. m.	*father*	(453)
ܐܒܗܘܬܐ	n. f.	*family, fatherhood, parentage*	(1)
		ܐܒܕ	
ܐܒܕ	v.	*perish*; Aph^cel ܐܘܒܕ *destroy, lose*	(87)
ܐܒܕܢܐ	n. m.	*loss, perdition, waste*	(21)
ܐܒܝܕܐ	pass. ptc. m.	*perished, lost*	(4)
		ܐܒܠ	
ܐܒܝܠܐ	pass. ptc. m.	*mourner*	(1)
ܐܒܠ	v.	Ethp^cel *grieve, mourn*	(8)
ܐܒܠܐ	n. m.	*mourning, grief, sadness*	(7)
		ܐܓܘܢܐ	
ܐܓܘܢܐ	n. m.	*contest, conflict*	(10)
		ܐܓܪ	
ܐܓܝܪܐ	pass. ptc. m.	hired *servant, hireling*	(6)
ܐܓܪ	v.	*hire*	(4)
ܐܓܪܐ	n. m.	*pay, reward, recompense*	(31)
		ܐܓܪܐ	
ܐܓܪܐ	n. m.	*roof, housetop*	(10)
		ܐܓܪܬܐ	
ܐܓܪܬܐ	n. f.	*letter, epistle*	(28)
		ܐܕܢܐ	
ܐܕܢܐ	n. f.	*ear*	(45)

7. Words Arranged by Root

Syriac	Cat.	Meaning	
		¹ܐܘ	
ܐܘ	particle	*O! Oh!*	(17)
		²ܐܘ	
ܐܘ	particle	*or, else, rather than*	(296)
		ܐܘܢܓܠܝܘܢ	
ܐܘܢܓܠܝܘܢ	n. m.	*Gospel*	(30)
		ܐܙܠ	
ܐܙܠ	v.	*depart, go*	(447)
		ܐܚܐ	
ܐܚܐ	n. m.	*brother*	(360)
ܐܚܘܬܐ	n. f.	*brotherhood*	(2)
ܐܚܝܢܐ	adj.	*cousin; f. kinswoman, kinsman*	(10)
ܚܬܐ	n. f.	*sister*	(22)
		ܐܚܕ	
ܐܘܚܕܢܐ	n. m.	*dominion, possession, sovereignty*	(5)
ܐܚܕ	v.	*take, hold;* Aphᶜel ܐܘܚܕ *cause to take, let out, w/ ܢܘܪܐ kindle, apprehend, maintain, close* (a door)	(168)
ܐܚܝܕܐ	pass. ptc. m.	*holder, closed*	(11)
		ܐܚܪ	
ܐܚܪ	v.	Aphᶜel ܐܘܚܪ *tarry, delay*	(11)
ܐܚܪܝܐ	adj.	*last, extreme*	(53)
ܐܚܪܢܐ	adj.	*another*	(295)
ܐܚܪܢܐܝܬ	adv.	*contrariwise, otherwise*	(5)
ܚܪܬܐ	n. f.	*end*	(41)
ܘܚܪܐ	n. m.	*delay*	(1)
ܐܘܚܪܬܐ	n. f.	*delay, tarrying*	(1)
		ܐܝܟ	
ܐܝܟ	prep.	*as, according to*	(759)

Syriac	Cat.	Meaning	
ܐܝܟܡܐ	particle	*as, as long as*	(1)
		ܐܝܟܐ	
ܐܝܟܘ	particle	w/ ܐܝܟܐ *where is (he)?*	(10)
ܐܝܟܐ	particle	*where*	(109)
		ܐܝܟܡ	
ܐܝܟܢܐ	prep.	*as, how*	(308)
		ܐܝܠܢ	
ܐܝܠܢܐ	n. m.	*tree*	(26)
		ܐܝܡܟܐ	
ܐܝܡܟܐ	particle	*whence?*	(26)
		ܐܝܡܡܐ	
ܐܝܡܡܐ	n. m.	*daytime*	(30)
		ܐܝܢ	
ܐܝܢ	particle	*yes, so, truly, yea*	(34)
		ܐܝܢܐ	
ܐܝܢܐ	pron. f.	*who, what, which*	(858)
ܐܝܢܐ	pron.	*who, which, what*	(6)
		ܐܝܬ	
ܐܝܬ	sub.	*is, are*	(1100)
ܐܝܬܘܬܐ	n. f.	*substance, essence*	(1)
ܠܝܬ	sub.	*is not*	(223)
		ܐܟܘܬ	
ܐܟܘܬ	prep.	*like as*	(20)
ܐܟܢܐ	prep.	*as, just as*	(2)
ܐܟܚܕܐ	particle	*as one, together*	(25)
		ܐܟܠ	
ܐܟܘܠܐ	adj.	*gluttonous*	(2)
ܐܟܠ	v.	*eat, consume,* w/ ܩܪܨܐ *accuse;* Aphᶜel *feed*	(178)
ܐܟܠ ܩܪܨܐ	n. m.	*accuser, calumniator*	(19)

7. Words Arranged by Root

Syriac	Cat.	Meaning	
ܐܟܠܐ	n. c.	*weevil*	(3)
ܡܐܟܘܠܬܐ	n. f.	*food*	(28)
ܡܐܟܠ ܩܪܨܐ	idiom	*accusation*	(4)
ܡܐܟܠܐ	n. m.	*food*	(3)

ܐܟܣܢܝܐ

ܐܟܣܢܝܐ	adj.	*guest, stranger*	(15)

ܐܠܐ

ܐܠܐ	particle	*but, but rather*	(799)

ܐܠܗ

ܐܠܗܐ	n. m.	*God, a god*	(1389)
ܐܠܗܘܬܐ	n. f.	*Godhead, divinity*	(3)
ܐܠܗܝܐ	adj.	*divine*	(2)
ܐܠܗܬܐ	n. f.	*goddess*	(3)

ܐܠܘ

ܐܠܘ	particle	*if*	(57)

¹ܐܠܦ

ܐܠܦܐ	num.	*thousand*	(48)

²ܐܠܦ

ܐܠܦܐ	n. f.	*ship, boat*	(45)
ܐܠܦܪܐ	n. m.	*mariner*	(1)

ܐܠܨ

ܐܘܠܨܢܐ	n. m.	*oppression, affliction, tribulation*	(59)
ܐܠܘܨܐ	n. m.	*oppressor*	(1)
ܐܠܝܨܐ	pass. ptc. m.	*urgent, narrow, strait, afflicted, requisite*	(3)
ܐܠܨ	v.	*urge, constrain*	(41)

¹ܐܡ

ܐܘܡܬܐ	n. c.	*people, nation*	(10)
ܐܡܐ	n. f.	*mother*	(93)

Syriac	Cat.	Meaning	
		ܐܡ²	
ܐܲܡܗ݂ܬܐ	n. f.	*handmaid*, female bond-*servant*	(10)
		ܐܡܝܢ	
ܐܲܡܝܢ	particle	*Amen, verily*	(147)
		ܐܡܢ	
ܐܲܡܝܢܐ	adj.	*constant*	(10)
ܐܲܡܝܢܐܝܬ	adv.	*assiduously, constantly*	(10)
ܐܡܢ	v.	Ethpᶜel *be constant, be firm*	(1)
		ܐܡܪ¹	
ܐܡܲܪ	v.	*say, speak, announce, affirm*	(2553)
		ܐܡܪ²	
ܐܸܡܪܐ	n. m.	*lamb*, young *sheep*	(39)
		ܐܡܬܝ,	
ܐܸܡܲܬ݂ܝ	particle	*when?*	(57)
		ܐܢ	
ܐܸܢ	particle	*if*	(680)
ܐܸܢܕܹܝܢ	particle	*but if*	(3)
ܐܸܢܗܘ	particle	*if*	(2)
ܐܸܢ	particle	*even if*	(32)
		ܐܢܐ	
ܐܸܢܐ	pron. c.	*I*	(1728)
		ܐܢܚ	
ܐܢܚ	v.	Ethpaᶜal ܐܸܬܲܢܲܚ *groan, sigh deeply, murmur*	(7)
ܐܲܢܲܚܬܐ	n. f.	*groaning*	(3)
		ܐܢܫ	
ܐ݇ܢܵܫܐ	n. c.	*man, mankind*	(709)
ܐ݇ܢܵܫܘܬܐ	n. f.	*humanity, mankind*	(3)
ܟܠܢܫ	n. c.	w/ ܟܠ *every one*	(96)
ܒܲܪܢܵܫܐ	n. c.	w/ ܒܲܪ *human*	(231)

7. Words Arranged by Root

Syriac	Cat.	Meaning	
		ܐܢܬ	
ܐܰܢܬ	pron. m.	*thou*	(1401)
		ܐܢܬܬܐ	
ܐܰܢܬܬܐ	n. f.	*woman, wife*	(238)
		¹ܐܣܐ	
ܐܶܫܬܐܣܬܐ	n. f.	*foundation*	(22)
ܐܣܬܐ	n. f.	*wall*	(1)
		²ܐܣܐ	
ܐܣܝ	v.	Paᶜel ܐܰܣܝ *heal*	(74)
ܐܣܝܐ	n. m.	*physician*	(7)
ܐܣܝܘܬܐ	n. f.	*healing, cure*	(8)
		ܐܣܛܪܛܝܐ	
ܐܣܛܪܛܝܐ	n. f.	*army, soldiery, band* of troops	(1)
ܐܣܛܪܛܝܓܐ	n. m.	*prefect, praetor*	(5)
ܐܣܛܪܛܝܘܛܐ	n. m.	*soldier*	(21)
		ܐܣܟܡܐ	
ܐܣܟܡܐ	n. m.	*form, fashion, figure*	(12)
		ܐܣܪ	
ܐܣܘܪܐ	n. m.	*bond, fetter, chain*	(20)
ܐܣܘܪܝܐ	n. m.	*bondage, captivity*	(1)
ܐܣܝܪܐ	pass. ptc. m.	*prisoner, w/* ܕܝ *sergeant, bound*	(57)
ܐܣܪ	v.	*bind, fasten*	(66)
ܐܣܪܐ	n. m.	*belt, girdle, zone*	(4)
ܡܐܣܪܢܐ	n. f.	*bundle*	(1)
		ܐܦ	
ܐܦ	particle	*also, even*	(765)
ܐܦܟܢ	particle	w/ ܐܦ	(1)
ܐܦܠܐ	particle	w/ ܐܦ *not even*	(86)

Syriac	Cat.	Meaning	
		ܐܦܐ	
ܐܲܦܵܐ	n. f.	*face*, w/ ܢܣܒ *hypocrite*, w/ ܠܚܡ	(143)
		presence-bread	
		ܐܘܪܚ	
ܐܘܿܪܚܵܐ	n. f.	*way, road, highway, journeying*	(105)
		ܐܪܟ	
ܐܲܪܟܘܼ	n. f.	*principality*	(6)
ܐܲܪܟܘܿܢܵܐ	n. m.	*ruler, magistrate, captain*	(14)
		ܐܪܡܠܬܐ	
ܐܲܪܡܲܠܬܵܐ	n. f.	*widow*	(27)
		¹ܐܪܥ	
ܐܲܪܥܵܐ	n. f.	*earth, land, country, soil, ground*	(272)
ܐܲܪܥܵܢܵܝܵܐ	adj.	*terrestrial, mundane, earthly*	(3)
		²ܐܪܥ	
ܐܘܿܪܥܵܐ	n. m.	*meeting*	(7)
ܐܲܪܥ	v.	*encounter, meet*	(11)
		ܐܫܕ	
ܐܲܫܸܕ	v.	*pour out*	(25)
		ܐܫܟܚ	
ܐܸܫܟܲܚ	v.	*find, happen, be able*	(448)
		¹ܐܬܐ	
ܐܵܬܵܐ	n. f.	*miraculous* token, *sign*	(82)
ܐܸܓܲܪܬܵܐ	n. f.	*letter*	(1)
		²ܐܬܐ	
ܐܸܬܵܐ	v.	*come;* Aph°el ܐܲܝܬܝܼ *bring*	(966)
ܡܲܬܝܵܢܵܐ	n. m.	*arrival, presence, advent*	(1)
ܡܲܬܝܵܢܘܼܬܵܐ	n. f.	*coming, advent*	(24)
		ܐܬܪ	
ܐܲܬܪܵܐ	n. m.	*region, place, country, respite,* available	(116)
		space or room	

Syriac	Cat.	Meaning	
ܒܵܬܲܪ	prep.	*after, behind*	(256)
ܒܵܬܲܪܟܸܢ	particle	*afterwards*	(15)
ܠܒܸܣܬܲܪ	particle	*backwards*	(2)

ܒ

ܒ	prep.	*in, by, into, among, at, with, against*	(824)

ܒܐܫ

ܒܐܫ	v.	Ethp^{c}el ܐܸܬܒܐܸܫ w/ ܥܠ *be offended;* Aph^{c}el ܐܲܒܐܸܫ *ill-treat*	(9)
ܒܝܼܫܵܐ	adj.	*evil, wrong*	(185)
ܒܝܼܫܵܐܝܼܬ	adv.	*badly, sorely*	(12)
ܒܝܼܫܘܼܬܵܐ	n. f.	*wickedness, wrong-doing*	(13)

ܒܕܪ

ܒܲܕܲܪ	v.	*scatter, disperse, spend, waste, scare away*	(19)

ܒܗܪ

ܒܗܪ	den.	Shaph^{c}el *glorify;* Eshtaph^{c}al *pride oneself*	(45)
ܡܲܒܗܪܵܢܵܐ	adj.	*boastful*	(2)
ܡܲܒܗܪܵܢܘܼܬܵܐ	n. f.	*pride*	(1)
ܫܘܼܒܗܵܪܵܐ	n. m.	*glorying, vainglory, vaunting*	(24)

ܒܗܬ

ܒܗܸܬ	v.	*be ashamed;* Aph^{c}el ܐܲܒܗܸܬ *shame*	(37)
ܒܗܸܬܬܵܐ	n. f.	*shame*	(11)

ܒܙܚ

ܒܲܙܚ	den.	Pa^{c}el *mock, deride*	(16)
ܒܘܼܙܵܚܵܐ	n. m.	*mocking, jeering*	(2)
ܡܒܲܙܚܵܢܵܐ	n. m.	*mocker*	(1)

ܒܚܪ

ܒܲܚܝܼܪܵܐ	ap f	*tried, approved*	(1)
ܒܘܼܚܵܪܵܐ	n. m.	*proof* (by trial), *scrutiny*	(3)

Syriac	Cat.	Meaning	
ܒܚܢ	v.	*prove, examine, inspect*	(7)

ܒܛܠ

ܒܛܝܠܐ	adj.	*idle, vain, useless*	(6)
ܒܛܝܠܐܝܬ	adv.	*carefully, deligently, punctiliously*	(4)
ܒܛܝܠܘܬܐ	n. f.	*eagerness, diligence*	(1)
ܒܛܠ	v.	*be idle, cease,* w/ ܥܠ *care;* Pa^cel ܒܛܠ *annul*	(56)
ܒܛܠܐ	adj.	*idle, vain, useless*	(4)
ܒܛܠܐܝܬ	adv.	without *cause*	(1)

ܒܛܢ

ܒܛܢ	v.	*conceive*	(4)
ܒܛܢܐ	n. m.	*conception*	(1)
ܒܛܝܢܬܐ	adj.	*pregnant*	(8)

ܒܝܐ

ܒܘܝܐܐ	n. m.	*comfort, encouragement*	(23)
ܒܝܐ	v.	Pa^cel ܒܝܐ *comfort, encourage*	(28)
ܡܒܝܐܢܐ	n. m.	*comforter, consoler, exhorter*	(1)

ܒܝܡ

| ܒܝܡ | n. f. | *judgement-seat, tribunal* | (11) |

ܒܝܬ

ܒܝܢܬ	prep.	*between, among*	(22)
ܒܝܢܝ	prep.	*between*	(49)
ܒܝܬ	prep.	*between*	(46)

ܒܟܐ

ܒܟܐ	v.	*weep*	(41)
ܒܟܝܐ	n. m.	*weeping*	(8)
ܒܟܝܬܐ	n. f.	*weeping*	(1)

ܒܟܪ

| ܒܘܟܪܐ | n. m. | *first-born* | (9) |
| ܒܘܟܪܘܬܐ | n. f. | *birthright,* right of *primogeniture* | (1) |

7. Words Arranged by Root

Syriac	Cat.	Meaning	
ܒܟܝܪܝܐ	adj.	*early* (rain season), the *first*	(1)

ܒܠܐ

ܒܠܐ	v.	become *old*	(5)
ܒܠܝܐ	adj.	*old, worn out*	(8)

ܒܠܥ

ܒܠܘܥܐ	n. m.	*fish-hook*	(1)
ܒܠܥ	v.	*swallow* up, *be struck, be beaten, be smitten*	(12)

ܒܢܐ

ܒܢܐ	v.	*build*	(47)
ܒܢܝܐ	n. m.	*builder*	(5)
ܒܢܝܢܐ	n. m.	*edification, building*	(20)

ܒܣܡ

ܒܣܐ	v.	*despise*; Aph^{c}el *despise, neglect*	(13)

ܒܣܡ

ܒܘܣܡܐ	n. m.	*pleasure, luxury, revelling*	(1)
ܒܣܝܡܐ	adj.	*pleasant, mild, kindly, sweet* (smell), *fair* (of speech)	(5)
ܒܣܝܡܐܝܬ	adv.	*gladly, readily*	(2)
ܒܣܝܡܘܬܐ	n. f.	*pleasantness, gentleness, kindliness, pleasure, gladness*	(13)
ܒܣܡ	v.	be *merry*; Pa^{c}el *anoint*; Ethpa^{c}al ܐܬܒܣܡ *live merrily, live joyfully, be rejoice*	(20)
ܒܣܡܐ	n. m.	*ointment, unguent, incense* (censings)	(21)

ܒܣܪ

ܒܣܪܐ	n. m.	*flesh*	(129)

ܒܣܬܪ

ܒܣܬܪܐ	particle	the *back, behind, backwards*	(16)

ܒܥܐ

ܒܥܐ	v.	*seek for, require, question, inquire into*	(313)
ܒܥܘܬܐ	n. f.	*prayer, petition*	(12)

Syriac	Cat.	Meaning	
ܫܘܟܠܐ	n. f.	*questioning, enquiry*	(7)

ܒܗܠ

Syriac	Cat.	Meaning	
ܒܥܝܠܬܐ	n. f.	*married woman*	(1)
ܒܥܠܐ	n. m.	*lord, husband, master*	(44)
ܒܥܠܕܒܒܐ	adj.	*enemy*	(38)
ܒܥܠܕܒܒܘܬܐ	n. f.	*enmity*	(6)
ܒܥܠܕܝܢܐ	n. m.	*adversary* (at law)	(1)

ܒܨܐ

Syriac	Cat.	Meaning	
ܒܨܐ	v.	*search, examine*	(10)

ܒܨܪ

Syriac	Cat.	Meaning	
ܒܨܝܪܐ	pass. ptc. m.	*inferior, less, least, worse*	(1)
ܒܨܝܪܐܝܬ	adv.	*less, a very* little, *scarcely*	(1)
ܒܨܝܪܘܬܐ	n. f.	mere *trifle, deterioration*	(2)
ܒܨܪ	v.	*decrease, be less, be inferior*	(17)

ܒܩܐ

Syriac	Cat.	Meaning	
ܒܩܐ	n. m.	*gnat*	(1)
ܒܘܩܢܐ	n. m.	*proof, probation*	(8)
ܒܩܐ	v.	*prove, examine*; Ethpaᶜal *consider*	(21)

¹ܒܪ

Syriac	Cat.	Meaning	
ܒܪܐ	n. m.	*outside*	(7)
ܒܪܝܐ	adj.	*outer, without*	(12)
ܠܒܪ	prep.	*outside*	(82)

²ܒܪ

Syriac	Cat.	Meaning	
ܒܪ ܚܐܪܐ	idiom	*freeman*	(1)
ܒܪ ܫܥܬܐ	idiom	*at once, straightway*	(1)
ܒܪܐ	n. m.	*son*	(786)
ܒܪܬܐ	n. f.	w/ ܩܠܐ *utterance, daughter, word*	(41)

ܒܪܐ

Syriac	Cat.	Meaning	
ܒܪܐ	v.	*create, make*	(15)

7. Words Arranged by Root

Syriac	Cat.	Meaning	
ܒ̇ܪܘܿܝܐ	n. m.	*Creator*	(2)
ܒ̇ܪܝܐ	n. m.	*creator*	(1)
ܒܪܝܼܬܐ	n. f.	*creation*	(22)

ܒܪܟ

ܒܘܿܪܟܐ	n. f.	*knee*	(14)
ܒܘܿܪܟܬܐ	n. f.	*blessing, benediction*	(18)
ܒܪܝܼܟܐ	pass. ptc. m.	*blessed*	(2)
ܒܪܸܟ	v.	*kneel*; Pacel ܒܲܪܸܟ *bless, bow*	(58)
ܡܒܲܪܟܐ	pass. ptc. m.	*blessed*	(5)

ܒܪܡ

ܒܪܲܡ	particle	*nevertheless, but, yet*	(32)

ܒܪܩ

ܒܪܲܩ	v.	*flash, gleam*	(3)
ܒܲܪܩܐ	n. m.	*lightning*	(8)

ܒܬ

ܒܬ	den.	*lodge, remain*	(3)
ܒܲܝܬܐ	n. m.	*house, abode*	(434)
ܒܲܝܬܘܼܬܐ	idiom	*stewardship*	(4)

ܒܬܠ

ܒܬܘܿܠܐ	n. m.	*virgin*	(1)
ܒܬܘܿܠܘܼܬܐ	n. f.	*virginity*	(2)
ܒܬܘܿܠܬܐ	n. f.	*virgin*	(14)

ܓܒܐ

ܓܒ̣ܐ	v.	*choose*; Pacel *gather, elect, collect (tribute or tax)*	(44)
ܓܲܒܝܐ	n. m.	*officer, collector* (of tribute), *exactor*	(3)
ܓܒ̣ܝܐ	pass. ptc. m.	*chosen, elect, approved*	(24)
ܓܒ̣ܝܘܼܬܐ	n. f.	*election*	(3)

Syriac	Cat.	Meaning	
ܟܢܫܐ	n. f.	*collection* (of alms)	(4)

²ܓܒܐ

ܓܒܐ	n. m.	*party, side, sect, part* (of a ship)	(22)

ܓܒܠ

ܓܒܝܠܬܐ	n. f.	*lump* (of dough), the thing *formed,* *mass* (of clay)	(6)
ܓܒܠ	v.	*form,* gave *shape to*	(4)

ܓܒܪ

ܓܒܪܐ	n. m.	*man, husband, person*	(319)
ܓܒܘܪܬܐ	n. f.	(pl.)*prodigies, power,* (pl.)*wonders*	(8)
ܓܒܪ	den.	Ethpaᶜal *be a man*	(1)

ܓܕܦ

ܓܕܦ	v.	Paᶜel ܓܕܦ *blaspheme*	(34)
ܓܘܕܦܐ	n. m.	*blasphemy*	(19)
ܡܓܕܦܢܐ	n. m.	*blasphemer*	(2)

ܓܗܢܐ

ܓܗܢܐ	n.	*hell, Gehenna*	(11)

ܓܘ

ܓܘ	prep.	*in, within*	(30)
ܓܘܐ	n. m.	*inside, common* (as adj	(6)
ܓܘܝܐ	adj.	*inner part* (of a person), *interior*	(2)
ܓܘܐ	n. m.	*bowels*	(1)

ܓܙܪ

ܓܙܘܪܬܐ	n. f.	*circumcision*	(33)
ܓܙܪ	v.	*cut, circumcise*	(20)
ܓܙܪܐ	n. m.	*flock*	(1)
ܓܙܪܬܐ	n. f.	*island*	(14)
ܓܙܝܪ	pass. ptc. m.	*circumcised*	(2)

7. Words Arranged by Root

Syriac	Cat.	Meaning	
		ܓܝܪ	
ܓܝܪ	particle	*for*	(1085)
		ܓܠܐ	
ܓܠܝܐܝܬ	particle	*openly*	(6)
ܓܠܐ	v.	*reveal, manifest*	(98)
ܓܠܘܬܐ	n. f.	*captivity, exile*	(4)
ܓܠܝܐ	ap f	*manifest, uncovered*	(2)
ܓܠܝܐܝܬ	adv.	*openly*	(9)
ܓܠܝܢܘܬܐ	n. f.	*manifestation, w/ ܐܦ confidence*	(7)
ܓܠܝܢܐ	n. m.	*manifestation, revelation, assurance, the Apocalypse*	(27)
ܓܠܝܠܐ	n. m.	*w/ ܐܦ boldness*	(1)
		ܓܡܪ	
ܓܡܘܪܐ	adj.	*finisher, perfecter*	(1)
ܓܡܘܪܬܐ	n. f.	live *coal, coal*	(2)
ܓܡܝܪܐ	pass. ptc. m.	*perfect, mature*	(11)
ܓܡܝܪܐܝܬ	adv.	*perfectly, fully*	(4)
ܓܡܝܪܘܬܐ	n. f.	*perfection*	(4)
ܓܡܪ	v.	*perfect, accomplish, mature, fulfil*	(40)
ܓܡܪܐ	n. m.	*perfection*	(3)
		ܓܢ	
ܓܢ	v.	Aphᶜel ܐܓܢ *descend upon*, make *rest, dwell*	(8)
ܓܢܘܢܐ	n. m.	bridal *chamber*	(3)
ܓܢܢܐ	n. m.	*gardener*	(1)
ܓܢܬܐ	n. f.	*garden*	(5)
		ܓܢܒ	
ܓܢܒ	v.	*steal*	(15)
ܓܢܒܐ	n. m.	*thief*	(17)

Syriac	Cat.	Meaning	
ܓܲܢܵܒ݂ܘܼܬ݂ܵܐ	n. f.	*theft*	(2)

ܓܠܠ

ܓܘܼܥܠܵܢܵܐ	n. m.	*deposit*	(2)
ܓܥܠ	den.	Ethp^cel ܐܸܬ݂ܓܥܸܠ *be entrusted*; Aph^cel *commit, commend*	(10)

ܓܪ

ܓܵܪ	v.	*commit adultery*	(19)
ܓܲܘܪܵܐ	n. m.	*adultery*	(6)
ܓܝܘܿܪܵܐ	n. m.	*proselyte*	(4)
ܓܲܝܵܪܵܐ	n. m.	*adulterer*	(9)

ܓܪܒ

ܓܲܪܒ݂ܵܐ	n. m.	*leper*	(9)
ܓܲܪܒ݂ܵܐ	n. m.	*leprosy*	(4)

ܕܒܚ

ܕܒܲܚ	v.	*sacrifice, immolate*	(7)
ܕܸܒ݂ܚܵܐ	n. m.	*sacrifice, victim*	(25)
ܕܸܒ݂ܚܬ݂ܵܐ	n. f.	*sacrifice*	(9)
ܕܲܒ݂ܚܘܼܬ݂ܵܐ	n. f.	*sacrificing, immolation*	(1)
ܡܲܕ݂ܒ݂ܚܵܐ	n. m.	*altar*	(24)
ܕܒ݂ܝܼܚܵܐ	pass. ptc. m.	*sacrificed* (meat)	(6)

ܕܒܪ

ܕܒܲܪ	v.	*lead, take*; Pa^cel ܕܲܒܲܪ *rule, guide, conduct*	(93)
ܕܲܒ݂ܪܵܐ	n. m.	open *country, desert*	(4)
ܕܘܼܒܵܪܵܐ	n. m.	*custom, manner, conduct, habit* of life	(6)
ܡܲܕ݂ܒܪܵܐ	n. m.	*wilderness, desert*	(19)
ܡܲܕ݂ܒܪܵܝܵܐ	adj.	*desert*	(1)
ܡܕܲܒܪܵܢܵܐ	n. m.	*ruler, guide, leader*	(8)

Syriac	Cat.	Meaning	
ܡܕܲܒܪܵܢܘܼܬ݂ܐ	n. f.	*administration, rule, direction, dispensation*	(4)

		ܕܓܠ	
ܕܲܓܸܠ	v.	Pa^cel *lie, speak falsely*	(10)
ܕܲܓܵܠܐ	adj.	*false, liar*	(38)
ܕܲܓܵܠܘܼܬ݂ܐ	n. f.	*falsity, lie*	(9)

		ܕܗܒ	
ܕܗܒ	den.	Aph^cel *gild*	(2)
ܕܲܗܒ݂ܐ	n. m.	*gold*	(40)

		ܕܘܟ	
ܕܘܼܟ݁ܐ	n. m.	*place*	(2)
ܕܘܼܟ݁ܬ݂ܐ	n. f.	*place*	(69)

		ܕܚܠ	
ܕܲܚܘܼܠܬ݂ܵܢܐ	adj.	*fearful, timorous, timid*	(2)
ܕܚܝܼܠܐ	pass. ptc. m.	*terrible*	(2)
ܕܚܝܼܠܐ	adj.	*afraid*	(6)
ܕܚܸܠ	v.	*fear;* Pa^cel *cause to fear*	(114)
ܕܚܸܠܬ݂ܐ	n. f.	*fear, awe*	(84)

		ܕܚܫܐ	
ܕܲܚܫܐ	n. m.	*guard, attendant, servant, officer*	(11)

		ܕܝܘܐ	
ܕܲܝܘܐ	n. m.	*devil, demon*	(31)
ܕܲܝܘܵܢܐ	adj.	*possessed* (with a demon), *demoniac*	(8)

		ܕܝܠ	
ܕܝܼܠ	particle	*own*	(223)

		ܕܝܢ	
ܕܹܝܢ	particle	*but, yet*	(1828)
ܡܲܕܹܝܢ	particle	*then, therefore*	(16)

Syriac	Cat.	Meaning	
		ܕܝܢܪܐ	
ܕܝܼܢܵܪܵܐ	n. m.	*denarius*	(20)
		ܕܝܬܩܐ	
ܕܝܵܬܹܩܹܐ	n. f.	*testament, covenant*	(31)
		ܕܟܐ	
ܕܘܼܟܵܝܵܐ	n. m.	*cleansing, purification*	(3)
ܕܟܐ	v.	*be pure*; Pa^cel ܕܲܟܝܼ *cleanse*	(68)
ܕܲܟܝܵܐ	adj.	*clean, pure*	(25)
ܕܲܟܝܵܐܝܼܬ	adv.	*purely, sincerely*	(3)
ܕܲܟܝܘܼܬܵܐ	n. f.	*purity*	(9)
ܬܲܕܟܝܼܬܵܐ	n. f.	*purification, excrement, cleansing*	(8)
		ܕܟܪ ¹	
ܕܸܟܪܵܐ	adj.	*male*	(11)
		ܕܟܪ ²	
ܕܘܼܟܪܵܢܵܐ	n. m.	*remembrance, memorial*	(7)
ܕܟܲܪ	v.	Ethp^cel ܐܸܬܕܟܲܪ *remember*; Aph^cel ܐܲܘܕܲܟ *remind, make mention of*	(33)
		ܕܠܚ	
ܕܘܼܠܵܚܵܐ	n. m.	*confusion, tumult*	(1)
ܕܠܲܚ	v.	*trouble, agitate, confuse*	(9)
		ܕܡ	
ܕܡܵܐ	n. m.	*blood*	(96)
		ܕܡܐ	
ܕܘܼܡܝܵܐ	n. m.	*likeness, form, image*	(3)
ܕܡܵܐ	v.	*resemble*; Pa^cel *liken to, compare*	(70)
ܕܡܘܼܬܵܐ	n. f.	*form, image, similitude, type, exemplar, pattern*	(64)
ܕܡܲܝܵܐ	n. m.	*price*	(14)
		ܕܡܟ	
ܕܡܸܟ	v.	*sleep*	(34)

7. Words Arranged by Root

Syriac	Cat.	Meaning	
ܕ݁ܡܰܟ݂ܳܐ	n. m.	*bed, sleep*	(2)
ܕ݁ܡܺܝܟ݂ܳܐ	n. m.	*asleep*	(2)

ܕ݁ܡܰܥ

ܕ݁ܶܡܥܬ݂ܳܐ	n. f.	*tear*	(11)

ܕ݁ܡܰܪ

ܕ݁ܘܡܳܪܳܐ	n. m.	*wonder, amazement*	(3)
ܕ݁ܡܰܪ	v.	Ethpaᶜal ܐܶܬ݁ܕ݁ܰܡܰܪ *marvel, be amazed*	(52)
ܬ݁ܶܕ݂ܡܽܘܪܬ݁ܳܐ	n. f.	*wonder, marvel, prodigy*	(15)

ܕ݁ܢ

ܕ݁ܳܢ	den.	*judge*	(118)
ܕ݁ܺܝܢܳܐ	n. m.	*judgement, sentence* (of judge)	(101)
ܕ݁ܰܝܳܢܳܐ	n. m.	*judge*	(27)
ܡܕ݂ܺܝܢ݇ܬ݁ܳܐ	n. f.	*city*	(223)

ܕ݁ܢܚ

ܕ݁ܢܰܚ	v.	*rise, shine*; Aphᶜel make *rise, dawn*	(12)
ܕ݁ܶܢܚܳܐ	n. m.	*dawn, dayspring, the Epiphany*	(1)
ܡܰܕ݂ܢܚܳܐ	n. f.	*east, Orient*	(9)

ܕ݁ܥܟ

ܕ݁ܥܶܟ݂	v.	*go out* (fire); Paᶜel *quench, extinguish*	(10)

ܕ݁ܪ

ܕ݁ܰܝܪܳܐ	n. f.	*dwelling, fold, habitation*	(1)
ܕ݁ܳܪܳܐ	n. m.	*generation*	(9)
ܕ݁ܳܪܬ݁ܳܐ	n. f.	*court, atrium*	(15)
ܡܕ݂ܰܝܪܳܐ	n. m.	*floor, loft*	(1)

ܕ݁ܪܟ

ܕ݁ܰܘܪܰܟ݂ܬ݁ܳܐ	n. f.	*pace, step*	(1)
ܕ݁ܪܰܟ݂	v.	Aphᶜel ܐܰܕ݂ܪܶܟ݂ *overtake, comprehend*	(18)
ܕ݁ܽܘܪܟ݁ܬ݁ܳܐ	n. f.	*treading out*	(1)

ܕ݁ܪܫ

ܕ݁ܽܘܪܳܫܳܐ	n. m.	*exercise*	(1)

Syriac	Cat.	Meaning	
ܕܪ̈ܘܫܐ	n. m.	*disputer, arguer, logician*	(1)
ܕܪܫ	v.	Pa^cel *train, debate, argue, question, dispute*	(13)
ܕܪܫܐ	n. m.	*disputation, argumentation*	(1)
		ܕܫ	
ܕܫ	v.	*trample*	(10)
		ܗܐ	
ܗܐ	particle	*lo! behold!*	(270)
		ܗܓܡܘܢܐ	
ܗܓܡܘܢܐ	n. m.	*governor, prefect*	(20)
ܗܓܡܢܘܬܐ	n. f.	*governorship, perfecture*	(2)
		ܗܕܡܐ	
ܗܕܡܐ	n. m.	*member, limb*	(38)
		¹ܗܘ	
ܗܘ	pron. m.	*he, it, (as enclitic)is*	(2141)
ܗܘܝܘ	pron.	w/ ܗܘ *i.e. that is to say*	(44)
ܗܘܢ	pron. m.	w/ ܢܐ	(68)
ܗܢܘ	pron. m.	w/ ܡܢ *who is this?*	(126)
ܗܢܘ	pron. m.	w/ ܡܢܐ *what is this?*	(16)
ܠܘ	pron. m.	w/ ܠܐ *no, not*	(34)
ܗܣܘ	pron. m.	w/ ܣ *it suffices*	(20)
		²ܗܘ	
ܗܘ	pron. m.	*that, those,* w/ ܕ *he who*	(1256)
		ܗܘܐ	
ܗܘܐ	v.	*be, (as enclitic)was, turn out*	(4006)
		ܗܝܕܝܢ	
ܗܝܕܝܢ	particle	*then, afterwards, next*	(169)
		ܗܝܟܠ	
ܗܝܟܠܐ	n. m.	*temple, sanctuary*	(117)

7. WORDS ARRANGED BY ROOT

Syriac	Cat.	Meaning	
		ܗܝܡܢ	
ܗܰܝܡܶܢ	v.	*believe, trust* in	(305)
ܗܰܝܡܳܢܘܼܬ݂ܐ	n. f.	*faith, belief*	(264)
ܡܗܰܝܡܢܐ	n. m.	*eunuch, faithful*	(10)
ܡܗܰܝܡܢܐ	n. m.	*believer, believing*	(46)
		ܗܟܘܬ	
ܗܳܟ݂ܘܳܬ	particle	*likewise, so*	(22)
		ܗܟܝܠ	
ܗܳܟ݂ܝܠ	particle	*therefore, hence*	(250)
		ܗܟܢ	
ܗܳܟ݂ܢܐ	particle	*thus*	(282)
		ܗܠܟ	
ܗܰܠܶܟ݂	v.	Paᶜel ܗܰܠܶܟ݂ *walk*	(110)
ܗܶܠܟ݂ܬ݂ܐ	n. f.	*walk, way, footsteps*	(1)
		ܗܢ	
ܗܳܢܐ	pron.	*this, these*	(1578)
		ܗܦܟ	
ܗܘܼܦܳܟ݂ܐ	n. m.	*conduct, behavior, ways, manner of life*	(11)
ܗܦܘܼܟ݂ܝܐ	n. m.	*overthrow*	(1)
ܗܦܰܟ݂	v.	*turn, return;* Ethpaᶜal *conduct oneself*	(91)
ܗܦܘܼܟ݂ܬ݂ܐ	n. f.	*answer, contrary principle*	(1)
		ܗܪ	
ܗܳܪ	v.	*suffer harm;* Aphᶜel *harm, hurt*	(15)
		ܗܪܟܐ	
ܗܳܪܟ݂ܐ	particle	*here, hence*	(51)
		ܗܫܐ	
ܗܳܫܐ	particle	*now*	(193)
		ܘܝ	
ܘܳܝ	particle	*woe! alas for!*	(48)

Syriac	Cat.	Meaning	
		ܙܒܘܪܐ	
ܐܙܒܘܪܐ	n. m.	*bowl, platter*	(14)
		ܙܒܢ	
ܙܒܢ	v.	*buy*; Pa‹el ܙܰܒܶܢ *sell*	(72)
		ܙܒܢܐ	
ܙܒܢܐ	n. m.	*time, season, period*	(227)
		ܙܕܘܩܝܐ	
ܙܳܕܽܘܩܳܝܐ	adj.	*Sadducee*	(14)
		ܙܕܩ	
ܙܰܕܝܩܐ	adj.	*righteous, just, worthy*	(47)
ܙܰܕܝܩܐܝܬ	adv.	*justly, worthily*	(1)
ܙܰܕܝܩܘܬܐ	n. f.	*righteousness, justness, uprightness*	(40)
ܙܕܩ	v.	Pa‹el ܙܰܕܶܩ *justify*; P‹al ܙܕܩ *it is right,*	(58)
		part.*fitting*; Pa‹el ܙܰܕܶܩ *approve*	
ܙܶܕܩܐ	n. m.	*justice, rectitude, propriety*	(1)
ܙܶܕܩܬܐ	n. f.	*alms, almsgiving, charity*	(14)
		ܙܗܪ	
ܙܰܗܝܪܐ	adj.	*cautious, wary*	(3)
ܙܰܗܝܪܐܝܬ	adv.	*cautiously, safely, warily, securely*	(3)
ܙܗܪ	v.	Ethp‹el take *heed*, w/ ܡܢ *beware of*, w/	(41)
		ܒ take *care of*; Pa‹el ܙܰܗܰܪ *warn*	
		ܙܘܓ	
ܙܘܓ	den.	*join together, marry, unite*	(6)
ܙܰܘܓܐ	n. m.	*yoke, pair, couple*	(4)
ܙܽܘܘܳܓܐ	n. m.	*marriage, wedlock*	(1)
		ܙܝܬܐ	
ܙܰܝܬܐ	n. m.	*olive*, w/ ܛܘܪܐ *Mount of Olives*	(19)
		ܙܟܐ	
ܙܟܐ	v.	*overcome*	(31)
ܙܟܘܬܐ	n. f.	*victory, justification*	(9)

7. Words Arranged by Root

Syriac	Cat.	Meaning	
ܢܲܨܝܼܚܵܐ	adj.	*victorious, innocent, pure*	(3)
ܙܡܪ			
ܙܡܝܼܪܬܵܐ	n. f.	*song, psalmody*	(2)
ܙܡܲܪ	v.	*sing, pipe*	(9)
ܙܡܵܪܵܐ	n. m.	*music, singing*	(5)
ܙܲܡܵܪܵܐ	n. m.	*musician, flute-player*	(1)
ܡܙܲܡܪܵܢܵܐ	n. m.	*psalm*	(7)
ܙܢ			
ܙܢ	den.	Pa‘el *arm*	(2)
ܙܲܝܢܵܐ	n. m.	*armour, arms*	(9)
ܙܢܐ			
ܙܢܝܼ	v.	commit *fornication*	(9)
ܙܲܢܵܝܵܐ	adj.	*fornicator, adulterer*	(10)
ܙܵܢܝܘܼܬܵܐ	n. f.	*fornication, adultery, harlotry*	(25)
ܙܵܢܝܼܬܵܐ	n. f.	*harlot, prostitute*	(12)
ܙܘܥ			
ܙܵܥ	v.	*be shaken, be confused;* Aph‘el ܐܲܙܝܼܥ *stir up, trouble, stir*	(44)
ܙܵܘܥܵܐ	n. m.	*earthquake, shaking, agitation, commotion*	(13)
ܙܥܩ			
ܙܥܲܩ	v.	*cry out*	(13)
ܡܙܲܥܩܵܢܵܐ	n. m.	*trumpeter*	(1)
ܙܥܪ			
ܙܥܘܿܪܵܐ	adj.	*little, least*	(66)
ܙܩܐ			
ܙܹܩܵܐ	n. f.	*wineskin, leather bag*	(12)
ܙܩܦ			
ܙܩܝܼܦܵܐ	n. m.	*cross, the Cross*	(26)
ܙܩܲܦ	v.	*crucify, lift up, elevate, erect*	(50)

Syriac	Cat.	Meaning	
ܙܪܥ			
ܙܳܪܘܿܥܳܐ	n. m.	*sower*	(6)
ܙܪܰܥ	v.	*sow*	(50)
ܙܰܪܥܳܐ	n. m.	*seed*	(50)
ܙܰܪܥܽܘܢܳܐ	n. m.	*grain, seed*	(4)
ܚܒ			
ܚܰܒ	v.	*be kindled*; Pa^cel *love*	(103)
ܚܰܒܽܘܚܳܐ	n. m.	*twig, stick*	(1)
ܚܰܒܺܝܒܳܐ	adj.	*beloved*	(65)
ܚܰܒܳܐ	n. f.	*stubble, straw, stalk*	(1)
ܚܽܘܒܳܐ	n. m.	*love, lovingkindness*	(125)
ܚܳܒ	v.	*be condemned, owe*; Pa^cel ܚܰܝܶܒ *condemn*	(48)
ܚܰܘܒܳܐ	n. m.	*debt, liability, wrong*	(3)
ܚܰܘܒܬܳܐ	n. f.	*debt*	(2)
ܚܽܘܝܳܒܳܐ	n. m.	*condemnation, judgement*	(5)
ܚܰܝܳܒܳܐ	adj.	*debtor*	(45)
ܚܰܝܳܒܽܘܬܳܐ	n. f.	*condemnation, judgement*	(3)
ܚܒܠ			
ܚܰܒܶܠ	v.	Pa^cel *corrupt, destroy, alter*	(35)
ܚܒܳܠܳܐ	n. m.	*corruption, decay*	(19)
ܡܚܰܒܠܳܢܳܐ	n. m.	*destroyer, corrupter*	(1)
ܡܶܬܚܰܒܠܳܢܽܘܬܳܐ	n. f.	*corruptibility*	(5)
ܡܚܰܒܠܳܐ	pass. ptc. m.	*corrupted*	(1)
ܚܒܪ			
ܚܰܒܪܳܐ	n. m.	*friend, companion, associate, comrade, neighbour*	(29)
ܚܒܫ			
ܚܒܽܘܫܝܳܐ	n. m.	*imprisonment, confinement, constraint*	(7)

Syriac	Cat.	Meaning	
ܚܒܫ	v.	*confine, include*	(9)
		ܚܓܪ	
ܚܓܝܪܐ	pass. ptc. m.	*lame*	(7)
ܚܓܪ	v.	*limp*	(1)
ܡܚܓܪܐ	pass. ptc. m.	*lame*	(2)
		ܚܕ	
ܚܕ	num. m.	*one*, (as adj)certain *one*, w/ ܚܕ ܚܕ *each one*	(739)
ܚܕ ܒܫܒܐ	idiom	*Sunday*	(1)
ܚܕܕܐ	pron. m.	*one another*	(16)
ܚܕܥܣܪ	num. f.	*eleven*	(9)
ܡܚܕܐ	particle	*immediately, at once*	(61)
		ܚܕܝ	
ܚܕܘܬܐ	n. f.	*joy, gladness*	(64)
ܚܕܝ	v.	*be glad, rejoice*; Pa^{c}el *gladden*	(76)
ܚܕܝܐ	adj.	*joyous*	(1)
ܚܕܝܐܝܬ	adv.	*gladly, readily*	(6)
		ܚܕܪ	
ܚܕܘܪܐ	adj.	*mendicant, vagrant*	(1)
ܚܕܪ	v.	*surround, wander, beg*; Aph^{c}el ܐܚܕܪ *hedge*	(14)
ܚܕܪܐ	n. m.	*surroundings, circle, vagrancy*	(22)
ܚܘܕܪܢܐܝܬ	adv.	*round about*	(1)
		ܚܕܬ	
ܚܕܬ	v.	Pa^{c}el ܚܕܬ *renew, restore*	(6)
ܚܕܬܐ	adj.	*new*	(59)
ܚܕܬܐܝܬ	adv.	*anew*	(1)
ܚܕܬܘܬܐ	n. f.	*newness*	(1)

Syriac	Cat.	Meaning	
ܡܘܕ̈ܝܐ	n. m.	renewal, Encaenia, Dedication (feast)	(3)
		ܚܘܐ	
ܚܘܐ	v.	Paᶜel ܚܰܘܺܝ show	(97)
ܬܚܘܝܬܐ	n. f.	example, appearance, demonstration	(9)
		ܚܘܕ	
ܒܠܚܘܕ	adv.	only, alone	(128)
ܠܚܘܕ	adj.	alone	(1)
		ܚܘܝܐ	
ܚܘܝܐ	n. m.	serpent	(13)
		ܚܘܪ	
ܚܘܪ	v.	be white; Paᶜel make white	(6)
ܚܘܪܐ	adj.	white	(21)
ܡܚܘܪܐ	ap f	whitened	(1)
		ܚܙܐ	
ܚܙܘܢܐ	n. m.	vision, spectacle	(3)
ܚܙܐ	v.	see, behold	(734)
ܚܙܘܐ	n. m.	appearance, aspect, apparition	(28)
ܚܙܝܐ	n. m.	observer, spectator, eye-witness	(3)
ܚܙܝܐ	n. m.	sight	(2)
ܚܙܝܬܐ	n. f.	sight, spectacle, aspect, appearance	(5)
ܡܚܙܝܐ	n. m.	sight, w/ ܥܝܢܐ eyeservice	(2)
ܡܚܙܝܬܐ	n. f.	mirror	(3)
		ܚܙܝܪ	
ܚܙܝܪܐ	n. m.	swine	(14)
		ܚܙܩ	
ܚܙܩ	v.	gird, journey	(9)
ܚܙܩܐ	n. m.	bond, belt, band	(2)
		ܚܛܐ	
ܚܛܐ	v.	sin, err	(39)
ܚܛܗܐ	n. m.	sin	(103)

7. WORDS ARRANGED BY ROOT

Syriac	Cat.	Meaning	
ܚܛܝܐ	adj.	*sinner*	(49)
ܚܛܝܬܐ	n. f.	*sin*	(87)

ܚܛܦ

ܚܛܘܦܐ	adj.	*ravenous, extortioner, rapacious*	(5)
ܚܛܘܦܝܐ	n. m.	*extortion, robbery*	(4)
ܚܛܦ	v.	*seize, snatch*	(17)

ܚܛܬܐ

ܚܛܬܐ	n. f.	*wheat*	(12)

ܚܝܐ

ܚܝܐ	v.	*live;* Aphᶜel ܐܚܝ *make* live, *save*	(165)
ܚܝܐ	adj.	*alive, living*	(89)
ܚܝܐ	n. m.	*life, salvation*	(177)
ܚܝܘܬܐ	n. f.	*living* creature, *animal*	(67)
ܚܝܬܐ	n. f.	w/ ܡܝܬܐ *resurrection, revivification*	(5)
ܡܚܝܢܐ	adj.	*life-giving, Saviour, preserver*	(16)

ܚܝܠ

ܚܝܠ	den.	Paᶜel ܚܝܠ *strengthen, confirm*	(18)
ܚܝܠܐ	n. f.	*power, mighty work, strength, virtue, force*	(150)
ܚܝܠܬܢܐ	adj.	*strong, mighty, robust, potentate*	(20)

ܚܟܡ

ܚܟܝܡܐ	adj.	*wise, prudent, cunning* (words)	(36)
ܚܟܝܡܐܝܬ	adv.	*wisely, prudently*	(2)
ܚܟܡ	v.	*know;* Paᶜel give *wisdom*	(4)
ܚܟܡܬܐ	n. f.	*wisdom*	(53)

ܚܠ

ܚܠܐ	n. m.	*vinegar*	(7)
ܚܠܐ	n. m.	*dust*	(6)
ܚܠܬܐ	n. f.	*sheath, scabbard*	(1)

Syriac	Cat.	Meaning	
		ܚܠܡ	
ܚܠܝܡܐ	adj.	*whole, healthy, sound, strong*	(20)
ܚܠܝܡܘܬܐ	n. f.	*health, strength*	(1)
ܚܠܡ	v.	Ethpᶜel ܐܬܚܠܡ *be cured*; Aphᶜel ܐܚܠܡ *cure*	(14)
		ܚܠܦ	
ܚܠܦ	v.	Paᶜel *change, transmute*; Shaphᶜel *change, alter*	(20)
ܚܠܦ	prep.	*for, instead*	(117)
ܡܫܚܠܦܐ	pass. ptc. m.	*different, diverse, various*	(11)
ܫܘܚܠܦܐ	n. m.	*change, variation*	(5)
ܐܚܠܘܦܐ	n. m.	*exchange*	(2)
		ܚܡܡ	
ܚܘܡܐ	n. m.	*heat*	(4)
ܚܡ	v.	*be hot*; Aphᶜel *burn*	(4)
ܚܡܝܡܐ	adj.	*hot*	(3)
		ܚܡܪ	
ܚܡܝܪܐ	n. m.	*leaven*	(14)
ܚܡܪܐ	n. m.	*wine*	(37)
		ܚܡܫ	
ܚܡܫܐ	num. f.	*five*	(49)
ܚܡܫܝܢ	num.	*fifty*	(8)
ܚܡܫܡܐܐ	num.	*five hundred*	(2)
ܚܡܫܬܥܣܪ	num. m.	*fifteen*	(4)
		ܚܡܬ	
ܚܡܬ	den.	Ethpaᶜal ܐܬܚܡܬ grow *angry*	(4)
ܚܡܬܐ	n. f.	*anger, wrath, fury*	(20)
ܚܡܬܢܐ	adj.	*wrathful, irascible, furious*	(1)

Syriac	Cat.	Meaning	
		ܚܢ	
ܚܢ	v.	have *compassion*; Ethpᶜel obtain *mercy*; Ethpaᶜal *implore*, *supplicate*	(9)
ܚܢܢܐ	n. m.	*compassion*, *mercy*, *favour*	(11)
ܐܬܚܢܢܬܐ	n. f.	*intercession*	(1)
		ܚܢܦ	
ܚܢܦܐ	adj.	*godless*, *Gentile*, *heathen*, *foreigner*, *profane*	(12)
		ܚܢܩ	
ܚܢܩ	v.	*choke*, *strangle*; Paᶜel *drown*	(12)
ܡܚܢܘܩܝܬܐ	n. f.	*noose*, *halter*	(1)
ܚܢܩܐ	n. m.	*strangle*	(2)
		ܚܣ	
ܚܣ	v.	*spare*, *pity*	(11)
ܚܘܣܢܐ	n. m.	*moderation*, *parsimony*	(2)
ܚܣ	particle	*God forbid*, *let it not be*	(16)
		ܚܣܐ	
ܚܘܣܝܐ	n. m.	*propitiation*	(4)
ܚܣܝܐ	den.	Paᶜel ܚܣܝ *absolve*, *free*, *exempt*	(3)
ܚܣܝܐ	adj.	*holy*, *pure*, *innocent*	(5)
ܚܣܝܘܬܐ	n. f.	*holiness*, *purity*	(1)
		ܚܣܕ	
ܚܣܕ	den.	Paᶜel ܚܣܕ *revile*, *reproach*, *upbraid*	(9)
ܚܣܕܐ	n. m.	*reproach*, *disgrace*, *opprobrium*	(6)
ܡܚܣܕܢܐ	adj.	*reviler*	(1)
		ܚܣܡ	
ܚܣܡ	v.	*envy*, *be jealous*	(8)
ܚܣܡܐ	n. m.	*envy*, *emulation*, *jealousy*	(16)
		ܚܣܢ	
ܚܣܝܢܐ	adj.	*strong*, *mighty*	(10)

Syriac	Cat.	Meaning	
ܚܣܢ	v.	*be strong, prevail*; Pa‘el *strengthen*	(3)
ܚܣܢܐ	n. m.	*stronghold*	(1)
ܡܚܣܢ	adv.	*scarcely, hardly*	(8)

ܚܣܪ

ܚܘܣܪܢܐ	n. m.	*loss, detriment*	(4)
ܚܣܝܪܐ	adj.	*lacking, deficient*	(21)
ܚܣܝܪܘܬܐ	n. f.	*want, need, defect*	(13)
ܚܣܪ	v.	*lack, lose*	(14)

ܚܦܛ

ܚܦܛ	v.	Pa‘el ܚܦܛ *exhort, incite, encourage*	(19)
ܚܦܝܛܐ	pass. ptc. m.	*diligent, careful, strenuous, busy, earnest*	(2)
ܚܦܝܛܐܝܬ	adv.	*diligently, eagerly*	(2)
ܚܦܝܛܘܬܐ	n. f.	*diligence, zest, earnestness, perseverance*	(10)

ܚܨܐ

| ܚܨܐ | n. m. | *back* (of the body), *loins* | (18) |
| ܚܨܐ | v. | *pluck out* | (4) |

ܚܨܕ

ܚܨܕ	v.	*reap*	(20)
ܚܨܕܐ	n. m.	*harvest*	(12)
ܚܨܘܕܐ	n. m.	*reaper*	(4)

ܚܪ

ܚܐܪܐ	adj.	*free, noble, freedman*	(18)
ܚܐܪܘܬܐ	n. f.	*freedom, liberty*	(10)
ܚܪܪ	v.	Pa‘el ܚܪܪ *set free*	(13)
ܚܘܪܪܐ	n. m.	*freedom, liberty, manumission, emancipation*	(1)
ܚܪ	v.	*look, behold*	(62)
ܚܘܪܐ	n. m.	*example, form, outline, pattern*	(1)

Syriac	Cat.	Meaning	
ܡܚܰܪܽܘܪܳܐ	n. m.	*set free*	(2)
		ܚܪܐ	
ܚܪܳܐ	v.	Ethp^cel *hold on to, affirm, strive, argue, contend*	(13)
ܚܶܪܝܳܢܳܐ	n. m.	*contention, strife, dispute, altercation, contradiction*	(22)
		ܚܪܒ	
ܚܽܘܪܒܳܐ	n. m.	*wilderness, plain, desolation*	(30)
ܚܪܶܒ	v.	*be desolate, devastate*	(3)
ܚܰܪܶܒ	v.	*lay waste*	(1)
ܚܰܪܒܳܐ	adj.	*desolate*	(4)
		ܚܪܒܐ	
ܚܰܪܒܳܐ	n. c.	*sword, slaughter, ploughshare*	(14)
		ܚܪܡ	
ܚܪܡ	v.	Aph^{c}el *vow, curse, anathematize*	(5)
ܚܶܪܡܳܐ	n. m.	*curse, anathema*	(7)
		ܚܪܦ	
ܚܰܪܺܝܦܳܐ	adj.	*sharp, incisive, keen, fervent*	(9)
ܚܰܪܺܝܦܳܐܺܝܬ	adv.	*suddenly, sharply*	(1)
		ܚܪܩ	
ܚܽܘܪܳܩܳܐ	n. m.	*gnashing*	(7)
ܚܰܪܶܩ	v.	Pa^{c}el *gnash*	(3)
		ܚܪܫ	
ܚܰܪܫܳܐ	adj.	*dumb, mute, deaf*	(16)
		ܚܪܫܐ	
ܚܰܪܳܫܳܐ	n. m.	*sorcerer*	(5)
ܚܰܪܫܳܐ	n. m.	*sorcery, enchantment*	(4)
ܚܰܪܳܫܽܘܬܳܐ	n. f.	*witchcraft, magic*	(1)
		ܚܫ	
ܚܰܫ	v.	*feel, suffer*	(35)

7. WORDS ARRANGED BY ROOT

Syriac	Cat.	Meaning	
ܚܰܫܳܐ	n. m.	*feeling, suffering, experience, affection, passion, lust*	(16)
ܚܳܫܽܘܫܳܐ	adj.	capable of *feeling*	(2)

ܚܫܒ

ܚܽܘܫܳܒܳܐ	n. m.	*reckoning, thought, idea*	(1)
ܚܽܘܫܒܳܢܳܐ	n. m.	*reckoning, calculation, account*	(7)
ܚܫܰܒ	v.	*think, reckon, deliberate*	(66)
ܡܰܚܫܰܒܬܳܐ	n. f.	*thought, reasoning, counsel*	(23)

ܚܫܚ

ܚܽܘܫܳܚܳܐ	n. m.	*use*	(2)
ܚܫܰܚ	v.	*be useful*; Ethpaᶜal ܐܶܬܚܰܫܰܚ *use, adapt, apply*	(13)
ܚܳܫܳܚܽܘܬܳܐ	n. f.	*advantage, usefulness, utility*	(3)
ܚܫܰܚܬܳܐ	n. f.	*use, usage, using, need*	(8)

ܚܫܟ

| ܚܶܫܽܘܟܳܐ | adj. | *dark, darkness* (dark place) | (52) |
| ܚܫܶܟ | v. | grow *dark*; Aphᶜel *darken*; Ettaphᶜal *be darkened* | (11) |

ܚܫܡ

| ܚܫܰܡ | den. | Aphᶜel eat *supper* | (4) |
| ܚܫܳܡܺܝܬܳܐ | n. f. | *supper*; pl. *feasts* | (15) |

ܚܬܡ

ܚܬܰܡ	v.	*seal, stamp, impress*	(10)
ܚܳܬܡܳܐ	n. m.	*seal*, token of *ratification*	(5)
ܚܬܺܝܡܳܐ	pass. ptc. m.	*sealed*	(2)

ܚܬܢ

| ܚܰܬܢܳܐ | n. m. | *bridegroom* | (15) |

ܚܬܪ

| ܚܰܬܺܝܪܳܐ | adj. | *proud* | (2) |
| ܚܬܺܝܪܽܘܬܳܐ | n. f. | *boasting, vaunting, swelling* | (2) |

Syriac	Cat.	Meaning	
ܚܬܪ	v.	Ethpᶜel *be puffed up*, *be proud*; Aphᶜel make *proud*	(7)
		ܛܒ	
ܛܒ	v.	Aphᶜel ܐܛܒ *inform*	(2)
ܛܒܐ	n. m.	*fame*, *rumour*, *report*	(9)
		ܛܒܥ	
ܛܒܥ	v.	Tr. *seal*, Int. *sink*; Paᶜel *drown*, Tr. *stamp*	(8)
ܛܒܥܐ	n. m.	*seal*, *stamp*	(13)
		ܛܗܡ	
ܛܘܗܡܐ	n. m.	*kin*, *family*, *birth*, *nationality*	(15)
		ܛܘܒ	
ܛܒܐ	adj.	*good*, w/ ܛܒ *much*	(214)
ܛܒܘܬܐ	n. f.	*goodness*	(2)
ܛܝܒ	v.	Paᶜel ܛܝܒ make *ready*	(70)
ܛܘܒܐ	n. m.	*blessedness*, *beatitude*, *happiness*	(48)
ܛܘܒܢܐ	adj.	*blessed*, *happy*	(4)
ܛܘܝܒܐ	n. m.	*preparedness*, *readiness*, *promptitude*, *preparation*	(2)
ܛܝܒܘܬܐ	n. f.	*grace*, *goodness*, *favour*, *kindness*, *graciousuess*	(154)
ܡܛܝܒܐ	pass. ptc. m.	*prepared*, *ready*	(1)
		ܛܘܪܐ	
ܛܘܪܐ	n. m.	*mountain*, *hill*	(66)
		ܛܠܠ	
ܛܠܠ	den.	Aphᶜel *overshadow*	(4)
ܛܠܠܐ	n. m.	*shadow*, *shade*	(3)
ܛܠܢܝܬܐ	n. f.	*shadow*, *shade*, *adumbration*, *type*	(5)
ܡܛܠܠܐ	n. m.	*shelter*	(5)
ܡܛܠܬܐ	n. f.	*booth*, *tabernacle*, *shade*, *shed*	(4)

Syriac	Cat.	Meaning	
ܛܰܠܠܟܳܢܳܐ	n. m.	*roof, rafter*	(2)

ܛܠܝ

ܛܰܠܝܳܐ	n. m.	*boy, youth, servant*; f. *girl*; f. *maid*	(80)
ܛܰܠܝܽܘܬܳܐ	n. f.	*youth, childhood*	(9)

ܛܠܡ

ܛܠܰܡ	v.	*reject, deny, wrong*	(15)

ܛܢܦ

ܛܡܐ	den.	Ethpaᶜal be considered *unclean*	(1)
ܛܰܡܐܐ	adj.	*unclean, impure*	(11)
ܛܰܡܐܘܬܐ	n. f.	*uncleaness, impurity, pollution*	(4)

ܛܢ

ܛܶܢ	v.	*be eager, be jealous*; Aphᶜel *provoke jealousy*	(12)
ܛܢܳܢܳܐ	n. m.	*jealousy, zeal*	(12)
ܛܰܢܳܢܳܐ	adj.	*zealot, zealous*	(6)

ܛܢܦ

ܛܢܶܦ	v.	*be soiled*; Paᶜel *soil, defile, pollute*	(2)
ܛܰܢܦܳܐ	adj.	*defiled, unclean, impure, filthy*	(31)
ܛܰܢܦܘܬܐ	n. f.	*uncleaness, impurity*	(14)

ܛܥܐ

ܛܽܘܥܰܝ	n. f.	*error, deception*	(7)
ܛܥܳܐ	v.	*wander, err, forget*; Aphᶜel ܐܛܥܺܝ *deceive*, go *astray*, lead *astray, delude*	(76)
ܛܥܝܘܬܐ	n. f.	*error, deception, mistake*	(10)
ܡܰܛܥܝܳܢܳܐ	adj.	*deceiver, impostor*	(7)
ܡܰܛܥܝܳܢܘܬܐ	n. f.	*error, deception*	(1)
ܛܰܥܝܳܐ	n. m.	*wandering, errant*	(2)

ܛܥܡ

ܛܥܶܡ	v.	*taste*; Ethpᶜel ܐܬܛܥܶܡ *be grafted*; Aphᶜel *graft, partake* (of)	(22)

7. Words Arranged by Root

Syriac	Cat.	Meaning	
ܛܥܢ			
ܛܥܢ	v.	bear, carry; Aphᶜel make *carry*	(12)
ܛܥܢܐ	n. m.	burden, load, cargo	(3)
ܛܪܦ			
ܛܪܦ	v.	smite, beat	(5)
ܛܪܦܐ	n. m.	leaf	(6)
ܛܫܐ			
ܛܘܫܝܐ	n.	w/ ܒ+ secretly	(6)
ܛܫܐ	v.	hide oneself, be hidden; Paᶜel ܛܫܝ hide	(22)
ܡܛܫܝܐܝܬ	adv.	secretly	(3)
ܝܐܐ			
ܝܐܝܐ	adj.	due, becoming, seemly, congruous, decorous	(11)
ܝܐܝܘܬܐ	n. f.	seemliness, beauty	(1)
ܝܒܠ			
ܝܒܠ	v.	Aphᶜel ܐܘܒܠ conduct, take, lead away; Ethpaᶜal ܐܬܝܒܠ be transmitted	(24)
ܝܘܒܠܐ	n. m.	progeny, course, succession	(1)
ܝܘܒܠܐ	n. f.	burden, load	(9)
ܝܒܫ			
ܝܒܝܫܐ	adj.	dry, withered	(9)
ܝܒܫ	v.	dry up, wither; Aphᶜel cause to *wither*	(12)
ܝܒܫܐ	n. m.	dry *land*, earth	(10)
ܝܕ			
ܐܝܕܐ	n. f.	hand, w/ ܒ through, w/ ܠܘܬ near	(362)
ܝܕܐ			
ܝܕܐ	v.	Aphᶜel ܐܘܕܝ confess, give *thanks*; Eshtaphᶜal ܐܫܬܘܕܝ profess, promise	(83)
ܡܘܕܝܢܐ	n. m.	promise	(13)
ܬܘܕܝܬܐ	n. f.	confession, thanksgiving, avowal	(17)

7. WORDS ARRANGED BY ROOT

Syriac	Cat.	Meaning	
		ܝܕܥ	
ܝܳܕܘܥܳܐ	n. m.	*acquaintance, familiar person*	(2)
ܝܺܕܺܝܥܳܐ	pass. ptc. m.	*apparent, known, certain* (one), *notable*	(12)
ܝܺܕܰܥܬܳܐ	n. f.	*knowledge, perception, concept*	(1)
ܝܺܕܰܥ	v.	*know*; Aph°el ܐܘܕܰܥ make *known*; Eshtaph°al ܐܫܬܰܘܕܰܥ *recognize*	(704)
ܝܺܕܰܥܬܳܐ	n. f.	*knowledge*	(49)
ܡܰܕܥܳܐ	n. m.	*knowledge, understanding, mind*	(18)
ܣܘܽܘܕܳܥܳܐ	n. m.	*acknowledgement, sign, indication, recognition*	(4)
ܝܺܕܥܳܐ	n. m.	*acquaintance*	(1)
		ܝܗܒ	
ܝܰܗܒ	v.	*give*	(534)
ܝܳܗܘܽܒܳܐ	n. m.	*giver*	(1)
ܡܰܘܗܰܒܬܳܐ	n. f.	*gift*	(46)
ܡܰܬܠܳܐ	n. m.	act of *giving*	(1)
		ܝܗܘܕ	
ܝܺܗܘܽܕܳܐܝܺܬ	adv.	*Judaically*	(2)
ܝܺܗܘܽܕܳܝܳܐ	adj.	*Jew*	(205)
ܝܺܗܘܽܕܳܝܘܽܬܳܐ	n. f.	*Judaism*	(2)
		ܝܘܡ	
ܝܰܘܡܳܐ	n. m.	*day*	(381)
ܝܰܘܡܳܢܳܐ	n. m.	*to-day*	(42)
		ܝܘܢܐ	
ܝܰܘܢܳܐ	n. c.	*dove*	(10)
		ܝܚܕ	
ܝܺܚܺܝܕܳܝܳܐ	adj.	*only, only begotten*	(8)
ܡܚܰܝܰܕܬܳܐ	ap f	*desolate, solitary, alone*	(1)
ܝܺܚܺܝܕܳܐ	n. m.	*only-begotten, single*	(1)

7. WORDS ARRANGED BY ROOT

Syriac	Cat.	Meaning	
		ܝܠܕ	
ܝܺܠܶܕ	v.	Aph^cel ܐܰܘܠܶܕ *beget*, *bear* (a child)	(120)
ܝܰܠܕܳܐ	n. m.	*birth, offspring, fruit* (of the vine)	(12)
ܝܰܠܽܘܕܳܐ	n. m.	*infant, child, babe*	(14)
ܝܳܠܽܘܕܳܐ	n. m.	*parent, begetter*	(1)
ܝܰܠܺܝܕܽܘܬܳܐ	n. f.	*origin, descent, ancestry, genealogy*	(1)
ܡܰܘܠܳܕܳܐ	n. m.	*birth*	(3)
ܝܰܠܕܳܐ	n. m.	*son*	(2)
		ܝܠܦ	
ܡܰܠܰܦ	pass. ptc. m.	*taught*	(4)
ܝܽܘܠܦܳܢܳܐ	n. m.	*teaching, instruction, doctrine*	(66)
ܝܺܠܶܦ	v.	*learn*; Pa^cel ܐܰܠܶܦ *teach*	(147)
ܡܰܠܦܳܢܳܐ	n. m.	*teacher*	(44)
ܡܰܠܦܳܢܽܘܬܳܐ	n. f.	*teaching, doctrine*	(2)
		ܝܡܐ	
ܝܺܡܳܐ	v.	*swear*; Aph^cel make *swear*, take an oath	(34)
ܡܰܘܡܳܬܳܐ	n. f.	*oath, curse*	(18)
		²ܝܡܐ	
ܝܰܡܳܐ	n. m.	*sea*	(108)
ܝܰܡܬܳܐ	n. f.	*lake*	(11)
		ܝܡܢ	
ܝܰܡܺܝܢܳܐ	n. f.	*right*	(52)
ܐܰܝܡܢܳܐ	n. f.	*south*	(9)
		ܝܣܦ	
ܝܣܦ	v.	Aph^cel ܐܰܘܣܶܦ *add, increase*	(25)
		ܝܨܦ	
ܝܰܨܺܝܦܳܐܝܺܬ	adv.	*carefully, anxiously*	(1)

Syriac	Cat.	Meaning	
ܡܲܪܢܝܼܬ݂ܵܐ	n. f.	diligence, solicitude, anxiety, importunity	(1)
ܡܪܚ	v.	be careful, be anxious, be solicitous	(30)
ܪܸܢܝܵܐ	n. f.	care, anxiety	(8)

ܝܩܕ

ܝܩܸܕ	v.	burn; Aphᶜel ܐܘܩܸܕ set (on fire)	(30)
ܝܲܩܕܵܐ	n. m.	burnt offering	(3)
ܝܲܩܕܵܢܵܐ	n. m.	burning, conflagration	(3)
ܝܲܩܕܵܐ	adj.	burning	(2)

ܝܩܪ

ܐܝܼܩܵܪܵܐ	n. m.	honour, glory, majesty	(39)
ܝܘܼܩܪܵܐ	n. m.	burden, load	(7)
ܝܲܩܝܼܪܵܐ	adj.	heavy, precious	(24)
ܝܲܩܝܼܪܵܐܝܼܬ݂	adv.	with difficulty, heavily	(2)
ܝܩܲܪ	v.	be heavy, be precious; Paᶜel honour; Aphᶜel make heavy	(41)
ܡܝܲܩܪܵܐ	pass. ptc. m.	honourable, precious	(1)

ܝܪܚ

| ܝܲܪܚܵܐ | n. m. | month | (21) |

ܝܪܬ

ܝܘܼܪܬܵܢܵܐ	n. m.	hereditary, inheritance, possession	(3)
ܝܼܪܸܬ݂	v.	inherit, heir	(18)
ܝܵܪܬܘܼܬ݂ܵܐ	n. f.	inheritance	(17)
ܝܵܪܬܵܐ	n. m.	heir	(16)

ܝܫܛ

| ܝܫܛ | v. | Aphᶜel ܐܘܫܸܛ stretch out | (12) |

ܝܬܒ

| ܝܼܬ݂ܸܒ݂ | v. | sit; Aphᶜel ܐܘܬ݂ܸܒ݂ seat, establish | (148) |
| ܡܲܘܬܒ݂ܵܐ | n. m. | seat | (6) |

Syriac	Cat.	Meaning	
ܬܰܘܬܳܒܳܐ	adj.	*settler, stranger, sojourner*	(8)
ܬܰܘܬܳܒܽܘܬܳܐ	n. f.	*sojourning*	(1)
ܝܳܬܒܳܐ	n. m.	*inhabitant*	(1)

ܝܬܪ

ܝܽܘܬܪܳܢܳܐ	n. m.	*lucre, advantage, profit, gain, abundance*	(12)
ܝܰܬܝܪܳܐ	adj.	*more, excessive, greater, better, excelling*	(100)
ܝܰܬܝܪܳܐܝܺܬ	adv.	*abundantly, especially, exceedingly*	(78)
ܝܰܬܝܪܽܘܬܳܐ	n. f.	*abundance, excellence, superiority*	(7)
ܝܬܰܪ	v.	*gain, remain over, abound*; Pac̄el make *abound*, w/ ܡܢ *prefer*; Aphc̄el ܐܰܘܬܰܪ *benefit*	(80)
ܡܝܰܬܪܳܢܳܐ	adj.	*profitable, useful*	(1)
ܡܝܰܬܪܳܐ	pass. ptc. m.	*excellent, eminent*	(5)
ܡܝܰܬܪܽܘܬܳܐ	n. f.	*excellence, virtue*	(3)
ܝܽܘܬܳܪܳܐ	n. m.	*remainder*	(5)

ܟܐ

ܟܳܐ	particle	*here*	(11)

ܟܐܐ

ܟܐܳܐ	v.	*rebuke, reprove*	(29)
ܟܐܳܬܳܐ	n. f.	*reproof, rebuke*	(1)

ܟܐܒ

ܟܐܶܒ	v.	*suffer, grieve*	(2)
ܟܐܒܳܐ	n. m.	*pain, suffering, disease*	(14)
ܟܐܺܒܳܐ	adj.	*painful*	(1)
ܡܰܟܐܒܳܐ	pass. ptc. m.	*afflicted*	(1)

ܟܐܦ

ܟܐܦܳܐ	n. f.	*stone, rock*	(69)

Syriac	Cat.	Meaning	
		ܟܒܪ	
ܟܒܰܪ	particle	*perhaps, long ago*	(17)
		ܟܒܫ	
ܟܒܰܫ	v.	*overcome, subdue*	(4)
ܟܽܘܒܫܳܐ	n. m.	*footstool*	(7)
		ܟܕ	
ܟܰܕ	particle	*when, after, while, where*	(1214)
		ܟܗܢ	
ܟܗܶܢ	den.	Pa‘el ܟܰܗܶܢ be a *priest*	(2)
ܟܳܗܢܳܐ	n. m.	*priest*	(121)
ܟܳܗܢܽܘܬܳܐ	n. f.	*priesthood*	(2)
ܟܳܗܢܳܝܳܐ	adj.	*priestly, sacerdotal*	(1)
		ܟܘܒܐ	
ܟܽܘܒܳܐ	n. m.	*thorn*	(14)
		ܟܘܟܒ	
ܟܰܘܟܒܳܐ	n. m.	*star, planet*	(28)
		ܟܘܡܪܐ	
ܟܽܘܡܪܳܐ	n. m.	*priest*	(28)
ܟܽܘܡܪܽܘܬܳܐ	n. f.	*priesthood*	(6)
ܟܽܘܡܪܳܬܳܐ	n. f.	*priestess*	(1)
		ܟܘܪܣܝܐ	
ܟܽܘܪܣܝܳܐ	n. m.	*throne, seat*	(59)
		ܟܝ	
ܟܺܝ	particle	*now, indeed, perhaps*	(16)
		ܟܝܠ	
ܟܳܠ	v.	Aph‘el *measure*	(6)
ܟܰܝܠܳܐ	n. m.	*measure*	(1)
ܡܰܟܝܠܬܳܐ	n. f.	*measure*	(4)

7. Words Arranged by Root

Syriac	Cat.	Meaning	
ܟܟܪܐ	n. f.	*talent*	(12)

¹ ܟܠ

Syriac	Cat.	Meaning	
ܟܠܠ	v.	Ethpaʿal *be crowned*	(1)
ܟܠܝܠܐ	n. m.	*crown, wreath*	(19)
ܟܠܬܐ	n. f.	*bride, daughter-in-law*	(9)

² ܟܠ

Syriac	Cat.	Meaning	
ܟܠ، ܟܘܠ	particle	*all, every, whole, entirely*	(1400)
ܟܠ ܐܢܫ	idiom	*everyone*	(1)
ܟܠܕܡ	idiom	*always*	(52)
ܟܠܚܕ	idiom	*each one*	(5)
ܟܠܝܘܡ	idiom	*everyday*	(21)
ܟܠܡܕܡ	idiom	*everything*	(83)
ܟܠܥܕܢ	idiom	*always*	(1)
ܟܠܡܢ	idiom	*whoever*	(8)

ܟܠܐ

Syriac	Cat.	Meaning	
ܟܠܐ	v.	*hinder, forbid, restrain*	(25)
ܟܘܠܝܢܐ	n. m.	*hindrance, prohibition*	(1)
ܟܠܝܬܐ	n. f.	*obstacle*	(1)

ܟܠܝܪܟ

Syriac	Cat.	Meaning	
ܟܠܝܪܟܐ	n. m.	*capt of a thousand*	(20)

ܟܡܐ

Syriac	Cat.	Meaning	
ܟܡܐ	particle	*how much? how many?*	(73)

ܟܢ

Syriac	Cat.	Meaning	
ܟܐܢܐ	adj.	*upright, just, righteous*	(23)
ܟܐܢܐܝܬ	adv.	*rightly, justly*	(2)
ܟܐܢܘܬܐ	n. f.	*righteousness, uprightness, godliness, rectitude, justice*	(67)
ܟܘܘܢܐ	n. m.	*reproof*	(1)

Syriac	Cat.	Meaning	
ܩܘ	v.	*exist*; Paᶜel *reprove, rebuke*; Aphᶜel *create*	(19)
ܩܝܢܐ	n. m.	*nature*	(17)
ܩܝܢܐܝܬ	adv.	*naturally*	(1)
ܡܩܝܢܐ	pass. ptc. m.	*natural, created*	(1)
ܩܘ	particle	*afterwards*	(1)

ܟܢܐ

ܟܢܐ	v.	Ethpaᶜal ܐܬܟܢܝ *be named*	(6)
ܟܢܬܐ	n. m.	*companion, fellow* servant	(10)

ܟܢܫ

ܟܢܘܫܬܐ	n. m.	*congregation, assembly, synagogue*	(4)
ܟܢܘܫܬܐ	n. f.	*synagogue, council*	(76)
ܟܢܫ	v.	*assemble, gather*	(105)
ܟܢܫܐ	n. m.	*gathering* (of persons), *multitude, council, assembly, crowd*	(178)

ܟܣ

ܟܣ	v.	Ethpᶜel *be reproved*; Aphᶜel *rebuke, admonish, convict*	(12)
ܡܟܣܢܘܬܐ	n. f.	*reproof, rebuke*	(1)

ܟܣܐ

ܟܣܐ	n. m.	*cup*	(33)
ܟܣܝܐ	n. m.	w/ ܒ+ *secretly*	(8)
ܟܣܐ	v.	*cover, conceal, hide*	(31)
ܟܣܝܐܝܬ	adv.	*secretly*	(1)
ܐܟܣܝܬܐ	n. f.	*covering, garment*	(4)
ܟܣܝܐ	adj.	*hidden*	(7)

ܟܣܦ

ܟܣܦܐ	n. m.	*silver, money*	(39)

ܟܦܢ

ܟܦܢ	v.	*hunger*	(21)

Syriac	Cat.	Meaning	
ܟܦܢܐ	n. m.	hunger, famine	(14)
ܟܦܢܐ	adj.	hungry	(2)

ܟܦܪ

Syriac	Cat.	Meaning	
ܟܘܦܪܐ	n. m.	rubbish	(1)
ܟܦܘܪܐ	adj.	unthankful	(1)
ܟܦܰܪ	v.	deny, refuse	(44)
ܟܦܪܐ	n. m.	denier	(1)

ܟܪܐ

Syriac	Cat.	Meaning	
ܟܪܐ	v.	sorrow; Pa^cel ܟܪܝ shorten; Aph^cel ܐܟܪܝ make *sorry*	(28)
ܟܪܝܘܬܐ	n. f.	sorrowfulness, sadness	(10)
ܟܪܝܐ	adj.	sad	(3)

ܟܪܗ

Syriac	Cat.	Meaning	
ܟܘܪܗܢܐ	n. m.	sickness, infirmity, ailment, disease	(24)
ܟܪܗ	v.	be sick, be weak	(30)
ܟܪܝܗܐ	pass. ptc. m.	sick, weak (in faith), *infirm*	(29)
ܟܪܝܗܘܬܐ	n. f.	sickness, infirmity, frailty, weakness	(10)

ܟܪܙ

Syriac	Cat.	Meaning	
ܟܪܘܙܐ	n. m.	preacher	(4)
ܟܪܘܙܘܬܐ	n. f.	preaching, proclamation	(7)
ܟܪܙ	den.	Ethp^cel ܐܬܟܪܙ be preached; Aph^cel ܐܟܪܙ preach; Ethp^cel ܐܬܟܪܙ be proclaimed	(94)
ܡܟܪܙܢܐ	n. m.	preacher	(1)

ܟܪܟ

Syriac	Cat.	Meaning	
ܟܪܟ	v.	wrap; Ethp^cel ܐܬܟܪܟ go around; Aph^cel lead about	(39)
ܟܪܟܐ	n. m.	scroll, codex	(1)
ܟܪܟܐ	n. m.	walled *city*, *town*	(3)

Syriac	Cat.	Meaning	
		ܟܪܡ	
ܟܲܪܡܵܐ	n. m.	*vineyard*	(26)
		ܟܪܣ	
ܟܲܪܣܵܐ	n. f.	*belly, womb*	(27)
		ܟܫܠ	
ܟܫܠ	v.	Ethpᶜel *be offended*; Aphᶜel *make stumble*	(30)
ܟܘܼܫܠܵܐ	n. m.	*offense*	(4)
ܡܲܟܫܘܿܠܵܐ	n. m.	*offense, scandal*	(7)
		ܟܬܒ	
ܟܬܲܒ	v.	*write*	(231)
ܟܬܵܒܵܐ	n. m.	*book, writing, Scripture*	(102)
ܟܬܵܒܘܿܢܵܐ	n. m.	*booklet*	(4)
ܟܬܵܒܬܵܐ	n. f.	w/ ܐܝܼܕܵܐ *handwriting*	(2)
ܡܲܟܬܒܵܢܘܼܬܵܐ	n. f.	*enrollment, list, writing, rescript*	(1)
ܟܬܝܼܒܵܐ	pass. ptc. m.	*written*	(3)
		ܟܬܢܐ	
ܟܘܼܬܝܼܢܵܐ	n. f.	*coat*, linen *garment, tunic*	(11)
ܟܬܵܢܵܐ	n. m.	*linen sheet*	(11)
		ܟܬܪ	
ܟܬܲܪ	v.	Paᶜel ܟܲܬܲܪ *remain, abide, continue, wait*	(11)
		ܟܬܫ	
ܟܬܲܫ	v.	*strike*; Ethpaᶜal *strive, endeavor, fight*	(12)
ܐܲܟܬܘܿܫܵܐ	n. m.	*contest, strife, struggle*	(3)
		ܠ	
ܠ	prep.	*to, for*	(4234)
		ܠܐ	
ܠܵܐ	particle	*no, not*	(3140)

7. WORDS ARRANGED BY ROOT

Syriac	Cat.	Meaning	
		ܐܠܐ	
ܐܠܝ	v.	*toil, labour*; Aph^cel *tire*	(26)
ܐܠܝܘܬܐ	n. f.	*weariness, labour, fatigue, laboriousness*	(4)
ܐܠܝܐ	adj.	*weary, tired*	(1)
		ܠܒ	
ܠܒܒ	den.	Pa^cel ܠܒܒ *encourage*	(10)
ܠܒܐ	n. m.	*heart*	(168)
ܠܘܒܒܐ	n. m.	*encouragement, heartiness*	(2)
		ܠܒܫ	
ܠܒܘܫܐ	n. m.	*clothing, dress, apparel*	(21)
ܠܒܫ	v.	*put on, be clothed*; Aph^cel ܐܠܒܫ *clothe*	(50)
ܠܒܫܐ	n. m.	*clothes, garment*	(3)
		ܠܘܐ	
ܠܘܐ	v.	*accompany*; Pa^cel *escort*	(10)
ܠܘܝܬܐ	n. f.	*company*	(2)
		ܠܘܬ	
ܠܘܬ	prep.	*to, toward, against*	(602)
		ܠܚܡ	
ܠܘܚܡܐ	n. m.	*threat, intimidation*	(2)
ܠܚܡ	v.	*threaten, intimidate*	(4)
ܠܚܡܐ	n. m.	*bread*, w/ ܐܦܐ *shewbread*	(98)
		ܠܛ	
ܠܛ	v.	*curse*	(9)
ܠܘܛܬܐ	n. f.	*curse, malediction*	(7)
ܠܝܛܐ	pass. ptc. m.	*accursed*	(1)
		ܠܠܝ	
ܠܠܝܐ	n. m.	*night*	(68)

7. Words Arranged by Root

Syriac	Cat.	Meaning	
ܠܡܕ			
ܝܘܠܦܢܐ	n. m.	*doctrine, discipleship*	(1)
ܐܠܦ	den.	*teach, instruct*	(6)
ܬܠܡܝܕܐ	n. m.	*disciple*	(277)
ܠܥܣ			
ܠܥܣ	v.	*eat, chew*	(28)
ܠܥܙ			
ܠܫܢܐ	n. m.	*tongue, language*	(58)
ܡܐ			
ܕܠܡܐ	particle	*lest*	(87)
ܠܡܐ	pron.	*why*	(61)
ܡܐ	pron.	*what*	(236)
ܡܐܐ			
ܡܐܐ	num.	*one hundred*	(25)
ܡܐܬܝܢ	num.	*two hundred*	(9)
¹ܡܐܢ			
ܡܐܢ	v.	*be tired, be weary; Aphᶜel neglect, tedious*	(13)
²ܡܐܢ			
ܡܐܢܐ	n. m.	*vessel, garment, utensil, receptacle*	(56)
ܡܕܡ			
ܡܕܡ	n. c.	*something*	(492)
ܡܘܡ			
ܡܘܡܐ	n. m.	*spot, blemish*	(14)
ܡܚܐ			
ܡܚܐ	v.	*strike, gird*	(45)
ܡܚܘܬܐ	n. f.	*wound, plague, stroke*	(24)
ܡܚܠ			
ܡܚܝܠܐ	adj.	*weak*	(5)
ܡܚܝܠܘܬܐ	n. f.	*weakness, impotence*	(2)

7. Words Arranged by Root

Syriac	Cat.	Meaning	
ܡܟܫ	den.	grow *weak*	(5)

ܡܚܪ

ܡܚܪ	adv.	*tomorrow*	(12)

ܡܛܐ

ܡܛܐ	v.	*arrive, reach*; Pa^cel ܡܛܝ *attain*	(66)

ܡܛܠ

ܡܛܠ	prep.	*because*	(740)
ܡܛܠܗܢܐ	particle	*on this account*	(6)

ܡܛܪ

ܡܛܪ	v.	*rain*; Aph^cel ܐܡܛܪ *cause to* rain, *shower*	(1)
ܡܛܪܐ	n. m.	*rain*	(12)

ܡܝܐ

ܡܝܐ	n. m.	*water*	(94)

ܡܟ

ܡܟܘܟܐ	n. m.	*lowliness, humiliation*	(4)
ܡܟ	v.	*be humble*; Pa^cel ܡܟܟ *humble*	(19)
ܡܟܝܟܐ	adj.	*humble, lowly, mild, gentle*	(21)
ܡܟܝܟܘܬܐ	n. f.	*humility, meekness, lowliness, condescension, courtesy*	(15)

ܡܟܐ

ܡܟܐ	particle	of place:*hence,* w/ ܘܡܟܐ ܡܟܐ *here and there,* w/ ܡܢ *from this time*	(12)

ܡܟܝܠ

ܡܟܝܠ	particle	*therefore, now, henceforth*	(56)

ܡܟܣ

ܡܟܣܐ	n. m.	*tax collector, publican*	(26)
ܡܟܣܐ	n. m.	*tax, tribute, impost, toll*	(3)

ܡܠ

ܡܠ	v.	Pa^cel ܡܠܠ *speak*	(351)
ܡܠܝܠܐ	adj.	*reasonable, rational*	(1)

Syriac	Cat.	Meaning	
ܡܠܬܐ	n. f.	*word, case, cause, matter*	(409)
ܡܡܠܠܐ	n. m.	*speech, discourse, talk*	(9)

ܡܠܐ

ܡܘܠܝܐ	n. m.	*fullness, fulfilment, consummation*	(9)
ܡܠܐ	v.	*fill, complete*	(166)
ܡܠܐܐ	n. m.	*fullness*	(1)
ܡܠܝܐܝܬ	adv.	*fully, completely, perfectly*	(4)
ܡܠܝܬܐ	n. f.	*fullness, supplement, patch*	(3)
ܡܡܠܐ	n. m.	w/ ܠܒܐ *consolation*	(1)
ܡܡܠܝܐ	pass. ptc. m.	*full, complete, perfect*	(5)
ܡܘܡܠܝܐ	n. m.	*fullness, completion*	(4)
ܡܠܐ	n. m.	*flood*	(2)

ܡܠܐܟ

ܡܠܐܟܐ	n. m.	*messenger, angel*	(181)

ܡܠܚ

ܡܠܚ	v.	Ethp^{c}el *be salted*	(5)
ܡܠܚܐ	n. f.	*salt*	(9)
ܡܡܠܚܐ	pass. ptc. m.	*salty*	(1)

ܡܠܟ

ܡܘܠܟܢܐ	n. m.	*promise*	(38)
ܡܠܟ	v.	*counsel, promise;* Ethpa^{c}al *deliberate;* Aph^{c}el ܐܡܠܟ *reign*	(42)
ܡܠܟܐ	n. m.	*king; f. queen*	(130)
ܡܠܟܐ	n. m.	*counsel*	(11)
ܡܠܟܘܬܐ	n. f.	*kingdom, realm, reign*	(167)

ܡܢ[1]

ܡܢ	prep.	*from*	(2966)
ܡܢܫܠܝܐ	particle	*suddenly*	(1)

Syriac	Cat.	Meaning	
		ܡܢ ^{2}	
ܡܰܢ	pron.	*who*, w/ ܕ *he who*	(367)
		ܡܢ ^{3}	
ܠܡܳܢܳܐ	pron.	*why*	(52)
ܡܳܢܳܐ	pron.	*why, what*	(289)
		ܡܢܐ	
ܡܢܳܐ	v.	*number, reckon*	(5)
ܡܰܢܝܳܐ	n. m.	*mina* (monetary unit)	(10)
ܡܶܢܝܳܢܳܐ	n. m.	*number*	(18)
ܡܢܳܬܳܐ	n. f.	*part, portion*	(16)
		ܡܗܐ	
ܡܨܳܐ	v.	*be able*	(14)
		ܡܗܕ	
ܡܶܨܥܳܝܳܐ	n. m.	*mediator*	(6)
ܡܶܨܥܬܳܐ	n. f.	*middle, midst*	(29)
		ܡܪ	
ܡܽܘܪܳܐ	n. m.	*myrrh*	(3)
ܡܶܬܡܰܪܡܪܳܢܳܐ	adj.	*contentious, provoking*	(1)
ܡܰܪ	v.	*be bitter*; Aph^cel *make bitter*; Ethpalpal *grieve*	(4)
ܡܰܪܺܝܪܳܐ	adj.	*bitter*	(4)
ܡܰܪܺܝܪܳܐܝܬ	adv.	*bitterly*	(2)
ܡܰܪܺܝܪܽܘܬܳܐ	n. f.	*bitterness, acrimony*	(3)
ܡܪܳܪܳܐ	n. f.	*bitterness*	(1)
ܡܪܳܪܬܳܐ	n. f.	*gall*	(1)
ܡܪܬܳܐ	n. f.	*bitterness*	(1)
		ܡܪܐ	
ܡܳܪܝܳܐ	n. m.	*lord, master*	(755)
ܡܳܪܽܘܬܳܐ	n. f.	*dominion*	(8)

Syriac	Cat.	Meaning	
		ܡܪܚ	
ܡܪܰܚ	den.	Aphᶜel ܐܰܡܪܰܚ *dare*	(18)
ܡܰܪܚܳܐ	adj.	*bold, presumptuous, audacious*	(1)
ܡܰܪܚܳܐܺܝܬ	adv.	*boldly*	(1)
		ܡܫܚ [1]	
ܡܫܽܘܚܬܳܐ	n. f.	*measure, proportion*	(13)
ܡܫܰܚ	v.	*measure*	(5)
		ܡܫܚ [2]	
ܡܫܰܚ	v.	*anoint*	(14)
ܡܶܫܚܳܐ	n. m.	*ointment, oil, unguent*	(14)
ܡܫܺܝܚܳܐ	pass. ptc. m.	*Messiah, Annointed One, Christ*	(586)
ܡܫܺܝܚܽܘܬܳܐ	n. f.	*anointing, unction*	(3)
		ܡܘܬ	
ܡܺܝܬ	v.	*be dead, die*; Aphᶜel put to *death*	(171)
ܡܰܘܬܳܐ	n. m.	*death*	(125)
ܡܰܘܬܳܢܳܐ	n. m.	*plague, mortality*	(2)
ܡܳܘܬܳܢܽܘܬܳܐ	n. f.	*mortality*	(2)
ܡܺܝܽܘܬܳܐ	adj.	*dead*	(1)
ܡܺܝܬܳܐ	pass. ptc. m.	*dead*	(126)
ܡܺܝܬܽܘܬܳܐ	n. f.	*mortality, death*	(2)
		ܡܬܠ	
ܡܰܬܶܠ	v.	Aphᶜel ܐܰܡܬܶܠ use *parables*	(3)
ܡܰܬܠܳܐ	n. m.	*parable, proverb, similitude*	(46)
		ܡܬܡ	
ܡܡܰܬܽܘܡ	particle	*always, ever*	(20)
ܡܬܽܘܡ	particle	*always, ever*	(11)
		ܢܒܐ	
ܢܒܳܐ	v.	Ethpaᶜal ܐܶܬܢܰܒܺܝ *prophesy*	(29)

7. WORDS ARRANGED BY ROOT

Syriac	Cat.	Meaning	
ܢܒܺܝܐ	n. m.	*prophet*; f. *prophetess*	(167)
ܢܒܺܝܘܬܐ	n. f.	*prophecy*	(20)

ܢܓܕ

Syriac	Cat.	Meaning	
ܡܢܓܕܢܐ	n. m.	*scourger, torturer*	(1)
ܢܓܕ	v.	*lead, drag*; Pa°el ܢܓܶܕ *beat, scourge*; Ethpa°al *be beaten, draw, withdraw*	(29)
ܢܓܕܐ	n. m.	*stripe, weal, wound* (caused by scourging)	(4)
ܢܓܘܕܐ	n. m.	*guide, leader, conductor*	(3)

ܢܓܪ

Syriac	Cat.	Meaning	
ܡܓܪܢܘܬܐ	n. f.	*long suffering*	(11)
ܢܓܝܪܐ	adj.	w/ ܪܘܚܐ *long suffering*	(2)
ܢܓܝܪܘܬܐ	n. f.	w/ ܪܘܚܐ *long suffering*	(5)
ܢܓܪ	v.	Aph°el ܐܓܪ *be prolonged, make long,* w/ ܪܘܚܐ *be patient*	(12)
ܢܘܓܪܐ	n. m.	*long ago, protraction, delay*	(1)

¹ܢܗܪ

Syriac	Cat.	Meaning	
ܢܗܪܐ	n. m.	*river*	(15)

²ܢܗܪ

Syriac	Cat.	Meaning	
ܢܗܝܪܐ	adj.	*light, bright,* (pl.)*luminaries, illumined*	(16)
ܢܗܝܪܐܝܬ	adv.	*clearly*	(1)
ܢܗܪ	v.	*shine*; Pa°el *bring to light, explain*; Aph°el ܐܢܗܪ *light*	(29)
ܢܘܗܪܐ	n. m.	*light*	(68)

ܢܘܢܐ

Syriac	Cat.	Meaning	
ܢܘܢܐ	n. m.	*fish*	(29)

ܢܘܪ

Syriac	Cat.	Meaning	
ܡܢܪܬܐ	n. f.	*candlestick, lamp-stand*	(12)
ܢܘܪܐ	n. f.	*fire*	(81)

7. Words Arranged by Root

Syriac	Cat.	Meaning	
ܢܚ			
ܢܚ	v.	cease, rest; Aphᶜel ܐܢܝܚ give rest, put off, refresh	(40)
ܢܘܚܐ	n. m.	calm, rest	(1)
ܢܝܚܐ	n. m.	restful, quiet, rest, relief, calm	(9)
ܢܝܚܐ	pass. ptc. m.	quietness, restfulness, rest, relief	(1)
ܢܝܚܘܬܐ	n. f.	quietness, meekness, gentleness, mildness	(3)
ܢܝܚܬܐ	n. f.	rest, repose, leisure, recreation	(12)
ܢܚܬ			
ܡܚܬܬܐ	n. f.	descent	(2)
ܢܚܬ	v.	descend	(108)
ܢܚܬܐ			
ܢܚܬܐ	n. m.	garment	(27)
ܢܛܪ			
ܡܛܪܬܐ	n. f.	watch	(7)
ܢܛܘܪܐ	n. m.	gaoler, keeper, guard	(2)
ܢܛܘܪܬܐ	n. f.	custody, watching	(3)
ܢܛܪ	v.	guard, keep, reserve, observe	(130)
ܢܟܠ			
ܢܟܝܠܐ	pass. ptc. m.	deceitful, wily	(2)
ܢܟܝܠܘܬܐ	n. f.	deception, craftiness, deceit	(1)
ܢܟܠ	v.	deceive	(4)
ܢܟܠܐ	n. m.	deceit, guilt, trickery, guile, craft	(18)
ܢܟܘܠܬܢܐ	adj.	deceitful, crafty	(1)
ܢܟܣ			
ܢܟܣ	v.	kill, sacrifice, immolate	(7)
ܢܟܣܐ	n. m.	a possession; pl. goods	(8)
ܢܟܣܬܐ	n. f.	slaughter, sacrifice, victim, immolation	(4)

7. Words Arranged by Root

Syriac	Cat.	Meaning	
ܢܚܝܣܐ	pass. ptc. m.	*slaughtered*	(2)

ܟܚܕ

ܢܟܘܦܐ	n. m.	*modesty*	(1)
ܢܟܦ	v.	*be modest*; Pa^cel make *modest*	(5)
ܢܟܦܐ	adj.	*modest, sober*	(9)
ܢܟܦܘܬܐ	n. f.	*modesty, sobriety*	(5)

ܟܚܪ

ܢܘܟܪܝܐ	adj.	*strange, foreign, alien*	(21)

ܢܡܘܣܐ

ܢܡܘܣܐ	n. m.	*law*	(224)

ܢܣܐ

ܡܢܣܝܢܐ	n. m.	*tempter*	(1)
ܢܣܐ	v.	Pa^cel *tempt, prove, try*	(40)
ܢܣܝܘܢܐ	n. m.	*trial, temptation*	(21)
ܢܣܝܢܐ	n. m.	*experience, experiment*	(1)

ܢܣܒ

ܢܣܒܐ	n. m.	*taking*, w/ ܐܦܐ *hypocrisy, acceptance*	(12)
ܢܣܒ	v.	*take, receive*, w/ ܐܦܐ *be a hypocrite*	(229)

ܢܦܠ

ܡܦܘܠܬܐ	n. f.	*fall, collapse*	(3)
ܢܦܠ	v.	*fall*	(157)

ܢܦܩ

ܡܦܩܐ	n. m.	w/ ܪܘܚܐ *defense, answer*	(11)
ܡܦܩܢܐ	n. m.	*exodus, a way out, departure, exit*	(4)
ܡܦܩܬܐ	n. f.	*exodus, departure*	(1)
ܢܦܩ	v.	*go out*, w/ ܪܘܚܐ *defend*; Ethpa^cal *be exercised*; Aph^cel ܐܦܩ *go out, make cast out, eject*	(405)
ܢܦܩܬܐ	n. f.	*expense, cost, outlay, payment*	(6)

Syriac	Cat.	Meaning	
ܢܦܫ			
ܢܝܳܚܳܐ	n. m.	*refreshment, relief, pause*	(2)
ܢܰܦܫܳܐ	n. f.	*soul, breath of life, self*	(422)
ܢܰܦܫܳܢܳܝܳܐ	adj.	*natural*	(3)
ܢܨܒ			
ܢܨܰܒ	v.	*plant*	(13)
ܢܶܨܒܬܳܐ	n. f.	*plant*	(1)
ܢܩܦ			
ܢܩܶܦ	v.	*cleave to, follow, adhere*	(41)
ܢܩܫ			
ܢܩܰܫ	v.	*knock*	(11)
ܢܫܒ			
ܢܶܫܒܳܐ	n. m.	*breeze, wind, blast*	(1)
ܢܫܰܒ	v.	*blow*	(9)
ܢܫܩ			
ܢܘܫܰܩܬܳܐ	n. f.	*kiss*	(6)
ܢܫܰܩ	v.	*kiss*	(13)
ܣܐܡܐ			
ܣܐܡܳܐ	n. m.	*silver, money*	(10)
ܣܐܢ			
ܣܐܘܢܳܐ	n. m.	*sandal, shoe*	(10)
ܣܐܶܢ	v.	*put on sandals*	(4)
ܣܒܥ			
ܣܒܰܥ	v.	*be full, be satisfied;* Pa‘el ܣܰܒܰܥ *satisfy*	(18)
ܣܰܒܥܳܐ	adj.	*full*	(1)
ܣܳܒܥܳܐ	n. m.	*fullness, plenty, satiety*	(1)
ܣܒܪ[1]			
ܣܒܰܪ	v.	*think, suppose;* Pa‘el *hope, consider*	(108)
ܣܰܒܪܳܐ	n. m.	*hope*	(59)

7. Words Arranged by Root   141

Syriac	Cat.	Meaning	
		ܣܒܪ^2	
ܡܣܒܪܢܘܬܐ	n. f.	*preaching*	(3)
ܡܣܒܪܢܐ	adj.	*evangelist*	(3)
ܡܣܝܒܪܢܘܬܐ	n. f.	*patience, endurance*	(31)
ܣܒܪ	den.	Pacel ܣܰܒܰܪ *preach, declare*; Paycel ܣܰܝܒܰܪ *bear, endure*; Ethpaycal *be nourished, be fed*	(115)
ܣܒܪܬܐ	n. f.	good *tidings, Gospel, message*	(48)
ܣܝܒܪܬܐ	n. f.	*food, sustenance*	(13)
		ܣܓܐ	
ܣܓܝ	v.	*increase*; Aphcel ܐܣܓܝ *multiply, be great*	(30)
ܣܓܝܐܐ	adj.	*much, many*	(439)
ܣܓܝܐܘܬܐ	n. f.	*abundance*	(1)
ܣܘܓܐܐ	n. m.	*multitude, abundance*	(21)
		ܣܓܕ	
ܣܓܕ	v.	*worship, pay homage*	(61)
ܣܓܘܕܐ	n. m.	*worshipper*	(2)
		ܣܗܕ	
ܣܗܕ	v.	*witness, testify*	(118)
ܣܗܕܐ	n. m.	*witness, martyr*	(30)
ܣܗܕܘܬܐ	n. f.	*testimony*	(67)
		ܣܗܪܐ	
ܣܗܪܐ	n. c.	*moon*	(10)
		ܣܘܟܐ	
ܣܘܟܬܐ	n. f.	*branch*	(13)
		ܣܚܐ	
ܣܚܐ	v.	*wash, swim*	(7)
ܣܚܘܐ	n. m.	*swimming*	(2)
ܣܚܝܐ	n. m.	*washing*	(1)

7. Words Arranged by Root

Syriac	Cat.	Meaning	
مَسِيݣُا	n. f.	*washing*, *laver* of baptism	(1)
مَسِه			
مَفومُبُا	n. m.	*destruction, demolition, overthrow, subversion, upsetting*	(3)
مَمَبو	v.	*overthrow, cast down*	(7)
مَيݣَ			
مَكُيُا	n. m.	*adversary*, as prop. n.*Satan*	(49)
مَبِد			
مَبُا	adj.	*old, aged*	(4)
مَبِخُوِاً	n. f.	*old age*	(2)
مَمَبِخُوِاً	n. f.	*abomination, pollution*	(1)
مَبِد	v.	Pa^cel مَبِد *defile*	(21)
مَفوَبُا	n. m.	*abomination, pollution*	(2)
مَمَبِخُا	pass. ptc. m.	*defiled*	(1)
مَبِه			
مَبِفُا	n. m.	*sword*	(14)
مَبِكَ			
مَحا	v.	Pa^cel *expect, look for*	(28)
¹مَحَل			
مَمَحَكُنُا	n. m.	*evil doer, offender*	(4)
مَجَكَ	den.	Aph^cel أَمَقَ *offend, wrong*	(14)
مَجلَا	adj.	*foolish*	(18)
مَجَكِدِاً	n. f.	*foolishness, transgression, error, trespass, wrong-doing, sin*	(21)
²مَحَل			
مَفوَݣُلا	n. m.	*understanding, intelligence, discernment*	(6)
مَفوَكُݣُنُا	adj.	*intelligent, prudent*	(3)
مَحَكَ	v.	Pa^cel make *understand*; Ethpa^cal أَمَݣَكَ *understand*	(49)

7. Words Arranged by Root

Syriac	Cat.	Meaning	
		ܣܟܢ	
ܣܟܢ	den.	Ethpalpal ܐܣܬܟܲܢ become *poor*	(1)
ܣܟܢܵܐ	adj.	*poor*	(38)
ܣܟܢܘܬܐ	n. f.	*poverty*	(3)
		ܣܠܐ	
ܣܠܝܚܐ	pass. ptc. m.	*despised, rejected, reprobate, contemptible*	(5)
ܣܠܝܚܢܘܬܐ	n. f.	*rejection, reprobation*	(1)
ܣܠܐ	v.	*despise, reject*	(20)
		ܣܠܩ	
ܣܘܠܩܐ	n. m.	*ascension*	(1)
ܣܠܩ	v.	*go up, ascend*; Aph°el ܐܣܩ *make ascend*	(134)
		ܣܡ	
ܣܡ	v.	*put, place*	(207)
ܣܝܡܬܐ	n. m.	w/ ܐܝܕܐ *laying on of hands*	(4)
ܣܝܡܬܐ	n. f.	*treasure, store*	(25)
ܣܡܐ	n. m.	*drug, poison, remedy, venom*	(2)
		ܣܡܐ	
ܣܡܝ	v.	*be blind*; Pa°el ܣܡܝ *blind*	(6)
ܣܡܝܐ	adj.	*blind*	(41)
		ܣܡܟ	
ܣܡܝܟܐ	pass. ptc. m.	*seated* (at meals), *guest*	(7)
ܣܡܟ	v.	*support, recline* to eat; Aph°el *cause to recline*	(46)
ܣܘܡܟܐ	n. m.	*pillar, steadfastness*	(1)
ܣܡܟܐ	n. m.	*seat* at a meal, *feast, company* at a meal	(14)

Syriac	Cat.	Meaning	
		ܣܡܐܠܐ	
ܣܡܐܠܐ	n. f.	*left*	(13)
		ܣܢܐ	
ܣܢܐ	v.	*hate*	(42)
ܣܢܝܐ	ap f	*hateful, shameful, detestable*	(3)
ܣܢܐܐ	n. m.	*enemy*	(2)
ܣܢܝܐܐ	adj.	*hated, hateful*	(7)
		ܣܢܩ	
ܣܢܘܩܐ	n. m.	*need, necessity*	(3)
ܣܢܝܩܘܬܐ	n. f.	*need, necessity, lack, want*	(5)
ܣܢܩ	v.	*need*	(22)
ܣܢܝܩܐ	pass. ptc. m.	*needy*	(1)
		¹ܣܥܪ	
ܣܘܥܪܢܐ	n. m.	*deed, visitation, event, happening, matter, affair*	(13)
ܣܥܘܪܐ	n. m.	*overseer, bishop*	(1)
ܣܥܪ	v.	*visit, do, effect*	(55)
		²ܣܥܪ	
ܣܥܪܐ	n. m.	*hair*	(16)
ܣܥܪܐ	n. f.	*barley*	(4)
		ܣܦ	
ܣܦܝܢܬܐ	n. f.	*boat, ship, sailing vessel*	(39)
ܣܦܢܐ	n. m.	*sailor*	(1)
		ܣܦܣܝܪ	
ܣܦܣܪܐ	n. f.	*sword*	(10)
		ܣܦܩ	
ܣܦܝܩܐܝܬ	adv.	*empty handed*	(1)
ܣܦܩ	v.	*be sufficient, be able, suffice*	(23)

7. Words Arranged by Root

Syriac	Cat.	Meaning	
ܣܦܪܐ			
ܣܦܪܐ	n. m.	*book, scroll, roll*	(14)
ܣܦܪܐ	n. m.	*scribe, lawyer*	(76)
ܣܪܩ			
ܣܪܝܩܐ	pass. ptc. m.	*vain, empty, vacant, void*	(11)
ܣܪܝܩܐܝܬ	adv.	*vainly*	(10)
ܣܪܝܩܘܬܐ	n. f.	*vanity, emptiness*	(5)
ܣܪܩ	v.	Pa‘el ܣܪܩ make *empty*, make *void*	(20)
ܣܬܘ			
ܣܬܐ	den.	Aph‘el *winter, weather* tempest	(5)
ܣܬܘܐ	n. m.	*winter, foul weather, tempest*	(8)
ܥܐܕܐ			
ܥܐܕܐ	n. m.	*feast, festival*	(6)
ܥܘܝܕܐ	n. m.	*feast, festival*	(24)
ܥܒܕ			
ܡܥܒܕܢܐ	n. m.	*worker, activator, affecter*	(1)
ܡܥܒܕܢܘܬܐ	n. f.	*operation, working, action, efficacy*	(4)
ܥܒܕ	v.	*do, make*; Shaph‘el ܫܥܒܕ *subdue, subject, act, perform, celebrate* (a feast)	(706)
ܥܒܕܐ	n. m.	*servant*	(141)
ܥܒܕܐ	n. m.	*deed, work*	(191)
ܥܒܕܘܬܐ	n. f.	*service, bondage*	(13)
ܥܒܘܕܐ	n. m.	*doer, maker*	(6)
ܫܘܥܒܕܐ	n. m.	*subjection*	(4)
ܥܒܝܕܐ	pass. ptc. m.	*make*	(1)
ܡܫܥܒܕܐ	pass. ptc. m.	*subjected*	(1)
ܥܒܪ			
ܡܥܒܪܢܘܬܐ	n. f.	*transgression*	(1)

Syriac	Cat.	Meaning	
ܥܒ݂ܰܪ	v.	*cross over*, w/ ܥܠ *transgress*, w/ ܡܢ *turn away from*; Aphᶜel ܐܥܒ݂ܰܪ *pass over*	(108)
ܥܒ݂ܳܪܳܐ	n. m.	*transgression*	(2)
ܥܒ݂ܳܪܳܐ	n. m.	*crossing*	(27)

ܥܒܪܝ

ܥܒ݂ܪܳܐܝܺܬ	adv.	in *Aramaic*, only in Rev.in *Hebrew*	(11)
ܥܒ݂ܪܳܝܳܐ	adj.	*Hebrew*	(4)

ܥܓܠ

ܥܓܠ	v.	Paᶜel ܥܰܓܶܠ *roll*	(6)
ܥܓܰܠ	particle	*quickly*	(32)
ܥܶܓܠܳܐ	n. m.	*calf*	(4)
ܥܶܓܠܬ݂ܳܐ	n. f.	*heifer*	(2)
ܥܽܘܓܠܳܐ	n. m.	*rolling, wallowing*	(1)

ܥܕ

ܥܰܕ	particle	*while, until*	(29)
ܥܰܕܠܳܐ	particle	*before*	(12)

ܥܕܟܝܠ

ܥܰܕܟ݁ܺܝܠ	particle	*yet, still*	(30)

ܥܕܡܐ

ܥܕ݂ܰܡܳܐ	prep.	*until*	(219)

ܥܕܢ

ܥܶܕܳܢܳܐ	n. m.	*moment, season, time, opportunity*	(24)

ܥܕܪ

ܡܥܰܕܪܳܢܳܐ	n. m.	*help, helper*	(10)
ܡܥܰܕܪܳܢܽܘܬ݂ܳܐ	n. f.	*help, aid, assistance*	(2)
ܥܰܕ݁ܰܪ	v.	*help, be of profit, advantage*	(26)
ܥܽܘܕ݁ܪܳܢܳܐ	n. m.	*help, advantage*	(4)

ܥܕܬܐ

ܥܺܕ݁ܬ݁ܳܐ	n. f.	*church, assembly, congregation*	(113)

Syriac	Cat.	Meaning	
		ܥܗܕ	
ܥܗܕ	v.	*remember*; Aph^c^el cause to *remember*	(35)
ܥܘܗܕܢܐ	n. m.	*remembrance*	(6)
		ܥܘܕ	
ܡܥܝܕܐ	pass. ptc. m.	*accustomed*	(9)
ܥܝܕܐ	n. m.	*custom, manner*	(12)
		ܥܘܠ [1]	
ܥܘܠܐ	n. m.	*child, babe,* a *suckling*	(4)
ܥܝܠܐ	n. m.	*colt, young animal*	(13)
		ܥܘܠ [2]	
ܥܘܠ	v.	Aph^c^el *wrong, cause harm*	(8)
ܥܘܠܐ	adj.	*unjust, unrighteous*	(14)
ܥܘܠܐ	n. m.	*unrighteousness, iniquity*	(39)
ܥܘܠܘܬܐ	n. f.	*unrighteousness, iniquity, depravity*	(1)
		ܥܘܪ	
ܥܘܝܪܐ	adj.	*blind*	(6)
ܥܘܝܪܘܬܐ	n. f.	*blindness*	(2)
ܥܘܪ	den.	Pa^c^el ܥܘܪ *blind*	(4)
		ܥܛܦ	
ܥܛܦ	v.	*turn*; Pa^c^el *clothe*	(17)
		ܥܝܢ	
ܡܥܝܢܐ	n. f.	*source, well, fountain*	(5)
ܥܝܢܐ	n. f.	*eye*	(155)
		ܥܠ [1]	
ܡܥܠܢܐ	n. m.	*entrance, ingress*	(4)
ܡܥܠܢܘܬܐ	n. f.	*entrance, introduction, access*	(1)
ܡܥܠܬܐ	n. f.	*entrance*	(2)
ܥܠ	v.	*enter*; Aph^c^el ܐܥܠ *bring in*	(264)
ܥܠܠܬܐ	n. f.	*produce, fruit, income*	(3)

Syriac	Cat.	Meaning	
ܥܶܠܬ݂ܳܐ	n. f.	*cause, occasion*	(33)

$$^2 \text{ܥܠ}$$

| ܥܰܠ | prep. | *on, about, concerning* | (1549) |

ܥܠܐ

ܥܠܳܐ	v.	Ethpaᶜal ܐܶܬ݂ܥܰܠܺܝ *be raised up;* Eshtaphᶜal *be arrogant up*	(9)
ܥܶܠܳܝܳܐ	adj.	*Most High, upper, exalted, lofty*	(5)
ܥܶܠܺܝܬ݂ܳܐ	n. f.	upper *room*	(6)
ܥܠܳܬ݂ܳܐ	n. f.	*altar*	(1)

ܥܠܒ

ܥܠܰܒ	v.	take *advantage, defraud*	(5)
ܥܳܠܽܘܒܳܐ	adj.	*unjust, covetous, avaricious*	(5)
ܥܳܠܽܘܒܽܘܬ݂ܳܐ	n. f.	*injustice, covetousness*	(6)

ܥܠܝܡ

| ܥܠܰܝܡܳܐ | n. m. | young *man, young man, youth* | (19) |
| ܥܠܰܝܡܬ݂ܳܐ | n. f. | young *woman, young woman* | (5) |

ܥܠܡ

ܥܳܠܡܳܐ	n. m.	*age, eternity, world*	(413)
ܥܳܠܡܳܢܳܝܽܘܬ݂ܳܐ	n. f.	*worldliness, secularity*	(1)
ܥܳܠܡܳܢܳܝܳܐ	adj.	*worldly, mundane*	(1)
ܠܥܳܠܡܥܳܠܡܺܝܢ	n. m.	*forevermore*	(1)

$$^1 \text{ܥܡ}$$

| ܥܰܡܳܐ | n. m. | *people, nation; pl. Gentiles* | (324) |

$$^2 \text{ܥܡ}$$

| ܥܰܡ | prep. | *with* | (723) |

ܥܡܕ

ܥܳܡܽܘܕܳܐ	n. m.	*baptizer*	(15)
ܥܳܡܽܘܕܽܘܬ݂ܳܐ	n. f.	*baptism, washing*	(31)
ܥܡܰܕ	v.	*be baptized;* Aphᶜel ܐܰܥܡܶܕ *baptize, sink*	(80)

7. Words Arranged by Root

Syriac	Cat.	Meaning	
		ܥܡܠ	
ܥܡܶܠ	v.	*toil, labour*; Aphᶜel *trouble*	(9)
ܥܰܡܠܐ	n. m.	*toil, labour*	(13)
		ܥܡܩ	
ܥܘܡܩܐ	n. m.	*depth, deep*	(10)
ܥܰܡܝܩܐ	adj.	*deep*	(2)
ܥܡܩ	v.	Paᶜel ܥܰܡܶܩ *dig* (deeply)	(1)
		ܥܡܪ	
ܡܥܡܪܐ	n. m.	*habitation, abode*	(2)
ܥܘܡܪܐ	n. m.	*habitation*, manner of *life, residence, sojourn*	(3)
ܥܳܡܘܪܐ	n. m.	*dweller, inhabitant*	(11)
ܥܡܰܪ	v.	*dwell*	(57)
		ܥܢܐ	
ܥܢܐ	v.	*answer*	(158)
ܥܳܢܐ	n. f.	*flock*	(16)
		ܥܢܢ	
ܥܢܳܢܐ	n. f.	*cloud*	(28)
		ܥܣܪ	
ܡܥܣܪܐ	n. m.	*tenth, tithe*	(6)
ܥܣܪܐ	num.	*ten*	(27)
ܥܰܣܪ	den.	Paᶜel ܥܰܣܰܪ *tithe*	(4)
ܥܣܪܝܢ	num.	*twenty*	(11)
		ܥܩ	
ܥܳܩ	v.	Aphᶜel *grieve, discourage*	(9)
ܥܰܩܝܩܐ	adj.	*grieved, sad, sorrowful*	(1)
ܥܰܩܬܐ	n. f.	*sorrow, distress*	(7)
		ܥܩܒ	
ܥܘܩܒܐ	n. m.	*investigation, inquiry*	(2)
ܥܩܒ	den.	Paᶜel ܥܰܩܶܒ *investigate, inquire, examine*	(8)

Syriac	Cat.	Meaning	
ܥܶܩܒܳܐ	n. f.	heel, ankle, footstep	(5)
		ܥܩܪ	
ܥܩܰܪ	v.	uproot	(3)
ܥܶܩܳܪܳܐ	n. m.	root	(20)
ܥܩܰܪ̈ܳܐ	adj.	barren	(5)
		ܥܪ	
ܥܪ	v.	Ettaphᶜal ܐܶܬܬܥܺܝܪ be awake; Aphᶜel wake up; Ettaphᶜal ܐܶܬܬܥܺܝܪ watch; Aphᶜel arouse	(41)
		ܥܪܒ	
ܡܰܥܪܒܳܐ	n. f.	setting of sun, west	(7)
ܥܪܶܒ	v.	set, go down	(1)
ܥܪܽܘܒܬܳܐ	n. f.	eve, day of preparation	(5)
		ܥܪܒܐ	
ܥܶܪܒܳܐ	n. m.	sheep	(23)
		ܥܪܛܠ	
ܥܰܪܛܶܠ	d m	naked, stripped, nude	(5)
ܥܰܪܛܶܠܳܝܳܐ	adj.	naked, bare, exposed	(10)
ܥܰܪܛܶܠܳܝܽܘܬܳܐ	n. f.	nakedness	(3)
		ܥܪܠ	
ܥܽܘܪܠܳܐ	adj.	uncircumcised	(1)
ܥܽܘܪܠܽܘܬܳܐ	n. f.	uncircumcision	(20)
		ܥܪܣܐ	
ܥܰܪܣܳܐ	n. f.	bed, pallet, bier	(28)
		ܥܪܩ	
ܥܪܽܘܩܝܳܐ	n. m.	flight	(2)
ܥܪܰܩ	v.	flee	(42)
		ܥܬܕ	
ܥܬܶܕ	v.	Paᶜel ܥܰܬܶܕ prepare	(121)
ܥܬܺܝܕܳܐ	ap f	express future shall, ready, prepared	(1)

7. Words Arranged by Root

Syriac	Cat.	Meaning	
ܟܕ݂ܡܝܐܝ݂ܬ	adv.	*readily*	(2)
ܥܬܩ			
ܥܬܝ݂ܩܐ	adj.	*old, ancient*	(12)
ܥܬܝ݂ܩܘܬܐ	n. f.	*antiquity, oldness*	(1)
ܥܬܩ	v.	grow *old*; Aph^cel ܐܥܬܩ make *old*	(2)
ܥܬܪ			
ܥܘܬܪܐ	n. m.	*wealth, riches*	(21)
ܥܬܝ݂ܪܐ	adj.	*rich, wealthy*	(35)
ܥܬܝ݂ܪܐܝ݂ܬ	adv.	*richly, abundantly, copiously*	(4)
ܥܬܪ	v.	grow *rich*; Aph^cel make *rich*	(12)
ܦܐܪܐ			
ܦܐܪܐ	n. m.	*fruit*	(81)
ܦܓܪ			
ܦܓܪܐ	n. m.	*body*	(176)
ܦܓܪܢܐ	adj.	*carnal, corporeal*	(3)
ܦܓܪܢܐܝ݂ܬ	adv.	*carnally, materially*	(1)
ܦܓܪܢܝܐ	adj.	*carnal*	(1)
ܦܘܡܐ			
ܦܘܡܐ	n. m.	*mouth, edge*	(86)
ܦܝܣ			
ܡܦܝܣܢܘܬܐ	n. f.	*persuasion*	(1)
ܡܫܬܡܥܢܘܬܐ	n. f.	*obedience*	(5)
ܦܝܣ	den.	Aph^cel ܐܦܝܣ *persuade, convince*	(66)
ܦܝܣܐ	n. m.	*compliance, persuasion, assurance, persuasiveness*	(7)
ܦܠܐܬܐ			
ܦܠܐܬܐ	n. f.	*comparison, parable*	(14)
ܦܠܓ			
ܡܦܠܓܢܐ	adj.	*divider*	(1)

Syriac	Cat.	Meaning	
ܦܘܠܓܐ	n. m.	*disputation, division, distinction, hesitation*	(7)
ܦܠܓ	v.	*divide, distribute;* Ethp^cel ܐܬܦܠܓ *divide, doubt*	(47)
ܦܠܓܐ	n. m.	*half, middle*	(10)
ܦܠܓܘܬܐ	n. f.	*half*	(4)
ܦܠܓܘܬܐ	n. f.	*division, portion, separation*	(12)
ܦܠܝܓܐ	pass. ptc. m.	*divided*	(1)

ܦܠܚ

ܦܘܠܚܢܐ	n. m.	*trade, occupation, work*	(10)
ܦܠܚ	v.	*work, labour;* Aph^cel make *serve, caltivate*	(66)
ܦܠܚܐ	n. m.	*servant, worshipper, soldier*	(22)
ܦܠܚܐ	n. m.	*husbandman, tiller, cultivator*	(18)
ܦܠܚܘܬܐ	n. f.	*service, warfare, military*	(3)

ܦܢܐ

ܦܘܢܝܐ	n. m.	*conversion, reconciliation, reversion*	(2)
ܦܢܐ	v.	*return;* Pa^cel ܦܢܝ *answer, give back;* Aph^cel ܐܦܢܝ *cause to* turn	(57)

ܦܣܣ

ܦܘܣܣܘܬܐ	n. f.	*permission, licence*	(1)
ܦܣ	v.	Aph^cel ܐܦܣ *allow, permit*	(26)
ܦܣܐ	n. f.	*lot, portion*	(8)

ܦܣܩ

ܦܘܣܩܐ	n. m.	*section*	(1)
ܦܣܘܩܬܐ	n. f.	*pl. w/* ܒ *briefly*	(1)
ܦܣܩ	v.	*cut off, cut down;* Pa^cel *break*	(34)
ܦܣܩܐ	n. m.	*cutting, w/* ܕܒܣܪܐ *mutilation* of the flesh	(1)

ܦܥܠ

ܦܥܠܐ	n. m.	*labourer, worker*	(13)

7. Words Arranged by Root

Syriac	Cat.	Meaning	
ܦܨܚ			
ܦܪܐ	v.	Paᶜel ܦܨܝ *deliver*	(21)
ܦܨܚ			
ܦܨܚܐ	n. m.	Feast of *Passover*	(28)
ܦܩܕ			
ܦܘܩܕܐ	n. m.	*commandment, precept, ordinance*	(6)
ܦܘܩܕܢܐ	n. m.	*commandment, edict, decree, precept*	(92)
ܦܩܕ	v.	*command*	(130)
ܦܩܚ			
ܦܩܚܐ	adj.	*expedient, profitable, better*	(25)
ܦܩܚ	v.	*blossom*	(2)
ܦܪܚ			
ܦܪܚ	v.	*fly*; Paᶜel ܦܪܚ *squander*	(7)
ܦܪܚܐܝܬ	adv.	*wastefully*	(1)
ܦܪܚܬܐ	n. f.	*bird*	(16)
ܦܪܥ			
ܦܘܪܥܢܐ	n. m.	*recompense, retribution*	(8)
ܦܪܘܥܐ	n. m.	*rewarder, recompenser*	(1)
ܦܪܥ	v.	*recompense*	(36)
ܦܪܨܘܦܐ			
ܦܪܨܘܦܐ	n. m.	*face, countenance, person, aspect*	(35)
ܦܪܩ			
ܦܘܪܩܢܐ	n. m.	*redemption, salvation, deliverance*	(23)
ܦܪܘܩܐ	n. m.	*Saviour, deliverer*	(11)
ܦܪܩ	v.	*depart, deliver, save*; Paᶜel *rescue, pursue*; Aphᶜel *go away, abstain from*	(54)
ܦܪܫ			
ܡܦܪܫܢܐ	n. m.	*discerner, judge*	(1)
ܦܘܪܫܢܐ	n. m.	*difference, separation, discrimination*	(6)
ܦܪܘܫܘܬܐ	n. f.	*discernment, discrimination*	(1)

Syriac	Cat.	Meaning	
ܦܪܝܫܐ	pass. ptc. m.	*Pharisee*	(102)
ܦܪܝܫܝܐ	adj.	*Pharisaic*	(1)
ܦܪܫ	v.	*separate, appoint*	(57)
ܡܦܪܫܐ	ap f	*diverse*	(1)

		ܦܫܛ	
ܦܫܛ	v.	Tr. *stretch out,* Int. *be straight*	(18)
ܦܫܝܛܐ	pass. ptc. m.	*simple, upright*	(5)
ܦܫܝܛܐܝܬ	adv.	*simply, freely*	(1)
ܦܫܝܛܘܬܐ	n. f.	*simplicity, directness*	(7)

		ܦܫܩ	
ܦܘܫܩܐ	n. m.	*interpretation*	(2)
ܦܫܝܩܐ	pass. ptc. m.	*easy, plain*	(1)
ܦܫܝܩܐܝܬ	adv.	*plainly, clearly*	(3)
ܦܫܩ	v.	Pa^cel *interpret, expound*	(22)

		ܦܬܓܡܐ	
ܦܬܓܡܐ	n. m.	*word*	(27)

		ܦܬܘܪܐ	
ܦܬܘܪܐ	n. m.	*table*	(19)

		ܦܬܚ	
ܦܬܝܚܐ	n. m.	w/ ܦܘܡܐ open *mouthed*	(1)
ܦܬܚ	v.	*open*	(84)
ܦܬܝܚܐ	pass. ptc. m.	*open*	(4)

		ܦܬܟܪܐ	
ܦܬܟܪܐ	n. m.	*idol, image*	(26)

		ܨܒܐ	
ܨܒܐ	v.	*will, desire*	(273)
ܨܒܘܬܐ	n. f.	*thing, matter, affair*	(33)

7. Words Arranged by Root

Syriac	Cat.	Meaning	
ܨܶܒܝܳܢܳܐ	n. m.	*will, desire*	(101)
ܨܒܬ			
ܨܒܬ	den.	*adorn*	(9)
ܨܶܒܬܳܐ	n. m.	*adornment*	(2)
ܬܶܨܒܺܝܬܳܐ	n. m.	*adornment*	(1)
ܡܨܰܒܬܳܐ	ap f	*adorned*	(1)
ܨܝܕ			
ܡܨܺܝܕܬܳܐ	n. f.	*net*	(16)
ܨܳܕ	v.	Ethp^cel *be captured*; Pa^cel *catch*	(2)
ܨܰܝܕܳܐ	n. m.	*catch*	(2)
ܨܰܝܳܕܳܐ	n. m.	*fisherman*	(5)
ܨܗܐ			
ܨܗܳܐ	v.	*be thirsty*	(15)
ܨܗܶܐ	pass. ptc. m.	*thirsty, aridity*	(1)
ܨܶܗܝܳܐ	n. m.	*thirst*	(1)
ܨܚܐ			
ܨܽܘܚܝܬܳܐ	n. f.	*reviling, insult, abuse*	(4)
ܨܰܚܝ	v.	Pa^cel *revile*	(10)
ܨܝܕ			
ܨܶܝܕ	prep.	*near, with, at*	(18)
ܨܠܐ			
ܨܠܳܐ	v.	*incline toward, heed*; Pa^cel ܨܰܠܺܝ *pray*	(100)
ܨܠܽܘܬܳܐ	n. f.	*prayer*	(49)
ܨܠܒ			
ܨܠܰܒ	v.	*crucify*	(8)
ܨܠܺܝܒܳܐ	n. m.	*cross*	(5)
ܨܠܡ			
ܨܰܠܡܳܐ	n. m.	*image, portrait, figure*	(15)

Syriac	Cat.	Meaning	
		ܨܘܡ	
ܨܳܡ	v.	*fast*	(24)
ܨܰܘܡܳܐ	n. m.	*fast*	(7)
		ܨܥܪ	
ܡܨܰܥܪܳܢܳܐ	n. m.	*despiser, reviler*	(4)
ܨܥܰܪ	v.	*be despised*; Pa^cel ܨܰܥܰܪ *despise*	(17)
ܨܶܥܪܳܐ	n. m.	*shame, dishonor, ignominy, disgrace*	(9)
		ܨܦܪܐ	
ܨܰܦܪܳܐ	n. m.	*daybreak, morning*	(23)
		ܨܪܐ	
ܨܪܳܐ	v.	*rend, burst*; Ethpa^cal w/ ܥܰܠ *break out against*	(11)
		ܩܒܠ	
ܠܘܩܒܰܠ	prep.	*against, near, toward,* w/ ܩܳܡ *resist, opposite to*	(65)
ܠܩܘܒܠܳܐ	adj.	*opposite*	(3)
ܡܩܰܒܠܳܐ	pass. ptc. m.	*acceptable*	(6)
ܡܩܰܒܠܳܢܳܐ	n. m.	*host, entertainer*	(2)
ܣܩܘܒܠܳܐ	adj.	*contrary, adverse*	(11)
ܩܘܒܠܳܐ	n. m.	w/ ܡܶܢ *far away*	(2)
ܩܒܶܠ	v.	*appeal to, accuse*; Pa^cel ܩܰܒܶܠ *receive, take*; Saph^cel *be present, oppose*	(200)
ܩܘܒܳܠܳܐ	n. m.	*acceptance, reception, feast*	(4)
		ܩܒܪ	
ܩܒܘܪܳܐ	n. m.	*tomb, sepulchre*	(32)
ܩܰܒܘܪܳܐ	n. m.	*grave digger*	(1)
ܩܒܘܪܬܳܐ	n. f.	*burial*	(1)
ܩܒܰܪ	v.	*bury*; Pa^cel *heap up*	(16)
ܩܰܒܪܳܐ	n. m.	*tomb, sepulchre, grave*	(26)

7. Words Arranged by Root

Syriac	Cat.	Meaning	
		ܩܕܡ	
ܠܘܩܕܡ	particle	*before, formerly*	(56)
ܩܕܝܡܘܬܐ	n. f.	w/ ܝܺܕܰܥܬ݂ܳܐ *foreknowledge, precedence*	(2)
ܩܕܝܡܐ	pass. ptc. m.	*before,* w/ ܡܢ *before, formerly*	(45)
ܩܕܡ	v.	*go before*	(52)
ܩܕܡ	prep.	*before*	(290)
ܩܕܡܝܐ	adj.	*first*	(2)
ܩܕܡܝܐ	adj.	*first, fore*	(103)
ܩܕܡܝܬ	adv.	*first*	(3)
ܩܘܕܡܐ	n. m.	*before, front*	(1)
		ܩܕܫ	
ܩܘܕܫܐ	n. m.	w/ ܒܝܬ *sanctuary,* w/ ܒܝܬ *holy place*	(5)
ܩܕܝܫܐ	adj.	*holy, saint*	(148)
ܩܕܝܫܘܬܐ	n. f.	*holiness, sanctification*	(14)
ܩܕܫ	v.	Paᶜel ܩܰܕܶܫ *consecrate, sanctify*	(26)
ܩܘܕܫܐ	n. m.	*holiness*	(99)
		ܩܘܐ	
ܩܘܐ	den.	Paᶜel ܩܰܘܺܝ *abide, remain*	(98)
		ܩܘܫܬܐ	
ܩܘܫܬܐ	n. m.	*truth, verity*	(31)
		ܩܛܠ	
ܩܛܘܠܐ	n. m.	*murderer, slayer*	(8)
ܩܛܠ	v.	*kill*	(124)
ܩܛܠܐ	n. m.	*murder, slaughter*	(11)
ܩܛܝܠܐ	pass. ptc. m.	*stain*	(1)
		ܩܛܪ	
ܩܛܝܪܐ	n. m.	*violence, necessity, force*	(12)
ܩܛܝܪܢܐ	adj.	*violent*	(1)

Syriac	Cat.	Meaning	
ܩܛܪ	v.	Ethpaʿal *be joined together*	(1)
ܩܛܪܐ	n. m.	*bond, fetter*	(1)

ܩܛܪܓ

ܩܛܪܓܢܐ	n. m.	*accuser*	(4)
ܩܛܪܓܢܘܬܐ	n. f.	*accusation*	(2)
ܩܛܪܓ	v.	*accuse*	(10)

ܩܝܣܐ

ܩܝܣܐ	n. m.	*timber, tree, wood*	(15)

ܩܠ

ܩܠܐ	n. m.	*voice*	(153)

ܩܠ²

ܩܠ	v.	*lessen*; Aphᶜel *lighten, make light of*	(2)
ܩܠܝܠܐ	adj.	*little, light, swift*	(69)

ܩܡ

ܩܘܡܩܐ	n. m.	*sustenance, food, support*	(1)
ܩܡ	v.	*rise, stand*; Paᶜel ܩܝܡ *establish*; Aphᶜel ܐܩܝܡ *cause to stand*	(550)
ܩܘܡܬܐ	n. m.	*fathom*	(2)
ܩܘܡܬܐ	n. f.	*stature*	(5)
ܩܝܘܡܐ	n. f.	*succourer, supporter*	(1)
ܩܝܡܐ	adj.	*remaining, abiding, lasting, valid*	(13)
ܩܝܡܐ	n. m.	*covenant, standing up, stand, pact*	(7)
ܩܝܡܬܐ	n. f.	*resurrection*	(36)

ܩܢܐ

ܩܢܐ	v.	*obtain*	(17)
ܩܢܝܢܐ	n. m.	*possession, goods, property, substance*	(19)

ܩܢܕܝܢܘܣ

ܩܝܢܕܘܢܘܣ	n. f.	*peril, danger*	(11)

ܩܢܛܪܘܢܐ

ܩܢܛܪܘܢܐ	n. m.	*centurion*	(25)

	Syriac	Cat.	Meaning	

ܩܢܝܐ

| ܩܲܢܝܵܐ | n. m. | *pen, cane, reed* | (12) |

ܩܢܘܡ

| ܩܢܘܡܐ | n. m. | *person, individual* (self), *substance* | (15) |

ܩܥܐ

| ܩܥܐ | v. | *cry aloud,* w/ ܥܠ *appeal to* | (81) |
| ܩܥܬܐ | n. f. | *cry, clamor* | (2) |

ܩܨܡ

| ܩܨܐ | v. | *break* (bread) | (18) |
| ܩܨܝܐ | n. m. | *fragment* | (10) |

ܩܪܐ

ܩܘܩܝܐ	n. m.	*crowing*	(1)
ܩܪܐ	v.	*call, read,* w/ ܥܠ *appeal to*	(330)
ܩܪܝܢܐ	n. m.	*calling, vocation, reading, lesson*	(10)
ܩܪܝܬܐ	n. f.	*calling, vocation*	(7)
ܩܪܝܐ	pass. ptc. m.	*called, being by vocation*	(12)

ܩܪܒ

ܩܘܪܒܐ	n. m.	*approach, access*	(1)
ܩܘܪܒܢܐ	n. m.	*offering, gift*	(31)
ܩܪܒ	v.	*draw near, touch, come;* Paᶜel ܩܲܪܒ *bring near, bring near, offer;* Aphᶜel *fight*	(244)
ܩܪܒܐ	n. m.	*war, battle, fighting*	(19)
ܩܪܝܒܐ	adj.	*at hand, near, neighbour*	(54)
ܩܪܝܒܘܬܐ	n. f.	*nearness, access, approach*	(1)

ܩܪܝܬܐ

| ܩܪܝܬܐ | n. f. | *village, field* | (67) |

ܩܪܢܐ

| ܩܲܪܢܐ | n. f. | *horn, corner* | (22) |

Syriac	Cat.	Meaning	
ܡܳܙܠ	n. m.	w/ ܐܰܟܠ *accuse*	(15)
ܪܩܘܩܙ			
ܩܳܪܩܦܬܐ	n. f.	*head, skull*	(11)
ܣܒ			
ܩܰܫܝܫܐ	n. m.	*elder*	(84)
ܩܰܫܝܫܘܬܐ	n. f.	*office of an elder*	(2)
ܩܫܐ			
ܩܫܝ	v.	Paᶜel *harden*	(6)
ܩܰܫܝܐ	adj.	*hard, strong, rough*	(15)
ܩܰܫܝܐܝܬ	adv.	*sharply, severely*	(2)
ܩܰܫܝܘܬܐ	n. f.	*hardness, difficulty, severity*	(7)
ܪܒ			
ܪܒ	v.	Ethpalpal *be magnified*, made *great*	(2)
ܪܰܒܐ	adj.	*great, chief*, w/ suffix*master*	(395)
ܪܒ ܒܝܬܐ	idiom	*steward*	(9)
ܪܒ ܟܘܡܪܐ	n. m.	high *priest*	(3)
ܪܒܘܟܐ	n. m.	*master*	(1)
ܪܶܒܘܬܐ	n. f.	*myriad, thousand*	(12)
ܪܰܒܘܬܐ	n. f.	*greatness*, w/ ܟܘܡܪܘܬܐ high *priesthood*	(16)
ܪܰܒܝ	n. m.	*rabbi, master*	(18)
ܪܘܪܒܐܝܬ	adv.	*greatly*	(4)
ܪܒ	v.	*shout*; Aphᶜel *cause an uproar*	(1)
ܪܘܒܐ	n. m.	*uproar*	(4)
ܪܒܐ			
ܡܪܰܒܝܢܐ	n. m.	*nurse, guardian, rearer*	(2)
ܪܒܐ	v.	*grow up, increase*; Paᶜel ܪܒܝ *nourish*, cause *increase*	(35)
ܪܶܒܝܬܐ	n. f.	*usury, interest*	(2)
ܬܰܪܒܝܬܐ	n. f.	*increase, enlargement, progress*	(3)

7. Words Arranged by Root

Syriac	Cat.	Meaning	
ܐܲܪܒܥܵܐ	num. f.	*four*	(59)
ܐܲܪܒܥܝܼܢ	num.	*forty*	(25)
ܐܲܪܒܲܥܡܵܐܐ	num.	*four hundred*	(2)
ܐܲܪܒܲܥܸܣܪܸܐ	num. f.	*fourteen*	(7)
ܡܪܲܒܥܵܝܵܐ	adv.	*foursquare*	(1)
ܪܒܝܼܥܵܝܵܐ	adj.	*fourth*	(5)
ܪܘܼܒܥܵܐ	n. m.	*measure* (liquid)	(1)
ܪܘܼܒܥܵܐ	n. m.	*fourth part*	(1)

ܪܓ

Syriac	Cat.	Meaning	
ܪܓ	v.	*desire, covet, lust*	(24)
ܪܓܬܵܐ	n. f.	*lust*	(26)
ܪܓܬܵܐ	n. f.	*desire, lust*	(18)

ܪܓܙ

Syriac	Cat.	Meaning	
ܪܓܙ	v.	*be angry*; Aph^cel *provoke*	(17)
ܪܘܓܙܵܐ	n. m.	*anger, wrath, indignation*	(38)

ܪܓܠ

Syriac	Cat.	Meaning	
ܪܓܠܵܐ	n. f.	*foot*	(100)
ܪܓܠܵܐ	n. m.	foot *soldier*	(1)
ܪܓܠܬܵܐ	n. f.	*brook*	(1)

ܪܓܡ

Syriac	Cat.	Meaning	
ܪܓܡ	v.	*stone*	(20)

ܪܕܐ

Syriac	Cat.	Meaning	
ܪܕܝܵܐ	n. m.	*journey*	(1)
ܪܕܘܬܵܐ	n. f.	*chastisement, instruction*	(8)
ܪܕܝܬܵܐ	n. f.	*flow, voyage, passage*	(3)
ܪܕܐ	v.	*journey, flow, chastise, instruct;* Aph^cel make *flow, supply*	(63)
ܪܕܘܝܵܐ	n. m.	*instructor*	(1)

Syriac	Cat.	Meaning	
		ܪܕܦ	
ܪܳܕܽܘܦܳܐ	n. m.	*persecutor*	(3)
ܪܕܽܘܦܝܳܐ	n. m.	*persecution*	(7)
ܪܕܺܝܦܽܘܬܳܐ	n. f.	*persecution*	(3)
ܪܕܰܦ	v.	*follow, persecute*	(34)
		ܪܗܒ	
ܡܣܰܪܗܒܳܐܺܝܬ	adv.	*hastily*	(1)
ܣܽܘܪܗܳܒܳܐ	n. m.	*rashness, hastiness*	(1)
ܪܗܶܒ	v.	*agitate*; Ethp^cel *be frightened*; Saph^cel *hurry*	(11)
ܡܣܰܪܗܒܳܐ	pass. ptc. m.	*hasty*	(3)
		ܪܗܛ	
ܪܗܶܛ	v.	*run*	(46)
ܪܶܗܛܳܐ	n. m.	*course*	(3)
		ܪܘܐ	
ܪܘܺܝ	v.	become *drunk*	(10)
ܪܰܘܳܝܳܐ	adj.	*drunkard*	(3)
ܪܰܘܳܝܽܘܬܳܐ	n. f.	*drunkenness*	(4)
		ܪܘܙ	
ܪܘܶܙ	v.	*be glad, rejoice*	(9)
ܪܘܳܙܳܐ	n. m.	*gladness, exultation*	(1)
		ܪܘܚ	
ܪܘܰܚ	v.	*be ample*; Pa^cel *be enlarged*; Aph^cel *relieve*	(2)
ܪܽܘܚܳܐ	n. c.	*spirit, wind, breath*	(478)
ܪܽܘܚܳܢܳܐ	adj.	*spiritual*	(6)
ܪܽܘܚܳܢܳܐܺܝܬ	adv.	*spiritually*	(2)
ܪܽܘܚܳܢܳܝܳܐ	adj.	*spiritual*	(6)
ܪܰܘܚܳܐ	n. f.	*relief, relaxation, easing*	(1)

7. Words Arranged by Root

Syriac	Cat.	Meaning	
ܪܘܝܚܐ	pass. ptc. m.	*ample, large*	(1)
ܪܙܐ			
ܐܪܙܐ	n. m.	*mystery*	(28)
ܪܚܡ			
ܡܪܚܡܢܐ	adj.	*merciful, compassionate*	(7)
ܡܪܚܡܢܘܬܐ	n. f.	*compassion, mercy, pity, kindliness*	(3)
ܪܚܝܡܐ	pass. ptc. m.	*beloved*	(1)
ܪܚܡ	v.	*love,* have *mercy;* Ethpaᶜal ܐܬܪܚܡ *have mercy;* Paᶜel ܪܚܡ *have compassion*	(119)
ܪܚܡܐ	n. m.	*friend*	(29)
ܪܚܡܐ	n. m.	*bowels, mercy*	(39)
ܪܚܡܘܬܐ	n. f.	*friendship*	(1)
ܪܚܡܬܐ	n. f.	*love, friendship*	(6)
ܪܚܡܬܢܐ	adj.	*merciful*	(1)
ܪܚܩ			
ܪܘܚܩܐ	n. m.	*far place,* far *place,* w/ ܡܢ *from afar*	(15)
ܪܚܝܩܐ	adj.	*far, distant, remote*	(23)
ܪܚܩ	v.	Ethpaᶜal *keep away from;* Aphᶜel ܐܪܚܩ *remove, depart*	(6)
ܪܛܢ			
ܪܛܢ	v.	*murmur*	(13)
ܪܛܢܐ	n. m.	*murmuring*	(5)
ܪܫ			
ܪܫܐ	n. m.	*head, beginning; pl. chiefs*	(181)
ܪܫܝܐ	adj.	*best, choicest, excellent*	(4)
ܪܫܝܬܐ	n. f.	*beginning, (pl)first fruits*	(28)
ܪܫܢܘܬܐ	n. f.	*principality, sovereignty*	(1)
ܪܫܢܐ	n. m.	*chief*	(4)

Syriac	Cat.	Meaning	
		ܪܟܒ	
ܡܲܪܟܲܒ݂ܬ݂ܐ	n. f.	chariot	(5)
ܪܟܸܒ݂	v.	mount, ride; Ethpaᶜal be constructed; Aphᶜel make ride	(11)
ܪܘܟ݂ܒܐ	n. m.	band, fastening	(1)
		ܪܟܫ	
ܪܲܟ݂ܫܐ	n. m.	horse	(10)
		ܪܡ	
ܡܪܵܘܡܐ	n. m.	height	(6)
ܡܪܲܡܡܐ	pass. ptc. m.	high, most high	(5)
ܪܡ	v.	be high; Aphᶜel ܐܲܪܝܡ exalt	(58)
ܪܵܘܡܐ	n. m.	height, high place	(6)
ܪܘܡܪܵܡܐ	n. m.	exaltation, high estate	(1)
ܪܵܡܐ	adj.	high, w/ ܩܵܠܐ loud voice	(39)
ܪܡܬ݂ܐ	n. f.	hill	(2)
		ܪܡܐ	
ܪܡܐ	v.	put, place, cast	(136)
ܬܐܪܡܝܬ݂ܐ	n. f.	foundation	(8)
		ܪܡܫܐ	
ܪܲܡܫܐ	n. m.	evening	(19)
		ܪܢܐ	
ܪܢܐ	v.	meditate, think, consider, plan	(15)
ܪܸܢܝܐ	n. m.	consideration, care, concern	(2)
		¹ܪܥܐ	
ܡܲܪܥܝܬ݂ܐ	n. f.	flock	(7)
ܪܥܐ	v.	feed, tend	(19)
ܪܵܥܝܐ	n. m.	shepherd, pastor	(20)
ܪܸܥܝܐ	n. m.	pasture	(1)

7. Words Arranged by Root

Syriac	Cat.	Meaning	
		²ܪܥܐ	
ܪܢܐ	den.	Ethpaꜥal ܐܬܪܥܝ *think*	(43)
ܪܶܢܝܳܢܐ	n. m.	*mind, conscience,* w/ ܣܰܟܠ *fool,* *thought, idea, conception*	(77)
ܬܰܪܥܺܝܬܐ	n. f.	*mind, thought, imagination*	(14)
		³ܪܥܐ	
ܪܥܝ	v.	Paꜥel ܪܰܥܝ *reconcile*	(8)
ܬܰܪܥܽܘܬܐ	n. f.	*reconciliation*	(5)
		ܪܥܡ	
ܪܽܘܥܳܡܐ	n. m.	*quarrel, complaint, grumbling,* *murmuring, muttering*	(1)
ܪܰܥܡܐ	n. m.	*thunder*	(12)
		ܪܩ	
ܪܽܘܩܐ	n. m.	*spittle*	(1)
ܪܩ	v.	*spit*	(9)
ܪܰܩܐ	particle	*fool*	(1)
		ܪܩܕ	
ܪܩܶܕ	v.	*dance;* Aphꜥel *mourn*	(10)
		ܪܫܐ	
ܪܫܐ	v.	*blame,* find *fault, accuse*	(9)
ܪܶܫܝܳܢܐ	n. m.	*accusation, blame,* w/ ܠܐ *blameless*	(13)
		ܪܫܡ	
ܪܽܘܫܡܐ	n. m.	*mark*	(7)
ܪܫܰܡ	v.	*engrave,* w/ ܩܕܡ *foreordain, mark*	(8)
		ܪܫܥ	
ܪܽܘܫܥܐ	n. m.	*wickedness, ungodliness*	(4)
ܪܰܫܺܝܥܐ	adj.	*impious, wicked, ungodly*	(11)
ܪܫܥ	v.	Aphꜥel act *wickedly*	(1)
		ܪܬ	
ܪܬ	v.	*tremble*	(5)

Syriac	Cat.	Meaning	
ܪܰܬܺܝܬܳܐ	n. c.	*trembling, tremor*	(5)
		ܫܐܕܐ	
ܫܺܐܕܳܐ	n. m.	*demon*, evil *spirit*	(48)
		ܫܐܠ	
ܫܶܐܠ	v.	*ask, inquire*, w/ ܫܠܳܡܳܐ *salute*; Aph^{c}el *lend*	(243)
ܫܶܐܠܬܳܐ	n. f.	*request, petition*	(3)
		ܫܒܐ	
ܫܒܳܐ	v.	lead *captive*	(6)
ܫܶܒܝܳܐ	n. m.	*captivity*	(2)
ܫܒܺܝܬܳܐ	n. f.	*captivity*	(1)
ܫܰܒܝܳܐ	n. m.	*captive*	(4)
		ܫܒܚ	
ܡܫܰܒܚܳܐ	pass. ptc. m.	*praiseworthy, excellent*	(3)
ܫܒܚ	den.	Pa^{c}el ܫܰܒܰܚ *praise, glorify, commend*	(95)
ܫܒܺܝܚܳܐ	adj.	*praiseworthy*	(2)
ܫܽܘܒܚܳܐ	n. m.	*glory, glorification, praise*	(89)
ܬܶܫܒܽܘܚܬܳܐ	n. f.	*praise, glory*	(99)
		ܫܒܛܐ	
ܫܰܒܛܳܐ	n. m.	*rod, sceptre, tribe*, w/ ܫܰܒ ܠܰܚ *magistrates, staff*	(19)
		ܫܒܥ	
ܫܒܺܝܥܳܝܳܐ	adj.	*seventh*	(1)
ܫܰܒܥܳܐ	num. f.	*seven*	(100)
ܫܰܒܥܺܝܢ	num.	*seventy*	(6)
		ܫܒܩ	
ܫܒܰܩ	v.	*forgive, leave, allow*	(217)
ܫܽܘܒܩܳܢܳܐ	n. m.	*remission, forgiveness, repudiation, release*	(19)

7. Words Arranged by Root 167

Syriac	Cat.	Meaning	
ܡܛܠܩܐ	ap f	*repudiated*	(3)
		ܫܒܬܐ	
ܫܒܬ	den.	Aph^cel *rest*	(1)
ܫܒܬܐ	n. f.	*Sabbath*	(69)
		ܫܓܫ	
ܫܓܘܫܐ	n. m.	*rioter*	(1)
ܫܓܘܫܝܐ	n. m.	*riot, uproar, tumult, commotion*	(13)
ܫܓܫ	v.	*stir up, trouble*	(17)
		ܫܕܐ	
ܫܕܐ	v.	*throw, cast*	(38)
		ܫܕܪ	
ܫܕܪ	v.	Pa^cel ܫܕܪ *send*	(235)
		ܫܘܐ	
ܫܘܐ	v.	*worthy, be equal*; Ethp^cel *agree*; Pa^cel *spread, wipe*; Aph^cel ܐܫܘܝ *smooth*	(86)
ܫܘܝܐ	ap f	*equal, the same*	(1)
ܫܘܝܐܝܬ	adv.	*equally, similarly*	(2)
ܫܘܝܘܬܐ	n. f.	*equality, similarity*	(4)
		ܫܘܠ	
ܡܫܘܠܬܐ	n. f.	*basin*	(1)
ܫܘܠ	v.	Aph^cel ܐܫܝܓ *wash*	(24)
		ܫܘܥ	
ܫܘܥܐ	n. m.	*rock*	(14)
		ܫܘܩ	
ܫܘܩܐ	n. m.	*street, marketplace, square, bazaar*	(27)
		ܫܘܬܦ	
ܫܘܬܦ	v.	*be partaker*	(27)
ܫܘܬܦܐ	n. m.	*partaker, partner*	(14)
ܫܘܬܦܘܬܐ	n. f.	*partnership, fellowship, participation, communion*	(16)

Syriac	Cat.	Meaning	
		ܫܚܢ	
ܫܘܚܢܐ	n. m.	*boil, ulcer*	(4)
ܫܚܢ	v.	*warm*	(7)
		ܫܛ	
ܫܛ	v.	*despise*, treat w/ *contempt*	(10)
ܫܛܐ	pass. ptc. m.	*contemptable*	(1)
		ܫܛܐ	
ܫܛܐ	v.	become *foolish*; Aph^{c}el ܐܫܛܝ make *foolish*	(3)
ܫܛܝܘܬܐ	n. f.	*foolishness, folly, infatuation*	(9)
ܫܛܝܐ	n. m.	*fool*	(2)
		ܫܝܘܠ	
ܫܝܘܠ	n. f.	*sheol, place of the dead*	(15)
		ܫܝܢ	
ܫܝܢ	v.	Pa^{c}el ܫܝܢ make *peace, reconcile*	(4)
ܫܝܢܐ	n. m.	*peace, tranquility*	(14)
		ܫܫܠܬܐ	
ܫܫܠܬܐ	n. f.	*chain*	(12)
		ܫܟܢ	
ܡܫܟܢܐ	n. m.	*tabernacle, habitation, tent*	(17)
ܫܟܢ	v.	*dwell, lodge*	(1)
		ܫܠܐ	
ܫܠܐ	v.	*cease, be quiet*; Pa^{c}el ܫܠܝ *quiet, stop*	(20)
ܫܠܘܐ	n. m.	w/ ܕܠܐ without *ceasing*	(2)
ܫܠܝܐ	n. m.	*calm, silence*, w/ ܡܢ *suddenly, cessation, lull, quietness*	(16)
ܫܠܝܐ	adj.	*calm, tranquil*	(1)
		ܫܠܚ	
ܫܠܚ	v.	*send*	(18)

7. Words Arranged by Root

Syriac	Cat.	Meaning	
ܡܫܬܠܚܢܐ	pass. ptc. m.	*apostle, sent one*	(86)
ܡܫܬܠܚܢܘܬܐ	n. f.	*Apostleship*	(5)

ܫܠܛ

ܡܫܠܛܐ	ap f	having *authority*	(3)
ܫܘܠܛܢܐ	n. m.	*power, authority, dominion*	(80)
ܫܠܛ	v.	Ethpaʿal have *power*, have *authority*; Aphʿel ܐܫܠܛ give *authority*	(7)
ܫܠܝܛܐ	adj.	*lawful, permitted,* (pl) *magistrates,* (pl) *rulers*	(53)
ܫܠܝܛܢܐ	n. m.	*ruler*	(8)

ܫܠܡ

ܡܫܡܠܝܐ	adj.	*perfect, complete*	(5)
ܡܫܠܡܢܐ	n. m.	*betrayer, traitor*	(10)
ܡܫܠܡܢܘܬܐ	n. f.	*tradition*	(8)
ܫܘܠܡܐ	n. m.	*end, consummation, fulfilment, fulness*	(16)
ܫܠܡ	v.	*die,* w/ ܠ *obey, agree, follow;* Ethpʿel ܐܫܬܠܡ *be delivered up;* Paʿel ܫܠܡ *complete;* Aphʿel ܐܫܠܡ *deliver up, be completed*	(200)
ܫܠܡܐ	adj.	*whole, entire, perfect*	(2)
ܫܠܡܐ	n. m.	*peace,* w/ ܝܗܒ *salute, salutation*	(164)
ܫܠܡܘܬܐ	n. f.	*peace, agreement, concord*	(2)

ܫܡ

ܫܡܐ	n. m.	*name*	(244)
ܫܡܗ	den.	*name, call*	(7)
ܫܡܫ	den.	*name*	(5)

ܫܡܝܐ

ܫܡܝܐ	n. c.	*heaven, sky*	(309)
ܫܡܝܢܐ	adj.	*heavenly, celestial* (bodies)	(6)

Syriac	Cat.	Meaning	
		ܫܡܥ	
ܫܽܡܥܳܐ	n. m.	*hearing, obedience*	(5)
ܫܡܰܥܬܳܐ	n. f.	*hearing, obedience*	(10)
ܫܳܡܽܘܥܳܐ	adj.	*obedient, compliant*	(2)
ܫܳܡܽܘܥܽܘܬܳܐ	n. f.	*obedience*	(7)
ܫܳܡܽܘܥܳܐ	n. m.	*hearer*	(4)
ܫܡܰܥ	v.	*hear, obey;* Aph^cel *cause to* hear	(494)
ܫܶܡܥܳܐ	n. m.	*hearing, report*	(9)
		¹ܫܡܫ	
ܫܶܡܫܳܐ	n. c.	*sun*	(33)
		²ܫܡܫ	
ܡܫܰܡܫܳܢܳܐ	n. m.	*minister, servant, attendant*	(41)
ܫܰܡܶܫ	v.	Pa^cel ܫܰܡܶܫ *minister, serve*	(60)
ܬܶܫܡܶܫܬܳܐ	n. f.	*ministration, service, attendance*	(52)
		ܫܢܐ	
ܫܢܳܐ	v.	*be mad;* Pa^cel ܫܰܢܺܝ *depart, remove*	(35)
ܫܰܢܝܽܘܬܳܐ	n. m.	*madness, wildness*	(1)
ܫܳܢܺܝܬܳܐ	n. f.	*mad*	(1)
		²ܫܢܐ	
ܫܶܢܳܐ	n. f.	*tooth, ivory, tusk*	(14)
		ܫܢܩ	
ܫܽܘܢܳܩܳܐ	n. m.	*torment*	(3)
ܫܰܢܶܩ	v.	Pa^cel *torment*	(16)
ܬܰܫܢܺܝܩܳܐ	n. m.	*torment*	(7)
		ܫܢܬܐ	
ܫܰܢܬܳܐ	n. f.	*year*	(72)
		ܫܥܐ	
ܫܽܘܥܺܝܬܳܐ	n. f.	*fable, story, talk*	(5)
ܫܥܳܐ	v.	Ethp^cel *play;* Ethpa^cal ܐܶܫܬܰܥܺܝ *narrate*	(30)
ܫܶܥܝܳܐ	n. m.	*jesting, play*	(1)

7. Words Arranged by Root   171

Syriac	Cat.	Meaning	
ܐܶܫܬܰܥܝܐ	n. f.	*narrative, account*	(3)

ܫܥܐ

| ܫܳܥܬܐ | n. | *hour* | (142) |

ܫܦܪ

ܫܘܦܪܐ	n. m.	*beauty, elegance, grace*	(1)
ܫܰܦܝܪܐ	adj.	*beautiful, good, well*	(108)
ܫܦܰܪ	v.	*please*	(31)
ܫܰܦܪܐ	n. m.	*daybreak, dawn*	(4)

ܫܩܐ

| ܫܩܐ | v. | Aphᶜel ܐܰܫܩܝ *water*, give to *drink* | (14) |

ܫܩܠ

ܡܫܰܩܠܐ	pass. ptc. m.	*proud*	(1)
ܫܩܰܠ	v.	*take up, bear*	(160)
ܫܩܳܠܛܰܥܢܐ	idiom	*diligence, care*	(1)
ܫܩܳܠܐ	n. m.	*taking away, acceptance, diligence,* w/ ܛܰܥܢܐ *care*	(1)
ܫܩܳܠܐ	n. m.	w/ ܡܶܕܶܡ *magistrate, orderly*	(2)
ܫܩܳܠܬܐ	n. f.	*carrying, bearer*	(2)

ܫܪ

ܫܰܪ	v.	*be strong*; Paᶜel ܫܰܪܝ *establish*; Aphᶜel ܐܰܫܰܪ *strengthen, believe*	(35)
ܫܰܪܝܪܐ	adj.	*true, steadfast*	(65)
ܫܰܪܝܪܐܝܬ	adv.	*truly*	(36)
ܫܰܪܝܪܘܬܐ	n. f.	*steadfastness*	(1)
ܫܪܳܪܐ	n. m.	*truth*	(94)
ܡܫܰܪܪܐ	ap f	*firm, sure*	(1)

ܫܪܐ

| ܫܶܪܝܢܐ | n. m. | *lodging* | (5) |
| ܡܫܰܪܝܐ | pass. ptc. m. | *sick, paralytic* | (14) |

Syriac	Cat.	Meaning	
ܡܫܪܝܬܐ	n. f.	*encampment*	(10)
ܫܘܪܝܐ	n. m.	*beginning*	(12)
ܫܪܐ	v.	*loosen, lodge*; Pa^cel ܫܪܝ *begin*; Ethpa^cal ܐܬܫܪܝ *be loosened, eat* a meal	(249)
ܫܪܘܬܐ	n. f.	*meal, breakfast, dinner*	(3)
ܫܪܝܐ	n. m.	*release*	(2)

ܫܪܒ

| ܫܪܒܬܐ | n. f. | *generation, tribe, family, stock, line* | (74) |

ܫܪܓ

| ܫܪܓܐ | n. m. | *light, lamp, wick* | (16) |
| ܫܪܓܓ | den. | Ethp^cel *imagine* | (1) |

ܫܪܟ

| ܫܪܟܐ | n. m. | *residue, rest, remainder* | (40) |
| ܫܪܟܢܐ | n. m. | *remnant* | (2) |

ܫܬ

ܫܬܐ	num. f.	*six*	(26)
ܫܬܝܢ	num.	*sixty*	(9)
ܫܬܝܬܝܐ	adj.	*sixth*	(1)
ܫܬܡܐܐ	num.	*six hundred*	(1)
ܫܬܥܣܪ	num.	*sixteen*	(1)

ܫܬܐ

ܡܫܬܘܬܐ	n. f.	*festivity*, wedding *feast, symposium*	(14)
ܡܫܬܝܐ	n. m.	*drink*	(5)
ܐܫܬܝ	v.	*drink*	(82)

ܫܬܩ

| ܫܬܩ | v. | keep *silent, be still*; Pa^cel ܫܬܩ *silence* | (24) |
| ܫܬܩܐ | n. m. | *silence* | (1) |

ܬܐܘܪܝܐ

| ܬܐܪܬܐ | n. f. | *conscience* | (27) |

7. WORDS ARRANGED BY ROOT

Syriac	Cat.	Meaning	
		ܬܒ	
ܬܒ	v.	*return, repent*; Aphᶜel ܐܬܝܒ *answer, vomit*	(38)
ܬܘܒ	particle	*again, furthermore*	(192)
ܬܝܒܘܬܐ	n. f.	*repentance*	(23)
ܬܝܘܒܐ	n. m.	*vomit*	(1)
		ܬܒܥ	
ܬܒܘܥܐ	n. m.	*avenger*	(2)
ܬܒܥ	v.	*avenge, require*	(17)
ܬܒܥܬܐ	n. f.	*vengeance, vindication*	(8)
		ܬܓܪ	
ܬܐܓܘܪܬܐ	n. f.	*merchandise, barter, trade*	(9)
ܬܓܪ	den.	Ethpaᶜal ܐܬܬܓܪ make *gain, trade*	(8)
ܬܓܪܐ	n. m.	*merchant*	(5)
		ܬܗܪ	
ܬܗܪ	v.	*marvel, be amazed*	(9)
ܬܗܪܐ	n. m.	*amazement, astonishment*	(1)
		ܬܘܪܐ	
ܬܘܪܐ	n. m.	*ox, steer*	(14)
		ܬܚܘܡܐ	
ܬܚܘܡܐ	n. m.	*boundary, border, confine*	(15)
		ܬܚܬ	
ܬܚܝܬ	prep.	*under*	(73)
ܬܚܬܝ	den.	bring *low*	(2)
ܬܚܬܝܐ	adj.	*low*	(3)
		ܬܟܠ	
ܬܘܟܠܢܐ	n. m.	*trust, confidence*	(10)
ܬܟܝܠܐܝܬ	adv.	*confidently*	(2)
ܬܟܠ	v.	Ethpᶜel *be confident*	(23)

Syriac	Cat.	Meaning	
ܬ̇ܠܝܬܳܝܳܐ	n. m.	third	(15)
ܬܠܳܬܳܐ	num. f.	three	(126)
ܬܠܳܬܺܝܢ	num.	thirty	(11)
ܬܠܳܬ ܡܳܐܐ	num.	three hundred	(1)
ܬܡܰܗ	v.	be astonished; Aphᶜel ܐܰܬܡܰܗ astonish	(26)
ܬܶܡܗܳܐ	n. m.	amazement, stupor	(5)
ܬܰܡܺܝܗܳܐ	adj.	astonished	(2)
ܬܰܡܳܢ	particle	there	(206)
ܬܡܺܝܢܳܝܳܐ	adj.	eighth	(1)
ܬܡܳܢܝܳܐ	num. m.	eight	(12)
ܬܡܳܢܺܝܢ	num.	eighty	(2)
ܬܡܳܢܰܥܣܰܪ	num. f.	eighteen	(3)
ܬܢܳܢ	particle	here	(14)
		¹	
ܬܶܢܳܢܳܐ	n. m.	smoke	(12)
		²	
ܬܰܢܺܝܢܳܐ	n. m.	dragon, monster	(14)
ܬܘܽܩܰܠܬܳܐ	n. f.	offense, stumbling block	(14)
ܬܩܶܠ	v.	stumble, hinder	(10)
ܬܩܶܢ	v.	be restored; Paᶜel restore, prepare; Aphᶜel ܐܰܬܩܶܢ establish	(22)
ܬܰܩܢܳܐ	adj.	honest, good, correct, firm	(2)
ܬܰܩܢܽܘܬܳܐ	n. f.	integrity, rectitude	(1)

Syriac	Cat.	Meaning	
		ܬܪܝ	
ܬܪܝܢ	num. m.	*two*	(204)
ܬܪܥܣܪ	num. m.	*twelve*	(75)
		ܬܪܢܓܠܬܐ	
ܬܪܢܓܘܠܬܐ	n. f.	*hen*	(2)
ܬܪܢܓܠܐ	n. m.	*cock*	(13)
		ܬܪܣܐ	
ܬܘܪܣܝܐ	n. m.	*nourishment, food*	(2)
ܬܪܣܐ	v.	*nourish, support, feed*	(10)
		ܬܪܥ	
ܬܪܥ	v.	*flow, open*	(1)
ܬܪܥܐ	n. m.	*door, gate, portal*	(77)
ܬܪܥܐ	n. m.	*doorkeeper*	(1)
		ܬܪܨ	
ܬܘܪܨܐ	n. m.	*correction*	(2)
ܬܪܝܨܐ	pass. ptc. m.	*straight, upright*	(5)
ܬܪܝܨܐܝܬ	adv.	*rightly, uprightly*	(7)
ܬܪܨ	v.	Tr. *direct*, Tr. make *straight*, Int. *rush*	(9)
		ܬܫܥ	
ܬܫܥ	num.	*nine*	(15)
ܬܫܥܝܢ	num.	*ninety, lot, portion*	(4)
		ܬܬܐ	
ܬܬܐ	n. f.	*fig, fig tree*	(21)

Chapter 8

Compound Words

Sequence.

This list is arranged in alphabetical order.

Format.

The list consists of four columns:

- **Column 1: Syriac Lexical Entry.**
  Gives the Syriac form of the proper noun in vocalized *Serto* (Western) script.

- **Column 2: Category.**
  Gives the grammatical category of the lexical entry.

- **Column 3: Compound.**
  Gives the compound components of the Syriac word.

- **Column 4: English Meanings.**
  Gives the English meanings of the lexical entry. At the right side of this column, the frequency of the lexical entry is given in italic in parenthesis.

8. Compound Words

How to use the list.

This list shows compounds words in Syriac. Noting the compound forms can make memorization easier.

Syriac	Cat.	Compound	Meaning	
ܐܟܚܕܐ	particle	ܐܝܟ + ܚܕܐ	*as one, together*	(25)
ܐܟܠܩܪܨܐ	n. m.	ܐܟܠ + ܩܪܨܐ	*accuser, calumniator*	(19)
ܐܦܢ	particle	ܐܦ + ܐܢ	*even if*	(32)
ܒܠܚܘܕ	adv.	ܒ + ܠ + ܚܘܕ	*only, alone*	(128)
ܒܥܠܕܒܒܐ	adj.	ܒܥܠܐ + ܕܒܒܐ	*enemy*	(38)
ܒܬܪ	prep.	ܒ + ܐܬܪ	*after, behind*	(256)
ܒܬܪܟܢ	particle	ܒܬܪ + ܟܢ	*afterwards*	(15)
ܕܠܡܐ	particle	ܕ + ܠܐ + ܡܐ	*lest*	(87)
ܟܠܝܘܡ	idiom	ܟܠ + ܝܘܡ	*always*	(52)
ܟܠܝܘܡ	idiom	ܟܠ + ܝܘܡ	*everyday*	(21)
ܟܠܡܕܡ	idiom	ܟܠ + ܡܕܡ	*everything*	(83)
ܟܠܢܫ	n. c.	ܟܠ + ܐܢܫ	w/ ܟܠ *every one*	(96)
ܠܒܪ	prep.	ܠ + ܒܪ	*outside*	(82)
ܠܘܩܒܠ	prep.	ܠ + ܩܘܒܠܐ	*against, near, toward,* w/ ܩܘܡ *resist, opposite to*	(65)
ܠܘܩܕܡ	particle	ܠ + ܩܘܕܡ	*before, formerly*	(56)
ܠܡܐ	pron.	ܠ + ܡܐ	*why*	(61)
ܠܡܢܐ	pron.	ܠ + ܡܢܐ	*why*	(52)
ܡܬܘܡ	particle	ܡ + ܡܬܘܡ	*always, ever*	(20)
ܩܕܠ	particle	ܩܕܡ + ܠ	*before*	(12)
ܫܬܐܣܬܐ	n. f.	ܫܬ + ܐܣܬܐ	*foundation*	(22)
ܬܪܥܣܪ	num. m.	ܬܪܝܢ + ܥܣܪ	*twelve*	(75)

Chapter 9

Semitic Cognate List

Sequence.

This list is arranged in alphabetical order.

Format.

The list consists of four columns:

- **Column 1: Syriac Lexical Entry.**
  Gives the Syriac form of the proper noun in vocalized *Serto* (Western) script.

- **Column 2: Hebrew form.**
  Gives a Hebrew cognate.

- **Column 3: Arabic form.**
  Gives an Arabic cognate.

- **Column 4: Category.**
  Gives the grammatical category of the lexical entry.

- **Column 5: English Meanings.**
  Gives the English meanings of the lexical entry. At the right side of this column, the frequency of the lexical entry is given in italic in parenthesis.

179

How to use the list.

This list shows where Syriac words are cognates with Hebrew and Arabic words, and the words remain similar in form allowing easy memorization for students. Listed are only Syriac words that occur more than 30 times in the Syriac New Testament. Hebrew and Arabic cognates are shown if they are words that a student is likely to know. For Hebrew words, these are those that occur thirty or more times in the Hebrew Bible, or have a more common Arabic cognate such as חָבַב, أَحَبّ and ܚܒܒ.

Student already familiar with Hebrew or Arabic can use this list to quickly expand their Syriac vocabulary, for many cognates are very similar in meaning. The list reveals many examples of the Canaanite shift, where the Proto-NorthWest-Semitic ā (long a) vowel retained in Syriac and Arabic turned into ō (long o) in Canaanite languages such as Hebrew. For example ܡܟܠܬܐ and سلام, but שָׁלוֹם. Likewise, ܠܐ and لا, but לֹא. An appendix to this section list Syriac words which are etymologically linked to Hebrew words, but where a consonantal shift has occurred between the languages.

Semitic Cognate Words

Syriac	Hebrew	Arabic	Cat.	Meaning	
ܐܒܐ	אָב	أب	n. m.	father	(453)
ܐܒܕ	אָבַד		v.	perish, destroy, lose	(87)
ܐܒܪܗܡ	אַבְרָהָם	ابراهيم	pr. n.	Abraham	(75)
ܐܓܪܐ		أجر	n. m.	pay, reward, recompense	(31)
ܐܕܢܐ		إذن	n. f.	ear	(45)
ܐܘ	אוֹ	أو	particle	or, else, rather than	(296)
ܐܘܢܓܠܝܘܢ		إنجيل	n. m.	Gospel	(30)
ܐܘܪܚܐ	אֹרַח		n. f.	way, road, highway, journeying	(105)
ܐܘܪܫܠܡ	יְרוּשָׁלַם	أورشليم	pr. n.	Jerusalem	(143)
ܐܚܐ	אָח	أخ	n. m.	brother	(360)

9. SEMITIC COGNATE LIST

Syriac	Hebrew	Arabic	Cat.	Meaning	
ܐܚܪܝܐ	אַחֵר	آخير	adj.	last, extreme	(53)
ܐܚܪܢܐ	אַחֵר	آخر	adj.	another	(295)
ܐܝܕܐ	יָד	يد	n. f.	hand, through, near	(362)
ܐܝܟܢܐ	אֵיךְ		prep.	as, how	(308)
ܐܝܡܡܐ	יוֹמָם		n. m.	daytime	(30)
ܐܝܣܪܐܝܠ	יִשְׂרָאֵל	اسرائيل	pr. n.	Israel	(77)
ܐܟܠ	אָכַל	أكل	v.	eat, consume, accuse, feed	(178)
ܐܠܗܐ	אֱלֹהִים	الله	n. m.	God, god	(1389)
ܐܠܘ	לוּ	لو	particle	if	(57)
ܐܠܝܐ	אֵלִיָּה	اليا	pr. n.	Elijah	(31)
ܐܠܦܐ	אֶלֶף		num.	thousand	(48)
ܐܡܐ	אֵם	أم	n. f.	mother	(93)
ܐܡܝܢ	אָמֵן	آمين	particle	Amen, verily	(147)
ܐܡܪ	אָמַר	أمر (= قال)	v.	say, speak, announce, affirm	(2553)
ܐܡܬܝ	מָתַי	متى	particle	when?	(57)
ܐܢ	אָם	أن	particle	if	(680)
ܐܢܐ	אֲנִי	أنا	pron. c.	I	(1728)
ܐܢܫܐ	אֱנוֹשׁ	أنسان	n. c.	man, mankind	(709)
ܐܢܬ	אַתָּה	انت	pron. m.	thou	(1401)
ܐܣܝܪܐ	אָסִיר	أسير	pass. ptc. m.	prisoner, sergeant, bound	(57)
ܐܣܪ	אָסַר	أسر	v.	bind, fasten	(66)
ܐܦ	אַף	أف	particle	also, even	(765)
ܐܦܐ	פָּנֶה	أنف (= وجه)	n. f.	face, hypocrite, presence-bread	(143)
ܐܦܢ	אַף		particle	even if	(32)
ܐܪܒܥܐ	אַרְבַּע	أربعة	num. f.	four	(59)

9. Semitic Cognate List

Syriac	Hebrew	Arabic	Cat.	Meaning	
ܐܰܪܥܳܐ		أرض	n. f.	earth, land, country, soil, ground	(272)
ܐܷܫܬܝ	שָׁתָה		v.	drink	(82)
ܐܳܬܐ	אוֹת		n. f.	miraculous, sign	(82)
ܐܳܬܐ	אָתָה	أتى	v.	come, bring	(966)
ܒ	בְּ	بِ	prep.	in, by, into, among, at, with, against	(824)
ܒܗܪ		بهر	den.	glorify, pride	(45)
ܒܗܬ		بهث	v.	ashamed, shame	(37)
ܒܛܠ	בָּטֵל	بطل	v.	idle, cease, care, annul	(56)
ܒܝܢ	בֵּין	بين	prep.	between	(49)
ܒܝܫܐ		بئس	adj.	evil, wrong	(185)
ܒܝܬ	בֵּין	بين	prep.	between	(46)
ܒܝܬܐ	בַּיִת	بيت	n. m.	house, abode	(434)
ܒܟܐ	בָּכָה	بكى	v.	weep	(41)
ܒܢܐ	בָּנָה	بنى	v.	build	(47)
ܒܣܪܐ	בָּשָׂר		n. m.	flesh	(129)
ܒܥܠܕܒܒܐ	בַּעַל		adj.	enemy	(38)
ܒܪܟ	[ברד]	برك (= سجد)	v.	kneel, bless, bow	(58)
ܒܢܝܢܫܐ	אֱנוֹשׁ		n. c.	human	(231)
ܓܒܐ		جبى (= إختار)	v.	choose, gather, elect, collect	(44)
ܓܒܪܐ	גִּבּוֹר		n. m.	man, husband, person	(319)
ܓܕܦ	[גדף]	جدّف	v.	blaspheme	(34)
ܓܠܐ	גָּלָה	جلى	v.	reveal, manifest	(98)
ܓܠܝܠܐ	גָּלִיל	الجليل	pr. n.	Galilee	(63)
ܘܒܪ		دبّر	v.	lead, take, rule, guide, conduct	(93)
ܕܓܠܐ		دجّال	adj.	false, liar	(38)

9. Semitic Cognate List

Syriac	Hebrew	Arabic	Cat.	Meaning	
ܕܰܗܒܳܐ		ذهب	n. m.	gold	(40)
ܕܰܘܺܝܕ	דָּוִד	داؤد	pr. n.	David	(60)
ܕܟܰܪ		ذكر	v.	remember, remind, mention	(33)
ܕܳܢ	דִּין	دان	den.	judge	(118)
ܗܳܐ	הֵן	ها	particle	lo! behold!	(270)
ܗܰܘ	הוּא	ذلك	pron. m.	that, those, who	(1256)
ܗܽܘ	הוּא	هو	pron. m.	he, it, is	(2141)
ܗܘܳܐ	הָיָה		v.	be, was, turn	(4006)
ܗܳܢܰܘ	הוּא		pron.	i.e. that is to say	(44)
ܗܰܝܟܠܳܐ	הֵיכָל	هيكل	n. m.	temple, sanctuary	(117)
ܗܰܝܡܶܢ	[אמן]	آمن	v.	believe, trust	(305)
ܗܰܝܡܳܢܽܘܬܳܐ	אֱמוּנָה		n. f.	faith, belief	(264)
ܗܳܟܰܢܳܐ	כֹּה	هكذا	particle	thus	(282)
ܗܰܠܶܟ	הָלַךְ		v.	walk	(110)
ܗܳܢܳܐ	הוּא		pron. m.	w/ ܗܰܘ	(68)
ܗܦܰܟ	הָפַךְ		v.	turn, return, conduct	(91)
ܙܰܕܺܝܩܳܐ	צַדִּיק	صدّيق	adj.	righteous, just, worthy	(47)
ܙܰܕܺܝܩܽܘܬܳܐ	צְדָקָה		n. f.	righteousness, justness, uprightness	(40)
ܙܕܶܩ	צָדֵק		v.	justify, right, fitting, approve	(58)
ܙܥܽܘܪܳܐ	זָעִיר	صغير	adj.	little, least	(66)
ܙܪܰܥ	זָרַע	زرع	v.	sow	(50)
ܙܰܪܥܳܐ	זֶרַע	زرع	n. m.	seed	(50)
ܚܶܒ	חָבַב	أحبّ	v.	kindled, love	(103)
ܚܰܒܺܝܒܳܐ	חָבַב	حبيب	adj.	beloved	(65)
ܚܰܕ	אֶחָד	واحد	num. m.	one, one, each one	(739)
ܚܰܕܬܳܐ		حديث	adj.	new	(59)
ܚܽܘܒܳܐ	חָבַב	حبّ	n. m.	love, lovingkindness	(125)

Syriac	Hebrew	Arabic	Cat.	Meaning	
ܚܙܐ	חָזָה		v.	see, behold	(734)
ܚܛܐ	חָטָא	أخطأ	v.	sin, err	(39)
ܚܛܝܬܐ	חַטָּאת	خطيئة	n. m.	sin	(103)
ܚܛܝܐ	חַטָּא	خاطئ	adj.	sinner	(49)
ܚܛܝܬܐ	חַטָּאת	خطيئة	n. f.	sin	(87)
ܚܝܐ	חַי	حيي	adj.	alive, living	(89)
ܚܝܐ	חַי	حياة	n. m.	life, salvation	(177)
ܚܝܐ	חָיָה	حي	v.	live, live, save	(165)
ܚܝܘܬܐ	חַיָּה	حيوان	n. f.	creature, animal	(67)
ܚܝܠܐ	חַיִל		n. f.	power, mighty work, strength, virtue, force	(150)
ܚܟܝܡܐ	חָכָם	حكيم	adj.	wise, prudent, cunning	(36)
ܚܟܡܬܐ	חָכְמָה	حكمة	n. f.	wisdom	(53)
ܚܡܪܐ	חֶמֶר	خمر	n. m.	wine	(37)
ܚܡܫܐ	חָמֵשׁ	خمسة	num. f.	five	(49)
ܚܪܬܐ	אַחֲרִית	آخرة	n. f.	end	(41)
ܚܫܒ	חָשַׁב	حسب	v.	think, reckon, deliberate	(66)
ܚܫܘܟܐ	חֹשֶׁךְ		adj.	dark, darkness	(52)
ܛܒܐ	טוֹב		adj.	good, much	(214)
ܛܘܒܐ	טוֹב	طوبى	n. m.	blessedness, beatitude, happiness	(48)
ܛܘܪܐ		طور (= جبل)	n. m.	mountain, hill	(66)
ܛܥܐ	תָּעָה		v.	wander, err, forget, deceive, astray, astray, delude	(76)
ܝܕܐ	[ידה]		v.	confess, thanks, profess, promise	(83)
ܝܕܥ	יָדַע		v.	know, known, recognize	(704)
ܝܕܥܬܐ	דַּעַת		n. f.	knowledge	(49)

9. SEMITIC COGNATE LIST

Syriac	Hebrew	Arabic	Cat.	Meaning	
ܝܗܒ	יָהַב	وهب	v.	give	(534)
ܝܗܘܕ	יְהוּדָה	يهوذا	pr. n.	Judea	(49)
ܝܗܘܕܝܐ	יְהוּדִי	يهوذي	adj.	Jew	(205)
ܝܘܡܐ	יוֹם	يوم	n. m.	day	(381)
ܝܘܡܢܐ	יוֹם	اليوم	n. m.	to-day	(42)
ܝܠܕ	יָלַד	ولد	v.	beget, bear	(120)
ܝܡܐ	יָם	يَمّ (= البحر)	n. m.	sea	(108)
ܝܡܝܢܐ	יְמִנִי	يمين	n. f.	right	(52)
ܝܩܪ	יָקַר	وقّر	v.	heavy, precious, honour, heavy	(41)
ܝܬܝܪܐ	[יתר]		adj.	more, excessive, greater, better, excelling	(100)
ܝܬܝܪܐܝܬ	[יתר]		adv.	abundantly, especially, exceedingly	(78)
ܝܬܪ	[יתר]		v.	gain, remain over, abound, abound, prefer, benefit	(80)
ܟܗܢܐ	כֹּהֵן	كاهن	n. m.	priest	(121)
ܟܘܪܣܝܐ	כִּסֵּא	كرسي	n. m.	throne, seat	(59)
ܟܠܢܫ	אֱנוֹשׁ		n. c.	every one	(96)
ܟܡܐ	מָה	كم	particle	how much? how many?	(73)
ܟܢܘܫܬܐ	כָּנַס	كنيس	n. f.	synagogue, council	(76)
ܟܣܐ	[כסה]		v.	cover, conceal, hide	(31)
ܟܣܐ	כּוֹס	كأس	n. m.	cup	(33)
ܟܣܦܐ	כֶּסֶף		n. m.	silver, money	(39)
ܟܦܪ	[כפר]	كفر	v.	deny, refuse	(44)
ܟܪܙ		كرز	den.	preached, preach, proclaimed	(94)
ܟܫܠ	כָּשַׁל		v.	offended, stumble	(30)

Syriac	Hebrew	Arabic	Cat.	Meaning	
ܟ݁ܬ݂ܰܒ݂	כָּתַב	كتب	v.	write	(231)
ܟ݁ܬ݂ܳܒ݂ܳܐ		كتاب	n. m.	book, writing, Scripture	(102)
ܠ	לְ	لـ	prep.	to, for	(4234)
ܠܐ	לֹא	لا	particle	no, not	(3140)
ܠܶܒ݁ܳܐ	לֵב		n. m.	heart	(168)
ܠܒ݂ܶܫ	לָבֵשׁ	لبس	v.	put on, clothed, clothe	(50)
ܠܰܚܡܳܐ	לֶחֶם		n. m.	bread, shewbread	(98)
ܠܺܠܝܳܐ	לַיְלָה	ليل	n. m.	night	(68)
ܠܡܳܐ	מָה	لمَ؟	pron.	why	(61)
ܠܡܳܢܳܐ		لمَ؟	pron.	why	(52)
ܠܶܫܳܢܳܐ	לָשׁוֹן	لسان (= لغة)	n. m.	tongue, language	(58)
ܡܳܐ	מָה	ما	pron.	what	(236)
ܡܕ݂ܺܝܢ݇ܬ݁ܳܐ		مدينة	n. f.	city	(223)
ܡܰܘܗܰܒ݂ܬ݁ܳܐ	יָהַב	موهبة	n. f.	gift	(46)
ܡܽܘܠܟ݁ܳܢܳܐ	מֶלֶךְ		n. m.	promise	(38)
ܡܽܘܫܶܐ	מֹשֶׁה	موسى	pr. n.	Moses	(82)
ܡܰܘܬ݁ܳܐ	מָוֶת	موت	n. m.	death	(125)
ܡܰܝܳܐ	מַי	ماء	n. m.	water	(94)
ܡܺܝܬ݂ܳܐ	מוּת	ميّت	pass. ptc. m.	dead	(126)
ܡܠܳܐ	מָלֵא	ملأ	v.	fill, complete	(166)
ܡܰܠܰܐܟ݂ܳܐ	מַלְאָךְ	ملاك	n. m.	messenger, angel	(181)
ܡܠܰܟ݂	מָלַךְ		v.	counsel, promise, deliberate, reign	(42)
ܡܰܠܟ݁ܳܐ	מֶלֶךְ	ملك	n. m.	king, queen	(130)
ܡܰܠܟ݁ܽܘܬ݂ܳܐ	מַלְכוּת	مملكة	n. f.	kingdom, realm, reign	(167)
ܡܶܠܬ݂ܳܐ	מִלָּה		n. f.	word, case, cause, matter	(409)
ܡܶܢ	מִן־	من	prep.	from	(2966)

9. SEMITIC COGNATE LIST

Syriac	Hebrew	Arabic	Cat.	Meaning	
ܡܢܐ	מָה		pron.	why, what	(289)
ܡܢܘ	מִי	مَن؟	pron. m.	who is this?	(126)
ܡܣܟܢܐ		مسكين	adj.	poor	(38)
ܡܥܡܘܕܝܬܐ		معمودية	n. f.	baptism, washing	(31)
ܡܫܝܚܐ	מָשִׁיחַ	المسيح	pass. ptc. m.	Messiah, Annointed One, Christ	(586)
ܡܫܡܫܢܐ		شمّاس	n. m.	minister, servant, attendant	(41)
ܡܝܬ	מוּת	مات	v.	dead, die, death	(171)
ܡܬܠܐ		مثل	n. m.	parable, proverb, similitude	(46)
ܢܒܝܐ	נְבִיא	نبي	n. m.	prophet, prophetess	(167)
ܢܘܗܪܐ	נְהָרָה	نور	n. m.	light	(68)
ܢܘܪܐ	תַּנּוּר	نار	n. f.	fire	(81)
ܢܚ	נוּחַ		v.	cease, rest, rest, put off, refresh	(40)
ܢܛܪ		نطر	v.	guard, keep, reserve, observe	(130)
ܢܡܘܣܐ		ناموس	n. m.	law	(224)
ܢܣܐ	[נסה]		v.	tempt, prove, try	(40)
ܢܦܠ	נָפַל		v.	fall	(157)
ܢܦܫܐ	נֶפֶשׁ	نفس	n. f.	soul, breath of life, self	(422)
ܣܓܕ	סָגַד	سجد	v.	worship, homage	(61)
ܣܗܕ	שָׁהֵד	شهد	v.	witness, testify	(118)
ܣܗܕܘܬܐ	שָׁהֵד	شهادة	n. f.	testimony	(67)
ܣܛܢܐ	שָׂטָן	شيطان	n. m.	adversary, Satan	(49)
ܣܡ	שׂוּם	وضع	v.	put, place	(207)
ܣܡܟ	סָמַךְ		v.	support, recline, recline	(46)
ܣܢܐ	שָׂנֵא		v.	hate	(42)
ܣܦܝܢܬܐ	סְפִינָה	سفينة	n. f.	boat, ship, vessel	(39)
ܣܦܪܐ	סֹפֵר		n. m.	scribe, lawyer	(76)

9. SEMITIC COGNATE LIST

Syriac	Hebrew	Arabic	Cat.	Meaning	
ܥܒܰܕ	עָבַד		v.	do, make, subdue, subject, act, perform, celebrate	(706)
ܥܰܒܕܳܐ	עֶבֶד	عبد	n. m.	servant	(141)
ܥܒܳܕܳܐ	עֲבֹדָה		n. m.	deed, work	(191)
ܥܒܰܪ	עָבַר	عبر	v.	cross over, transgress, turn away from, pass over	(108)
ܥܓܰܠ		عجلة	particle	quickly	(32)
ܥܕܰܡܳܐ	עַד		prep.	until	(219)
ܥܰܘܠܳܐ	עַוְלָה		n. m.	unrighteousness, iniquity	(39)
ܥܰܝܢܳܐ	עַיִן	عين	n. f.	eye	(155)
ܥܳܠܡܳܐ	עוֹלָם	عالم	n. m.	age, eternity, world	(413)
ܥܶܠܬܳܐ		علّة	n. f.	cause, occasion	(33)
ܥܰܡ	עִם		prep.	with	(723)
ܥܰܡܳܐ	עַם		n. m.	people, nation, Gentiles	(324)
ܥܡܰܕ		عمد	v.	baptized, baptize, sink	(80)
ܥܡܰܪ		عمر (= سكن)	v.	dwell	(57)
ܥܺܝܪ	עוּר		v.	awake, wake up, watch, arouse	(41)
ܦܺܐܪܳܐ	פְּרִי		n. m.	fruit	(81)
ܦܰܘܠܳܘܣ		بولس	pr. n.	Paul	(171)
ܦܘܡܳܐ	פֶּה	فم	n. m.	mouth, edge	(86)
ܦܺܝܠܰܛܳܘܣ		فيلاطوس	pr. n.	Pontius Pilate	(58)
ܦܠܰܚ	[פלח]	فلح (= عمل)	v.	work, labour, serve, caltivate	(66)
ܦܢܳܐ	פָּנָה		v.	return, answer, give back, turn	(57)
ܦܩܰܕ	פָּקַד		v.	command	(130)

9. SEMITIC COGNATE LIST

Syriac	Hebrew	Arabic	Cat.	Meaning	
ܦ̈ܪܝܫܐ		فريسي	pass. ptc. m.	Pharisee	(102)
ܦܪܫ	פְּרַס	فرش (= فرّق)	v.	separate, appoint	(57)
ܦܬܚ	פְּתַח	فتح	v.	open	(84)
ܨܠܘܬܐ		صلوة	n. f.	prayer	(49)
ܩܒܘܪܐ	קֶבֶר	قبر	n. m.	tomb, sepulchre	(32)
ܩܒܠ	[קבל]	قبل	v.	appeal to, accuse, receive, take, present, oppose	(200)
ܡܢ ܩܕܡ	[קדם]	قديما	pass. ptc. m.	before, before, formerly	(45)
ܩܕܝܫܐ	קָדוֹשׁ	قديس	adj.	holy, saint	(148)
ܗܘܐ	[קוה]		den.	abide, remain	(98)
ܩܘܕܫܐ	קֹדֶשׁ	قدوس	n. m.	holiness	(99)
ܩܘܪܒܢܐ	קָרְבָּן	قربان	n. m.	offering, gift	(31)
ܩܛܠ	קָטַל	قتل	v.	kill	(124)
ܩܝܡܬܐ	קום	قيامة	n. f.	resurrection	(36)
ܩܠܐ	קוֹל		n. m.	voice	(153)
ܩܠܝܠܐ	קַל	قليل	adj.	little, light, swift	(69)
ܩܡ	קום	قام	v.	rise, stand, establish, stand	(550)
ܩܣܪ		قيصر	pr. n.	Caesar	(35)
ܩܪܐ	קָרָא	قرأ	v.	call, read, appeal to	(330)
ܩܪܒ	קָרַב	قرب	v.	near, touch, come, near, bring near, offer, fight	(244)
ܩܪܝܒܐ	קָרֹב	قريب	adj.	hand, near, neighbour	(54)
ܩܪܝܬܐ	קִרְיָה	قرية	n. f.	village, field	(67)
ܩܫܝܫܐ		قسّيس	n. m.	elder	(84)
ܪܒܐ	רַב		adj.	great, chief, master	(395)

9. Semitic Cognate List

Syriac	Hebrew	Arabic	Cat.	Meaning	
ܪܒܐ	רָבַב	ربى	v.	grow up, increase, nourish, increase	(35)
ܪܓܠܐ	רֶגֶל	رجل	n. f.	foot	(100)
ܪܕܦ	רָדַף		v.	follow, persecute	(34)
ܪܗܛ	רוּץ		v.	run	(46)
ܪܘܚܐ	רוּחַ	روح	n. c.	spirit, wind, breath	(478)
ܪܚܡ	רָחַם	رحم (= أحب)	v.	love, mercy, mercy, compassion	(119)
ܪܫܐ	ראש	رأس	n. m.	head, beginning, chiefs	(181)
ܪܡ	רום		v.	high, exalt	(58)
ܫܐܠ	שָׁאַל	سأل	v.	ask, inquire, salute, lend	(243)
ܫܒܚ	[שבח]	سبّح	den.	praise, glorify, commend	(95)
ܫܒܥܐ	שֶׁבַע	سبعة	num. f.	seven	(100)
ܫܒܬܐ	שַׁבָּת	سبت (= أسبوع)	n. f.	Sabbath	(69)
ܫܘܒܚܐ	[שבח]	تسبحة	n. m.	glory, glorification, praise	(89)
ܫܘܠܛܢܐ		سلطان	n. m.	power, authority, dominion	(80)
ܫܠܝܚܐ	שָׁלַח	سليح	pass. ptc. m.	apostle, sent one	(86)
ܫܠܝܛܐ		متسلط	adj.	lawful, permitted, magistrates, rulers	(53)
ܫܠܡ	[שלם]	سلم	v.	die, obey, agree, follow, delivered up, complete, deliver, completed	(200)
ܫܠܡܐ	שָׁלוֹם	سلام	n. m.	peace, salute, salutation	(164)
ܫܡܐ	שֵׁם	إسم	n. m.	name	(244)
ܫܡܝܐ	שָׁמַיִם	سماء	n. c.	heaven, sky	(309)

9. SEMITIC COGNATE LIST

Syriac	Hebrew	Arabic	Cat.	Meaning	
ܫܡܥ	שָׁמַע	سمع	v.	hear, obey, hear	(494)
ܫܡܫ		شمّس	v.	minister, serve	(60)
ܫܡܫܐ	שֶׁמֶשׁ	شمس	n. c.	sun	(33)
ܫܢܬܐ	שָׁנָה	سنة	n. f.	year	(72)
ܫܥܬܐ		ساعة	n.	hour	(142)
ܫܪܟܐ	שְׁאֵרִית		n. m.	residue, rest, remainder	(40)
ܬܐܒ		تاب	v.	return, repent, answer, vomit	(38)
ܬܚܝܬ	תַּחַת	تحت	prep.	under	(73)
ܬܠܡܝܕܐ		تلميذ	n. m.	disciple	(277)
ܬܠܬܐ		ثلاثة	num. f.	three	(126)
ܬܪܝܢ		إثنان	num. m.	two	(204)
ܬܪܥܣܪ		اثناعشر	num. m.	twelve	(75)
ܬܫܒܘܚܬܐ	[שבח]	تسبحة	n. f.	praise, glory	(99)

Hebrew Cognates with Shift List

Shift ז → ד

Syriac	Cat.	Hebrew	Meaning	
ܐܚܕ	v.	אָחַז	take, hold, take, let, kindle, apprehend, maintain, close	(168)
ܕܚܠ	v.	זָחַל	fear, fear	(114)
ܕܒܚܐ	n. m.	זֶבַח	sacrifice, victim	(25)
ܕܚܠܬܐ	n. f.	זָחַל	fear, awe	(84)
ܕܟܪܐ	adj.	זָכָר	male	(11)
ܡܕܒܚܐ	n. m.	מִזְבֵּחַ	altar	(24)

9. Semitic Cognate List

Shift ע → צ

Syriac	Cat.	Hebrew	Meaning	
ܪܥܐ	den.	רָצָה	think	(43)
ܪܥܝܢܐ	n. m.	רָצוֹן	mind, conscience, fool, thought, idea, conception	(77)
ܬܪܥܝܬܐ	n. f.	רָצוֹן	mind, thought, imagination	(14)

Shift ת → שׁ

Syriac	Cat.	Hebrew	Meaning	
ܐܢܬܬܐ	n. f.	אִשָּׁה	woman, wife	(238)
ܐܝܬ	sub.	יֵשׁ	is, are	(1100)
ܒܗܬܬܐ	n. f.	בֹּשֶׁת	shame	(11)
ܝܬܒ	v.	יָשַׁב	sit, seat, establish	(148)
ܥܬܝܪܐ	adj.	עָשִׁיר	rich, wealthy	(35)
ܬܠܬܝܢ	num.	שְׁלֹשִׁים	thirty	(11)
ܬܘܪܐ	n. m.	שׁוֹר	ox, steer	(14)
ܬܡܢ	particle	שָׁם	there	(206)
ܬܪܥܐ	n. m.	שַׁעַר	door, gate, portal	(77)
ܬܘܒ	particle	שׁוּב	again, furthermore	(192)
ܬܠܝܬܝܐ	n. m.	שְׁלִישִׁי	third	(15)

Index

This index lists all the words covered in this book in alphabetical order.

. . . . 51	 52	. . . . 16, 81, 89, 181
. . . . 4, 88, 180	. . . . 5, 79, 89, 180	. . . . . 5, 81, 89, 181
. . . . . 11, 66, 88, 180	. . . . 30, 80, 89	 89
. . . . 27, 88	 89	. . . . . . 4, 121, 181
. . . . 88	 52	 52
. . . . 88	. . . . 15, 91	. . . . 3, 78, 89
. . . . 88	. . . . 40, 91	. . . . 9, 79, 90
. . . . 88	22, 50, 89, 180	. . . . 40, 79, 90
. . . . 88	 51	. . . . 5, 78, 90, 181
. . . . 44, 180	. . . . . 10, 94, 180	. . . . 24, 90
. . . . . 40, 50, 88	 94	. . . . . . 24, 79, 90
. . . . 51	 53	. . . . . 22, 90, 181
. . . . 88	. . . . . 44, 180	. . . . 21, 80, 90
. . . . 88	. . . . 4, 66, 89	. . . . 3, 78, 90
. . . . . 21, 88, 180	. . . . 4, 89, 180	 90
. . . . 40, 88	. . . . . 7, 66, 89, 191	 45
. . . . 46	 89	. . . . . . 44, 181
. . . . 23, 88	. . . . . . 38, 82, 89	 51
. . . . 17, 88, 180	. . . . . . 40, 81, 89	. . . . 19, 124
	. . . . 38, 67, 89	. . . . . 2, 80, 90, 192
		 90

193

ܐܟܐܢܐ 46
ܐܟܝܢܐ 51
ܐܟܘܠܐ 90
ܐܟܘܬܐ 28, 78, 90
ܐܟܪܢܐ 90
ܐܟܣܪܐ 25, 79, 90, 178
ܐܟܠ 7, 67, 90, 181
ܐܟܠ ܩܪܨܐ 29, 90
ܐܟܠܐ 91
ܐܟܠܘܣ 51
ܐܟܠܩܪܨܐ 178
ܐܟܡܐ 90
ܐܟܣܢܝܐ . . . 32, 50, 82, 91
ܐܠܐ 3, 80, 91
ܐܠܗܐ 2, 91, 181
ܐܠܗܘܬܐ 91
ܐܠܗܝܐ 91
ܐܠܗܢܐ 91
ܐܠܘ 15, 80, 91, 181
ܐܠܘܪܐ 91
ܐܠܝܢܐ 44, 181
ܐܠܝܪܐ 91
ܐܠܡܦܣ 47
ܐܠܦܐ 17, 91, 181
ܐܠܦܐ 17, 91
ܐܠܦܪܐ 91
ܐܠܨ 18, 67, 91
ܐܡܐ 11, 91, 181
ܐܡܗܬܗܘܢ 53
ܐܡܝܢ 8, 80, 92, 181
ܐܡܝܢܐ 40, 82, 92
ܐܡܝܢܐܝܬ 40, 85, 92
ܐܡܡ 92
ܐܡܪ 2, 67, 92, 181
ܐܡܪܐ 19, 92
ܐܡܬܐ 40, 92
ܐܡܬܝ . . . 15, 80, 92, 181
ܐܢ 3, 80, 92, 181
ܐܢܐ 2, 78, 92, 181
ܐܢܬ 92
ܐܢܕܪܐܘܣ 46
ܐܢܗܘ 92
ܐܢܫ 92
ܐܢܛܘܢܝܣ 46
ܐܢܫܐ 51
ܐܢܫܐ 3, 92, 181
ܐܢܫܘܬܐ 92
ܐܝܟ 2, 78, 93, 181
ܐܝܟܘܩܝܘܣ 51
ܐܝܟܢܐ 6, 93, 192
ܐܣܐ 13, 67, 93
ܐܣܛܘܟܘܬܐ 51
ܐܣܛܘܪܐ 28, 93
ܐܣܛܘܢܐ 93
ܐܣܛܝܪܐ 53
ܐܣܛܘܐ 51
ܐܣܛܘܐܡܣ 53
ܐܣܛܘܟܣܐ 51
ܐܣܛܘܡܟܐ 53
ܐܣܛܠܐ 50
ܐܣܛܘܡܣ 51
ܐܣܛܪܛܝܐ 53, 93
ܐܣܛܪܛܝܓܐ 51, 93
ܐܣܛܪܛܝܘܛܐ 27, 50, 93
ܐܣܛܪܢܐ 53
ܐܣܝܐ 45
ܐܣܝܐ 93
ܐܣܝܘܬܐ 93
ܐܣܝܪܐ 15, 82, 93, 181
ܐܣܦܘܠܐ 53
ܐܣܦܣܐ 36, 50, 93
ܐܣܦܘܓ 52
ܐܣܦܘܩܠܛܪܐ 53
ܐܣܦܪܐ 50
ܐܣܦܣ 53
ܐܣܦܪܝܪܐ 51
ܐܣܪ 14, 67, 93, 181
ܐܣܪܐ 52
ܐܣܪܐ 93
ܐܣܬܐ 93
ܐܣܬܘܪܐ 53
ܐܦ 3, 80, 93, 181
ܐܦܐ 8, 94, 181
ܐܦܛܪܘܦܐ 53
ܐܦܝܣܩܘܦܐ 53
ܐܦܠܐ 11, 80, 93
ܐܦܠܘ 47
ܐܦܠܝ 93
ܐܦܢ 21, 80, 92, 178, 181
ܐܦܣܩܘܢܝܬܐ 53

ܐܦܣܘܣ 45
ܐܦܣܝܛܘܢ 52
ܐܘܪܚܐ 15, 161, 181
ܐܘܪܚܢ 25, 161
ܐܘܪܚܬܐ 161
ܐܘܪܚܬ ܚܛܝܢ 161
ܐܘܪܐ 23, 163
ܐܘܓܐ 51, 94
ܐܘܓܘܢܐ 33, 50, 94
ܐܘܡܢܐ 45, 82
ܐܘܡܢܘܬܐ 24, 94
ܐܘܡܢܘܢ 52
ܐܘܠ 38, 67, 94
ܐܘܠܐ 5, 94, 182
ܐܘܠܢܢܐ 94
ܐܡܪ 25, 67, 94
ܐܡܪܢܐ 45
ܐܡܬܝ 12, 75, 172, 182
ܐܬܐ 12, 94, 182
ܐܬܐ 3, 67, 94, 182
ܐܬܘܬܐ 94
ܐܬܪܐ 9, 94

ܒ

ܒ 3, 79, 95, 182
ܒܐܫ 95
ܒܒܠ 46
ܒܕܪ 29, 72, 95
ܒܗܪ 18, 95, 182
ܒܗܬ 20, 63, 95, 182
ܒܗܬܬܐ 38, 95, 192
ܒܘܣܪܢܐ 95
ܒܘܝܐܐ 26, 96
ܒܘܙܐ 96
ܒܘܙܬܐ 96
ܒܘܚܢܐ 52
ܒܘܣܡܐ 97
ܒܘܥܐ 98
ܒܘܪܟܐ 33, 99
ܒܘܪܟܬܐ 30, 99
ܒܘܪܣܡܐ 52
ܒܚܢ 31, 95
ܒܚܢܐ 95
ܒܚܝܪܐ 95
ܒܚܪ 96
ܒܛܝܠܐ 96
ܒܛܝܠܐܝܬ 96
ܒܛܝܠܘܬܐ 96
ܒܛܠ 15, 64, 96, 182
ܒܛܠܐ 96
ܒܛܠܐܝܬ 96
ܒܛܢ 96
ܒܛܢܐ 96
ܒܛܢܬܐ 96
ܒܝܐ 23, 72, 96
ܒܝܢ 38, 50, 96
ܒܝܢܬ 26, 79, 96
ܒܝܢܝܬ 16, 79, 96, 182
ܒܝܫܐ 7, 82, 95, 182
ܒܝܫܐܝܬ 36, 85, 95
ܒܝܫܘܬܐ 35, 95
ܒܝܬ 17, 79, 96, 182
ܒܝܬ ܟܢܐ 46
ܒܝܬܝܐ 4, 99, 182
ܒܝܬܝܘܬܐ 99
ܒܟܐ 18, 69, 96, 182
ܒܟܝܐ 96
ܒܟܝܪܐ 97
ܒܟܬܐ 96
ܒܠܐ 97
ܒܠܘܥܐ 97
ܒܠܚܘܕ 8, 85, 112, 178
ܒܠܥܐ 97
ܒܠܥ 36, 72, 97
ܒܢܐ 17, 69, 97, 182
ܒܢܝܐ 97
ܒܢܝܢܐ 28, 97
ܒܣܡܐ 35, 69, 97
ܒܣܝܡܐ 97
ܒܣܝܡܐܝܬ 97
ܒܣܝܡܘܬܐ 35, 97
ܒܣܡ 28, 64, 97
ܒܣܡܐ 27, 97
ܒܣܪܐ 8, 97, 182
ܒܣܪܢܐ 31, 80, 97
ܒܥܐ 5, 69, 97
ܒܥܘܬܐ 36, 97
ܒܥܠܕܪܐ 98
ܒܥܠܐ 18, 98
ܒܥܠܕܒܒܐ 20, 82, 98, 178, 182
ܒܥܠܕܒܒܘܬܐ 98

196   INDEX

؟

Index

Left column:

ܚܰܕ݂ܝܳܐ . . . 15, 82, 111, 183
ܚܰܕ݂ܳܐܺܝܬ . . . 111
ܚܰܕ݂ܝܽܘܬ݂ܳܐ . . . 111
ܚܘܐ . . . 10, 70, 112
ܚܰܘܒܳܐ . . . 110
ܚܽܘܒܳܐ . . . 8, 110, 183
ܚܰܘܒܠܳܐ . . . 110
ܚܽܘܕܪܳܢܳܐܺܝܬ . . . 111
ܚܽܘܕܳܬ݂ܳܐ . . . 112
ܚܶܘܝܳܐ . . . 35, 112
ܚܽܘܝܳܒܳܐ . . . 110
ܚܽܘܣܳܐ . . . 114
ܚܽܘܣܳܝܳܐ . . . 115
ܚܽܘܣܳܢܳܐ . . . 115
ܚܽܘܣܪܳܢܳܐ . . . 116
ܚܘܰܪ . . . 112
ܚܰܘܪܳܐ . . . 116
ܚܶܘܳܪܳܐ . . . 27, 83, 112
ܚܽܘܪܒܳܐ . . . 22, 117
ܚܽܘܪܡܳܐ . . . 117
ܚܽܘܫܒܳܐ . . . 118
ܚܽܘܫܚܳܢܳܐ . . . 118
ܚܽܘܫܳܢܳܐ . . . 118
ܚܙܳܐ . . . 3, 70, 112, 184
ܚܶܙܘܳܐ . . . 23, 112
ܚܶܙܘܳܢܳܐ . . . 112
ܚܙܺܝܳܐ . . . 112
ܚܰܙܺܝܳܐ . . . 112
ܚܙܺܝܪܳܐ . . . 33, 112
ܚܙܰܩ . . . 112
ܚܙܽܩܳܐ . . . 112
ܚܙܽܬ݂ܳܐ . . . 112
ܚܛܳܐ . . . 19, 70, 112, 184
ܚܛܳܗܳܐ . . . 10, 112, 184
ܚܛܽܘܦܳܐ . . . 113
ܚܛܽܘܦܝܳܐ . . . 113
ܚܰܛܳܝܳܐ . . . 16, 82, 113, 184
ܚܛܺܝܬ݂ܳܐ . . . 11, 113, 184
ܚܛܰܦ . . . 30, 62, 113
ܚܶܛܬ݂ܳܐ . . . 36, 113
ܚܝܳܐ . . . 7, 70, 113, 184
ܚܰܝ̈ܶܐ . . . 7, 113, 184
ܚܰܝܳܐ . . . 11, 82, 113, 184
ܚܰܝܳܒܳܐ . . . 18, 82, 110
ܚܰܝܳܒܽܘܬ݂ܳܐ . . . 110
ܚܰܝܽܘܬ݂ܳܐ . . . 14, 113, 184
ܚܝܠ . . . 30, 113
ܚܰܝܠܳܐ . . . 8, 113, 184
ܚܰܝܠܬ݂ܳܢܳܐ . . . 28, 82, 113
ܚܰܝܢܬ݂ܳܐ . . . 113
ܚܰܟܺܝܡܳܐ . . . 20, 82, 113, 184
ܚܰܟܺܝܡܳܐܺܝܬ . . . 113
ܚܟܶܡ . . . 113
ܚܶܟ݂ܡܬ݂ܳܐ . . . 16, 113, 184
ܚܰܠܳܐ . . . 113
ܚܶܠܳܐ . . . 113
ܚܠܺܝܡܳܐ . . . 28, 82, 114
ܚܠܺܝܡܽܘܬ݂ܳܐ . . . 114
ܚܠܰܡ . . . 33, 65, 114
ܚܠܰܦ . . . 28, 65, 114
ܚܠܽܘܦ . . . 9, 79, 114
ܚܶܠܬ݂ܳܐ . . . 113
ܚܰܡ . . . 114
ܚܰܡܺܝܡܳܐ . . . 114
ܚܡܺܝܪܳܐ . . . 34, 114
ܚܰܡܪܳܐ . . . 20, 114, 184
ܚܰܡܫܳܐ . . . 17, 114, 184
ܚܰܡܫܺܝܢ . . . 114
ܚܰܡܶܫܡܳܐܐ . . . 114
ܚܰܡܫܰܥܶܣܪܳܐ . . . 114
ܚܡܬ . . . 114
ܚܶܡܬ݂ܳܐ . . . 28, 114
ܚܶܡܬ݂ܳܢܳܐ . . . 114
ܚܰܢ . . . 115
ܚܢܳܢܳܐ . . . 115
ܚܢܢܳܐ . . . 39, 115
ܚܰܢܦܳܐ . . . 36, 82, 115
ܚܢܰܩ . . . 36, 65, 115
ܚܽܣ . . . 31, 39, 74, 80, 115
ܚܣܳܐ . . . 115
ܚܣܝ . . . 115
ܚܶܣܝܳܐ . . . 115
ܚܰܣܝܳܐ . . . 115
ܚܰܣܝܽܘܬ݂ܳܐ . . . 115
ܚܰܣܺܝܢܳܐ . . . 40, 82, 115
ܚܰܣܺܝܪܳܐ . . . 27, 83, 116
ܚܰܣܺܝܪܽܘܬ݂ܳܐ . . . 35, 116
ܚܣܰܡ . . . 115
ܚܣܳܡܳܐ . . . 31, 115
ܚܣܶܢ . . . 116

ܚܦܝܐ 116
ܚܦܙ 34, 73, 116
ܚܦܛ 29, 65, 116
ܚܦܝܛܐ 116
ܚܦܝܛܐܝܬ 116
ܚܦܝܛܘܬܐ 40, 116
ܚܨܐ 116
ܚܨܐ 30, 116
ܚܨܕ 28, 62, 116
ܚܨܕܐ 37, 116
ܚܨܘܕܐ 116
ܚܪ 14, 74, 116
ܚܪܐ 35, 70, 117
ܚܪܒ 117
ܚܪܒܐ 34, 117
ܚܪܘܪܐ 116
ܚܪܝܢܐ 26, 117
ܚܪܝܦܐ 117
ܚܪܝܦܐܝܬ 117
ܚܪܡ 117
ܚܪܡܐ 117
ܚܪܦ 117
ܚܪܫ 35, 73, 116
ܚܪܫܐ 31, 83, 117
ܚܪܫܐ 117
ܚܪܫܘܬܐ 117
ܚܪܬܐ 19, 89, 184
ܚܫ 20, 75, 117
ܚܫܐ 31, 118
ܚܫܒ 14, 62, 118, 184
ܚܘܫܒܐ 16, 83, 118, 184
ܚܫܘܟܐ 118
ܚܫܟ 35, 73, 118
ܚܫܝܟܘܬܐ 118
ܚܫܟܬܐ 118
ܚܫܦ 39, 63, 118
ܚܫܡ 118
ܚܫܡܝܬܐ 32, 118
ܚܬܐ 26, 89
ܚܬܝܟܐ 118
ܚܬܝܬܐ 118
ܚܬܝܬܘܬܐ 118
ܚܬܡ 40, 62, 118
ܚܬܡܐ 118
ܚܬܢܐ 32, 118
ܚܬܪ 119

ܛ

ܛܒ 119
ܛܒܐ 6, 83, 119, 184
ܛܒܐ 119
ܛܒܘܬܐ 119
ܛܒܥ 119
ܛܒܥܐ 35, 119
ܛܘܒܐ 17, 119, 184
ܛܘܒܢܐ 119
ܛܘܗܡܐ 32, 119
ܛܘܝܒܐ 119
ܛܘܥܝ 120
ܛܘܦܝܪܘܢ 54
ܛܘܦܢܡܘܣ 54
ܛܘܦܣܐ 51
ܛܘܪܐ 14, 119, 184
ܛܘܥܝܐ 121
ܛܝܛܘܣ 46
ܛܝܛܪܒܐ 52
ܛܟܣ 13, 65, 119
ܛܟܣܘܬܐ 7, 119
ܛܟܣܐ 53
ܛܟܣܝܪܟܘܣ 45
ܛܠ 54
ܛܠܣ 54
ܛܠܣܐ 52
ܛܠܠ 119
ܛܠܠܐ 12, 120
ܛܠܠܘܬܐ 120
ܛܠܠܐ 119
ܛܠܡ 32, 62, 120
ܛܠܘܡܬܐ 119
ܛܡܐ 120
ܛܡܐܐ 39, 83, 120
ܛܡܐܘܬܐ 120
ܛܢ 37, 75, 120
ܛܢܢܐ 37, 120
ܛܢܢܐ 120
ܛܥܢ 120
ܛܥܢܐ 22, 83, 120
ܛܥܢܘܬܐ 34, 120
ܛܥܐ 13, 70, 120, 184

INDEX

INDEX

Left column:

Word	Page(s)
	54
	159
	135
	160
	161
	50
	161
	161
	161
	164
	135
	30, 136
	136
	136
	163
	163
	3, 135
	45, 46
	164
	135
	135
	135
	164
	164
	135
	135
	46
	135
	140
	166

Word	Page(s)
	147
	147
	32, 148
	22, 148, 187
	149
	149
	150
	139
	151
	151
	152
	39, 139
	139
	139
	154
	153
	154
	34, 70, 135
	155
	31, 155
	135
	156
	23, 135
	45
	156
	156
	47, 83
	45
	157
	157

Word	Page(s)
	8, 78, 106, 187
	31, 78, 106
	41, 135
	30, 135
	139
	37, 137
	134
	31, 135
	37, 139
	141
	141
	142
	142
	22, 141
	142
	143
	20, 83, 143, 187
	143
	143
	41, 140
	162
	162
	143
	145
	145
	147
	41, 146
	146
	147
	147

ܡܫܓܪܐ 167
ܡܫܘܚܐ 122
ܡܫܘܚܬܐ 35, 136
ܡܫܚ 34, 73, 136
ܡܫܚܐ 34, 136
ܡܫܟܢܐ 39, 83, 114
ܡܫܝܚܐ .. 3, 83, 136, 187
ܡܫܝܚܘܬܐ 136
ܡܫܬܝܐ 31, 168
ܡܫܠܡܐ 169
ܡܫܠܡܢܐ 169
ܡܫܠܡܢܐ 41, 169
ܡܫܠܡܢܘܬܐ 169
ܡܫܡܥܢܐ 134
ܡܫܡܫܐ 170
ܡܫܡܫܢܝܬܐ 41, 170
ܡܫܡܫܢܐ 19, 170, 187
ܡܫܢܝܐ 145
ܡܫܩܠܐ 171
ܡܫܪܐ 171
ܡܫܪܝܐ 34, 83, 171
ܡܫܪܝܐ 171
ܡܫܪܫܝܐ 41, 172
ܡܫܬܘܬܐ 34, 172
ܡܫܬܝܐ 172
ܡܫܬܡܫܢܐ 170
ܡܫܬܡܫܢܘܬܐ 170
ܡܬ 7, 74, 136, 187
ܡܬܘܡ 39, 81, 136
ܡܬܡܟܟܢܘܬܐ 110
ܡܬܛܦܫܢܘܬܐ 151
ܡܬܠ 136
ܡܬܠܐ 122
ܡܬܠܐ 17, 136, 187
ܡܬܟܒܪܢܘܬܐ 145
ܡܬܪܢܐ 53

ܢ

ܢܒܐ 23, 67, 136
ܢܒܝܐ 7, 137, 187
ܢܒܝܘܬܐ 28, 137
ܢܓܕ 23, 67, 137
ܢܓܕܐ 137
ܢܓܘܕܐ 137
ܢܓܝܪܐ 137
ܢܓܝܪܘܬܐ 137
ܢܓܪ 37, 67, 137
ܢܗܝܪܐ 31, 83, 137
ܢܗܝܪܐܝܬ 137
ܢܗܪ 23, 67, 137
ܢܗܪܐ 32, 137
ܢܘܓܪܐ 137
ܢܘܗܪܐ 13, 137, 187
ܢܘܦܠ 54
ܢܘܡܐ 138
ܢܘܟܦܐ 139
ܢܘܟܪܝܐ 27, 83, 139
ܢܘܦܐ 54
ܢܘܢܐ 23, 137
ܢܘܫܐ 54
ܢܘܪܐ 12, 137, 187
ܢܘܡܘܣܐ 140
ܢܚ 19, 74, 138, 187
ܢܚܬ 9, 67, 138
ܢܚܬܐ 24, 138
ܢܛܘܪܐ 138
ܢܛܘܪܬܐ 138
ܢܛܪ 8, 67, 138, 187
ܢܝܚܐ 138
ܢܝܚܐ 138
ܢܝܚܘܬܐ 138
ܢܝܫܐ 37, 138
ܢܟܘܠܬܢܐ 138
ܢܟܝܠܐ 138
ܢܟܠܘܬܐ 138
ܢܟܝܣܐ 139
ܢܟܠ 138
ܢܟܠܐ 30, 138
ܢܟܣ 138
ܢܟܣܐ 138
ܢܟܣܝܐ 138
ܢܟܦ 139
ܢܟܦܐ 139
ܢܟܦܘܬܐ 139
ܢܡܘܣܐ ... 6, 50, 139, 187
ܢܦܠ 19, 67, 139, 187
ܢܦܩ 6, 67, 139
ܢܦܫܢܐ 27, 139
ܢܦܫܢܝܐ 139
ܢܩܠܐ 140
ܢܩܘܫܐ 54

INDEX 207

.... 7, 67, 139, 187	.... 22, 141	.... 27, 142
.... 4, 67, 139	.... 14, 141, 187	 46
.... 139	.... 41, 141	.... 28, 70, 143
.... 4, 140, 187	.... 27, 141	.... 8, 63, 143
.... 140	 52	..... 6, 74, 143, 187
.... 35, 67, 140	 142	 143
.... 140	 142	 143
.... 45, 83	.... 35, 141	..... 19, 84, 143
.... 46	 142	 54
.... 19, 68, 140	 143	 143
.... 39, 68, 140	 144	... 17, 62, 143, 187
.... 140	.... 35, 144	...... 34, 143
.... 35, 68, 140	 162	 143
	 141	.... 36, 144
****	 141	.... 18, 70, 144, 187
..... 41, 50, 140	 141	 144
.... 140	 142	 144
.... 142	 142	 144
.... 30, 73, 140	.... 17, 142, 187	 144
.... 140	.... 27, 65, 142	 144
.... 9, 73, 140, 141	 142	.... 26, 66, 144
.... 15, 140	...... 36, 141	 144
...... 17, 141	 143	.... 16, 73, 144
.... 22, 70, 141	.... 25, 143	 144
..... 15, 62, 141, 187	.... 34, 142	.... 32, 144
.... 141	.... 23, 70, 142	.... 19, 144, 187
...... 4, 83, 141	 142	 144
...... 141	...... 17, 66, 142	 144
.... 47	.... 34, 142	...... 41, 144
.... 51	...... 30, 84, 142	.... 26, 63, 144
.... 9, 63, 141, 187		

ܥܩܒܐ 150
ܥܩܪ 150
ܥܩܪܐ 150
ܥܩܪܐ 28, 150
ܥܩܬܐ 149
ܥܪ 19, 74, 150, 188
ܥܪܒ 150
ܥܪܒܐ 26, 150
ܥܪܘܒܬܐ 150
ܥܪܘܩܐ 150
ܥܪܛܠ 150
ܥܪܛܠܝܐ 41, 84, 150
ܥܪܛܠܝܘܬܐ 150
ܥܪܩܐ 23, 150
ܥܪܩ 18, 62, 150
ܥܬܝܕ 9, 66, 150
ܥܬܝܕܐ 150
ܥܬܝܕܐܝܬ 151
ܥܬܝܩܐ 37, 84, 151
ܥܬܝܩܘܬܐ 151
ܥܬܝܪܐ 20, 84, 151, 192
ܥܬܝܪܐܝܬ 151
ܥܬܩ 151
ܥܬܪ 37, 73, 151

ܦ

ܦܐܪܐ 12, 151, 188
ܦܓܥܢܐ 54
ܦܓܪܐ 7, 151
ܦܓܪܢܐ 151
ܦܓܪܢܐܝܬ 151
ܦܓܪܢܝܐ 151
ܦܕܓܘܓܘܣ 46
ܦܘܠܓܐ 152
ܦܘܠܘܣ 44, 188
ܦܘܠܚܢܐ 41, 152
ܦܘܡܐ 11, 151, 188
ܦܘܢܝܐ 152
ܦܘܩܕܐ 153
ܦܘܩܕܢܐ 11, 153
ܦܘܪܣܐ 54
ܦܘܪܚܢܐ 153
ܦܘܪܩܢܐ 26, 153
ܦܘܪܫܢܐ 153
ܦܘܫܩܐ 154
ܦܘܬܐܡܐ 54
ܦܘܬܐܡܢܐ 54
ܦܝܠܣܘܦܘܣ 44, 188
ܦܝܠܢܩܘܣ 45, 46
ܦܝܠܣܘܦܐ 54
ܦܝܠܣܘܦܘܬܐ 54
ܦܝܢܟܐ 51
ܦܣ 14, 50, 151
ܦܣܩܐ 51, 151
ܦܥܪܐ 53
ܦܠܐܬܐ 34, 151
ܦܠܓ 17, 62, 152
ܦܠܓܐ 41, 152
ܦܠܓܘܬܐ 38, 152
ܦܠܓܘܬܐ 152
ܦܠܚ 14, 73, 152, 188
ܦܠܚܐ 30, 152
ܦܠܚܢܐ 27, 152
ܦܠܚܘܬܐ 152
ܦܠܚܝܐ 152
ܦܢܐ 15, 71, 152, 188
ܦܢܛܩܘܣܛܐ 52
ܦܢܩܝܬܐ 54
ܦܣ 24, 74, 152
ܦܣܐ 152
ܦܣܘܩܐ 152
ܦܣܝܩܬܐ 152
ܦܣܩ 21, 62, 152
ܦܣܩܐ 152
ܦܥܠܐ 36, 152
ܦܨܐ 27, 71, 153
ܦܨܝܢܐ 23, 153
ܦܩܕ 8, 62, 153, 188
ܦܩܚ 153
ܦܩܚܢܐ 25, 84, 153
ܦܪܓܠܐ 53
ܦܪܕܝܣܐ 51
ܦܪܘܩܐ 153
ܦܪܘܫܐ 39, 153
ܦܪܘܫܘܬܐ 153
ܦܪܚ 153
ܦܪܝܚܐܝܬ 153
ܦܪܝܫܐ 32, 153
ܦܪܛܘܢ 50
ܦܪܫ 10, 84, 154, 189
ܦܪܫܢܐ 154

INDEX

20, 73, 153	30, 79, 155	10, 84, 157 ......
20, 50, 153	155	157 ....
16, 62, 153	155	24, 66, 157 ......
51	46	10, 157, 189 ......
15, 62, 154, 189 ...	10, 72, 155	156 ....
30, 62, 154	155	156 ....
154	17, 155, 189	54 ....
154	155	157 ....
154	33, 155	10, 157, 189 .....
154	25, 74, 156	158 ....
154	31, 73, 156	54 ....
27, 66, 154	156	158 ....
24, 154	26, 156	158 ....
29, 154	124	54 ....
12, 73, 154, 189 ..	39, 71, 156	51 ....
154		159 ....
24, 154	****	22, 159, 189 ....
	52	53 ....
****	21, 156, 189	22, 157 ....
5, 71, 154	156	52, 158 ....
21, 154	156	53, 158 .....
10, 155	6, 62, 156, 189 ...	157 ....
155	32, 73, 156	157 ....
155	24, 156	38, 157 ....
155	18, 84, 157, 189 ..	157 ....
33, 71, 155	8, 84, 157, 189 ...	9, 62, 157, 189 ...
155	34, 157	39, 157 ....
155	16, 66, 157	158 ....
156	5, 79, 157	158 ....
46	157	41, 50, 75, 158 ..
41, 71, 155		

INDEX

ܐ‌ܘܟ‌ܡ‌ܟ‌ܐ 35, 165, 192

ܐ‌ܘ‌ܚ‌ܨ 13, 175, 178, 191

ܐ‌ܘ‌ܢ 175

ܐ‌ܡ‌ܟ‌ܘ‌ܣ‌ܟ‌ܐ . . 10, 166, 191

ܐ‌ܡ‌ܨ‌ܡ‌ܟ‌ܐ 16, 170

ܐ‌ܡ‌ܢ‌ܨ‌ܐ 170

ܐ‌ܡ‌ܟ‌ܒ 33, 175

ܐ‌ܡ‌ܟ‌ܝ 175

ܐ‌ܡ‌ܟ‌ܟ‌ܐ 171

ܐ‌ܟ‌ܐ‌ܐ 28, 175